WITTGENSTEIN

Wittgenstein

William Warren Bartley, III

Second edition ♦ Revised and Enlarged

Open ✺ Court
LaSalle, Illinois

OPEN COURT and the above logo are registered in the U. S. Patent and Trademark Office.

First edition published in the U.S.A. by J. B. Lippincott Company 1973

First printing of this edition 1985
Second printing 1988
Third printing 1994

Printed and bound in the United States of America.

Library of Congress Cataloging in Publication Data

Bartley, William Warren, 1934–
    Wittgenstein

    Bibliography: p.
    Includes index.
    1. Wittgenstein, Ludwig, 1889–1951. I. Title.
B3376.W564B37   1985   218   85-8962
ISBN: 0-87548-441-7

To the memory of my father
1895-1967

Contents

Foreword

It has been said that every great philosopher has given philosophy a new direction, but that only Wittgenstein has done this twice—first with his *Tractatus*, published right after World War I, and then again with the ideas that found their final form in his *Philosophical Investigations*, published posthumously after World War II. The early work influenced logical positivism, the later work the analytical philosophy that flourished in the English-speaking world for roughly a quarter of a century. No other philosopher has had nearly so great an influence on twentieth-century Anglo-American philosophy. Yet Wittgenstein was an Austrian who wrote his books in German. His life and personality were enigmatic—especially the decisive years during which he developed his later philosophy.

Knowing of W. W. Bartley's researches concerning the "lost" years in Wittgenstein's life, I invited him to write this book. I had no doubt that it would be interesting and important, but did not foresee the extent of Bartley's discoveries, which may strike some readers as sensational. Right from the start, we are swept up in the excitement of the author's quest for the man who, having published a book that made history, went on to teach at primary schools in three small Austrian villages while he changed his mind about many of his most influential ideas. The portrait that emerges from this account is human—all too human—but the author's respect for Wittgenstein is never in doubt. Though brief and written so that it can be understood by those with no previous knowledge of Wittgenstein's philosophy, this book is an important contribution to our understanding of the man and of the development of his thought.

Actually, I do not believe that every great philosopher has given philosophy a new direction. This one-dimensional metaphor gives us no idea of Plato's or Aristotle's importance, or of the significance of Spinoza, Hegel or Nietzsche. If a philosopher's ideas are promptly taken up by a school and developed only in one direction, this may well point to a lack of richness, of dimension, of profundity. It may be a mark of greatness in a philosopher if he feels distressed by his influence—as Wittgenstein did. He was not only one of the most influential philosophers of his century but also one of the most remarkable men of our time. Bartley does not see him merely as a link in a chain, nor does he concentrate on the human being to the exclusion of his thought. What he offers us is a concise intellectual biography of an extraordinary man.

WALTER KAUFMANN

[Note: Walter Kaufmann (1921-1980), Stuart Professor of Philosophy at Princeton University, was the editor of the series in which this book originally appeared.]

Preface

to the revised edition, 1985

THIS revised edition of *Wittgenstein* follows, in the main, the text of the German and Spanish translations of 1983. This text differs in some respects from that of the original American and English editions of the book, and also from that of the Italian and French translations.[1]

The most important addition has been the Afterword on Wittgenstein and homosexuality. This Afterword contains a reply to my critics; raises the question of the use of psychology and of psychological details in explaining the genesis and content of a philosophy; and rebuts some attempts to give a psychological explanation of Wittgenstein's philosophical ideas.

I have also taken this opportunity to correct minor errors throughout, to add a brief section on the question of the influence exerted on Wittgenstein by the Austrian school-reform movement, and greatly to expand the footnote and bibliographical references by citing the most important among the mass of new books and articles by and about Wittgenstein that have been published since the original

---

[1]This book was first published by J. B. Lippincott Co., Philadelphia and New York, in 1973. The following year Quartet Books Limited, of London, published a very slightly corrected British edition. Translations are as follows: Italian translation, *Wittgenstein: Maestro di Scuola Elementare*, Armando Armando, Rome, 1975; French translation, *Wittgenstein, une Vie*, Editions Complexe, Presses Universitaires de France, 1978; Spanish translation, *Wittgenstein*, Ediciones Catedra, Madrid, 1982; and German translation, *Wittgenstein: ein Leben*, Matthes & Seitz, Munich, 1983. A Japanese translation is in preparation.

appearance of this book. A new Bibliography is also provided.

The present little book on Wittgenstein is a small part of a larger work, as yet unfinished, which I hope one day to publish. This larger work, in several volumes, contains biographies and critical studies of the work of Sir Karl Popper and of F. A. von Hayek, as well as a longer study of Wittgenstein. The lives and work of these three figures are intimately connected. All three were born in Vienna during the period 1889-1902. Hayek and Wittgenstein were cousins; Hayek and Popper are close friends. The careers of all three lead out from Vienna to England. And all three are centrally—and very differently—concerned with the fundamental question of the scope and limits of rationality.

W. W. B.

The Hoover Institution
on War, Revolution and Peace,
Stanford University
February 1985

But I say unto you, That every idle word that men shall speak, they shall give account thereof in the day of judgment. For by thy words thou shalt be justified, and by thy words thou shalt be condemned.

—Matthew 12:36–37

Introduction

I

Ludwig Wittgenstein was born in Vienna in 1889 and died in Cambridge, England, in 1951. He was one of the half-dozen most influential philosophers of this century.

My presentation of his philosophy spans both his early and his later thought—the ideas of the *Tractatus Logico-Philosophicus* (1921 and 1922) as well as those developed in the posthumously published work, most importantly in *Philosophical Investigations*. The biographical focus, however, is much more restricted. I have not repeated well-known stories of Wittgenstein's life in Vienna, Manchester, and Cambridge before the First World War or after his return to professional philosophical activity in 1929. Rather, I have concentrated on the decade in his life following the First War. These are mystery years about which little has been written. I emphasize them here for two reasons: I may have something to say about them which will contribute to a better understanding of Wittgenstein; and I happen to believe that this transitional period is in many ways the most important of his life.

Since this study contains new information about Wittgenstein's development in the twenties that throws light on his later concerns, it will interest specialists. But I have tried to set down my account in such a way that readers who are not philosophers will be able to understand it too.

Thus I should report that the man with whom we are concerned was born into one of the most eminent families of Vienna's haute bourgeoisie. He was the youngest of eight children born to Karl Wittgenstein, creator of Austria's pre-war iron and steel industry and a great patron of culture, particularly of the visual arts and of music. As a child Ludwig was educated by private tutors, but when an adolescent he was sent to secondary school—to the K. K. Staats-Oberrealschule—in Linz. His ambition at that time was to become an engineer like his father, and in 1906 he enrolled in the Technische Hochschule in Berlin-Charlottenburg, where he spent three semesters. In 1908 he went to England to continue his engineering studies at Manchester University, where he did pioneering work in aeronautics. His mathematical work in engineering aroused his interest in the foundations of mathematics and in logic, and in 1911, on the advice of the great German logician Gottlob Frege (1848-1925), he went to Cambridge to consult Bertrand Russell. By 1 February 1912, he had withdrawn from Manchester University, and was a student at Trinity College, Cambridge.[1] During the two years following, he made a dazzlingly brilliant impression in Cambridge, gained the friendship of two of that University's most distinguished philosophers, G. E. Moore and Russell, and was elected to that most select of secret societies, The Apostles, to which Moore, Russell and

---

[1]Although Wittgenstein's interest in mathematical logic and in Russell's paradox, as well as his first contact with Russell himself, is usually put to 1911, the correspondence between Russell and Philip Jourdain suggests that it may have begun earlier. In his notebooks, Jourdain reports a long conversation with Russell that took place on 20 April 1909, writing: "Russell said that the views I gave in a reply to Wittgenstein (who had 'solved' Russell's contradiction) agree with his own." See I. Grattan-Guinness: *Dear Russell—Dear Jourdain: A Commentary on Russell's Logic, based on his correspondence with Philip Jourdain* (New York: Columbia University Press, 1977), pp. 112–115. Any such contact may have been entirely by correspondence, for Russell writes to Ottoline Morrell of taking Wittgenstein to "meet" Jourdain in 19 February 1913.

most of the male members of the Bloomsbury group already belonged.[2]

Wittgenstein spent the year immediately prior to the outbreak of the First World War in seclusion in Norway, working at logic in a hut he built for himself. When the war began, he volunteered for the Austrian army, where in due course he became an officer. During the war he completed the manuscript of a short philosophical work, *Tractatus Logico-Philosophicus*, now regarded as one of the greatest philosophical achievements of this century.

After the war he turned away from philosophy for a time: he took odd jobs as a gardener and hotel porter and spent six years as an elementary schoolteacher in Lower Austria. During the late twenties his interest in professional philosophy was rekindled, partly as a result of his friendship with Moritz Schlick, leader of the Vienna Circle, and in 1929 he returned to Cambridge, where he was soon awarded the doctorate and elected Fellow of Trinity College. In 1939 he succeeded Moore as Professor of Philosophy at Cambridge, and held this chair—with interruptions for civilian war service (as hospital orderly and laboratory technician) in Britain—until 1947, when he retired to devote more time to writing.

Although he wrote voluminously, the only philosophical work to be published in his lifetime, apart from a brief book review, was the *Tractatus* and a short article in the *Proceedings of the Aristotelian Society*. His literary executors have been publishing his other philosophical writings posthumously. The most important, *Philosophical Investigations*, was published in 1953. A number of his students have also published detailed notes from his lectures.

In appearance, Wittgenstein was of medium height, slender, with blue eyes and fair hair. His piercing glance and intense concentration, combined with fantastic presence,

---

[2]Concerning Wittgenstein's election to, and relationship with, The Apostles, see Paul Levy, *Moore: G. E. Moore and the Cambridge Apostles* (London: Weidenfeld & Nicolson, 1979), pp. 266-71.

gave him a most unusual charismatic quality which attracted fanatically devoted and loyal students to his side. By the mid-1930s he had succeeded, through teaching rather than publication, in forming a strong group of disciples.

Wittgenstein was baptized in the Roman Catholic faith and was given a Roman Catholic burial. Although his father and grandfather were prominent Viennese Protestants, his mother was Roman Catholic. During his First World War army duty, and in his subsequent work during the twenties as a schoolteacher, he continued to give his own religion as "Roman Catholic". In later years, while stating firmly that he was not an adherent to any organized religion, he nonetheless observed the rituals of organized religions when he encountered them. He avoided criticizing the Church and its clergy, had good friends among the clergy, and seriously contemplated entering monastic life himself. Some of his closest friends in Vienna were devout Roman Catholics, as were several of his favorite students in Cambridge. By descent, as opposed to persuasion, Wittgenstein was three-quarters Jewish. Outside the family the descent was not widely known; the matter is taken up briefly in an addendum at the back of this book.

II

Wittgenstein insisted that philosophical encounter with him produce moral change. In a moving part of his memoir of Wittgenstein, his student Norman Malcolm reports how bitterly Wittgenstein complained when this did not happen: "What is the use of studying philosophy", Wittgenstein asked, "if all that it does for you is to enable you to talk with some plausibility about some abstruse questions of logic, etc., & if it does not improve your thinking about the important questions of everyday life?"[3]

---

[3]Norman Malcolm, *Ludwig Wittgenstein: A Memoir* (London: Oxford University Press, 1966), p. 39.

My own interest in Wittgenstein was awakened when I
discovered that this man had actually gone about practising
what he preached—or, to be more accurate, had practised
what he once wrote could not be said but only shown. I had
had the good luck, during the course of an as yet uncompleted investigation into central European intellectual life following the collapse of the Habsburg monarchy, to stumble
upon material about the dark decade in Wittgenstein's life
from the end of the First World War until his return to
Cambridge in 1929. I learned some of the details of his life,
of his personal and intellectual milieux, during his years as
an elementary schoolteacher in three tiny mountain villages
in lower Austria. As details and anecdotes hitherto discon-
nected and unexplained gradually fell into place, an altogether startling image emerged of a man who had, contrary
to all accounts, *not* abandoned philosophy at all after the
First World War and the publication of the *Tractatus*, but
who was, rather, attempting to put into practice the ethical
portion of his earlier philosophy and at the same time beginning to formulate the concerns that were to dominate his
later philosophy.

I was led to the material just mentioned in a roundabout
way. In the course of my research—which initially related
more to the work of my own teacher and friend, Sir Karl
Popper, than to that of Wittgenstein—I had come upon some
information concerning two related topics: Otto Glöckel's
school-reform movement, now almost totally forgotten even
in Austria, and the philosophical and psychological ideas of
Karl Bühler. Bühler is hardly forgotten; indeed, a revival of
interest in his work has begun in recent years. Still, few
English or American psychologists know much about his
work, and he died in comparative obscurity in Los Angeles
in 1963. In the twenties and thirties, however, he had been
world-famous as one of the greatest psychologists of Europe
and a leading figure of the first Austrian Republic.

Certain similarities between some of the themes of
Glöckel's program and Bühler's theories on the one hand,
and ideas which infuse the later work of Wittgenstein on the
other, caused me to recall dimly that Wittgenstein had taught

elementary school in Austria in the twenties, and to wonder whether there might not be some connection. As it turned out, the connection was quite direct.

But when I began my work, the idea that there was any link between Glöckel, Bühler, and Wittgenstein was no more than the shakiest of hunches. So it was with some diffidence that I rented a car in Vienna one summer weekday morning for the long, and I feared unprofitable, drive to the remote villages of Trattenbach, Otterthal, and Puchberg, in the part of lower Austria known as Semmering or Neunkirchen, where Wittgenstein had taught from 1920 to 1926. I had no reason to suppose that anyone would remember him. Indeed, would any of the present inhabitants of these villages ever have known him? Trattenbach and Otterthal had, I had learned, been on the Russian front during the Second World War. And if anyone did remember Wittgenstein, would he or she talk about him? This part of Austria is not tourist country, and its peasants are sometimes suspicious and taciturn.

In the event, I did reach both Trattenbach and Otterthal that day; they are only about three miles apart and were until 1923 part of the same administrative community. But Puchberg had to be set aside for later visits—Trattenbach and Otterthal alone were to occupy me for weeks.

After the long climb into the hills above Gloggnitz, I pulled up to have lunch at one of the three simple inns in Otterthal. I had armed myself with the paperback edition of Malcolm's memoir of Wittgenstein, with its photo on the cover to jog failing memories, and also with a copy of Wittgenstein's letters to his friend Paul Engelmann, where Wittgenstein's German original faces the English translation and the villages are mentioned by name. So I could if necessary prove to doubters that such a man really had lived in these places. As I finished my tea, I began to look around for someone old enough to have been one of Wittgenstein's pupils, someone in his or her late fifties or early sixties. In a corner of the restaurant an old peasant woman with a bun of white hair, clad in a black dress, was busily scrubbing the floor. So I stepped over to her to ask if she might happen to remember anyone named Wittgenstein, or anyone who might have known him. I expected a bewildered apology; instead I got an explosive: "Wittgenstein! *Ludwig* Wittgenstein? Der Lehrer! Ach, freilich!" ("The teacher! Well, of course!").

The old woman asked me how he was—it turned out that she was in her early seventies—and I had to report that he had died in 1951. Not quite knowing where to begin, I pulled out Malcolm and Engelmann. The photo she declared a good likeness, while remarking that she hadn't, of course, seen him since 1926: "The trial, you know." Actually, I didn't know, but that was only one of the things I began to learn about that afternoon. Just about everyone in Trattenbach and Otterthal "knew about" Ludwig Wittgenstein (although they did not, except in one or two cases, know that he had "gone on" to become a philosopher) and many who had been his students, or whose brothers and sisters had attended his classes, still lived there.[4]

The central part of Otterthal consists of little more than a crossroads lined by small farmhouses. It was extraordinary to walk down the main road, calling out to peasants working in their gardens or sitting on their porches, and being given details in the most matter-of-fact way about a man whose name I had hitherto encountered only in books or in the conversation of philosophers and intellectuals. The remarks of these people who knew nothing of Wittgenstein's philosophy, and next to nothing of his later fame, convinced me that Ludwig Wittgenstein had been truly extraordinary.

Several hours after that first lunch I drove three miles westward down the road to Trattenbach. By then I knew that I would have to spend many days in these villages, despite my intention to do no more than look them over and take a few photographs before driving back to Vienna. I parked in front of a small general store not far from the village center and wandered in to buy some bananas. As I

---

[4]The trip reported here occurred in 1969. Since then the Wittgenstein Documentation Centre has been established in the neighbouring town of Kirchberg am Wechsel, and annual Wittgenstein congresses are held in these villages, so that the villagers now know of Wittgenstein's later achievements and reputation.

counted out the few schillings to the grocer I asked—by now routinely—whether he remembered a schoolteacher named Wittgenstein. The grocer stared at me, called for his wife to take over the store, and led me to a chair in the back room. Of course he remembered Wittgenstein: Wittgenstein had lived upstairs, in the attic of that grocery store, for nearly a year; and this grocer, Johann Scheibenbauer, had been one of his students from 1920 to 1922. It was strange, he remarked, that I had just bought bananas from him, for Ludwig Wittgenstein had given him *his* first banana—and his first orange—in those bleak postwar years when German Austria was starving. In order to feed his students, Wittgenstein had climbed for miles with packages of fruit bundled in a large knapsack on his back. In those days there was no public transportation to Trattenbach and Otterthal; those who went there hiked over twelve miles uphill through the forest from the train station at Gloggnitz, just as Wittgenstein had done.

Night had fallen before I was to take leave of Herr Scheibenbauer and those of his friends whom he had called in, in order to drive back to Vienna and make preparations for further trips and a longer stay in these villages.

III

An ulterior motive for focusing on a wholly Austrian decade in Wittgenstein's life (a decade during which he left Austria only four times—once for a two-week trip to Holland and northern Germany, once for a brief summer trip to England after an absence of over twelve years, and twice to work or holiday in Norway) is to remind those who have come to view Wittgenstein as a very English figure that in fact every decade in his life was an Austrian one, save that period of some nine years immediately before, during and after the Second World War when he was forced by circumstances quite beyond his control to remain in Britain. Any person who might be surprised by this statement would do well to reflect that the three Cambridge academic full terms are after all only eight weeks each in length, that Wittgenstein rarely arrived or lingered in Cambridge more than a few days before and after term, and that it was his habit, even in some of his most active Cambridge years, to spend twenty-five or twenty-six weeks each year in Vienna or on one of the family estates, such as the Hochreit, the country seat near Hohenberg in lower Austria that his father had bought in 1894.

If one accepts that the ways in which one styles oneself— the games one plays with one's own name—say a lot about who one is or would like to be, then how revealing it is to find out that Ludwig Wittgenstein characterized himself in the *Wiener Adreßbuch*, the Viennese City Directory, in each edition from 1933 to 1938, as "Dr Ludwig Wittgenstein, occupation: *architect*", a resident of Vienna, living, together with his sister Hermine and brother Paul, at the Palais Wittgenstein, Argentinierstraße 16. I had often heard of his schemes to become a monk, an architect, or an orchestral conductor but had hardly known how seriously to take them. Here is tangible evidence of Wittgenstein's ambivalence about his English academic attachments even during the very peak of his professional attainment in Cambridge.

Wittgenstein first went to Britain in 1908 and died there forty-three years later, a few days after his sixty-second birthday. Between 1908 and 1937 he spent a total of only about seven and one half years in England; from 1938 to 1946 he spent nine years there; from the beginning of 1947 until his death he was to spend only around twenty-one months on English soil.

Wittgenstein was not, then, one of those German-speaking intellectuals who emigrated from Germany or Austria when comparatively young and *settled* in one of the English-speaking countries. Because so many such persons exist who left Germany and Austria during the political and economic upheavals of the 1920s and 1930s, people are prone to classify Wittgenstein with these émigrés, with such persons as Rudolf Carnap and Herbert Feigl in America or Karl Popper and Friedrich Waismann in England. Wittgenstein was of an earlier generation and a different class, a member of the pre-First World War international haute bourgeoisie. Nor was English a language that he had to acquire as an adult; he grew up, like many other members of his class and others of his family, speaking fluent English and French as well as German.

In my research for this book I have, therefore, drawn principally on Austrian resources, on archives, and on people. In Vienna as well as in lower Austria I searched out Wittgenstein's former students; I tracked down the boy— then a widower in his middle sixties—whom Wittgenstein had tried hard to adopt in 1922. I had the pleasure of rounding up for an evening meal in a back room of a decrepit inn in Trattenbach most of Wittgenstein's living elementary school students there. It was during that evening reunion, in the midsummer of 1969, that one of Wittgenstein's old students, a peasant who had had no schooling since Wittgenstein had departed from Trattenbach in 1922, leaned across the table to say: "You know, there was an interesting thing that Lehrer Wittgenstein used to tell us about." And then out came the paradox of the liar![5] I have also talked with members of Wittgenstein's family and with other persons of exceptionally high culture in Vienna who had known Wittgenstein in one way or another. And I have gone to homosexual bars in Vienna and London in search of those who knew Wittgenstein in another way; and I was successful in that search. Some of the material gleaned from these encounters will be reported in the pages that follow. I have also consulted many persons in England and America, but I have deliberately refrained from consulting those who control the Wittgenstein archives, in order that this work be as independent as possible. They have complained sharply about this, but have produced nothing that conflicts with my own results. Thus, although they initially denied that he was homosexual, their own files proved to contain confirmation of my statements. (See the "Afterword, 1985".)

I hope that from my footwork—combing the streets of

---

[5]See Chapter 2, Section VII below.

the third district of Vienna, walking alone and rather apprehensively through the Prater late at night, trudging the dusty roads near Hütteldorf and in Neunkirchen, talking with those who remembered Wittgenstein, whether a toothless old school director in his attic room or some aging homosexual in his own special pub—there will emerge a more vivid picture of this period in the life of an extraordinary philosopher.

I could not begin to list the names of all who have aided me. Most of those who were especially helpful are named in the Acknowledgements. Any reader of the first chapter will understand without further ado why a few persons (to whom I am deeply indebted) asked that their names not be revealed. Those who are named have sometimes disagreed with my conclusions.

Whenever you are preoccupied with something, with some trouble or with some problem which is a big thing in your life—as sex is, for instance—then no matter what you start from, the association will lead finally and inevitably back to that same theme. Freud remarks on how, after the analysis of it, the dream appears so very logical. And of course it does .... An "Urszene" ... often has the attractiveness of giving a sort of tragic pattern to one's life. It is all the repetition of the same pattern which was settled long ago. Like a tragic figure carrying out the decrees under which the fates had placed him at birth. Many people have, at some period, serious trouble in their lives—so serious as to lead to thoughts of suicide. This is likely to appear to one as something nasty, as a situation which is too foul to be a subject of a tragedy. And it may then be an immense relief if it can be shown that one's life has the pattern rather of a tragedy—the tragic working out and repetition of a pattern.

—*Ludwig Wittgenstein*[1]

1 ◆ The Magic Carpet

I

One night in the early winter months of 1919, Ludwig Wittgenstein lay sleeping in Monte Cassino, in the camp north of Naples where he spent nine months as a prisoner of war following the fall of the Austro-Hungarian Monarchy. He dreamt as follows:

---

[1]*Lectures and Conversations on Aesthetics, Psychology and Religious Belief*, compiled from notes taken by Yorick Smythies, Rush Rhees, and James Taylor, ed. Cyril Barrett (Berkeley: University of California Press, 1967), pp. 50-51.

It was night. I was outside a house whose windows blazed with light. I went up to a window to look inside. There, on the floor, I noticed an exquisitely beautiful prayer rug, one which I immediately wanted to examine. I tried to open the front door, but a snake darted out to prevent me from entering; I tried another door, but there too a snake darted out to block my way. Snakes appeared also at the windows, and blocked my every effort to reach the prayer rug.

Wittgenstein awoke, and later referred to this as "the first dream".[2]

Wittgenstein had at that time read only a little Freud and was not to begin to read Freud with any care until later that year, after his return to Vienna. But his immediate interpretation of his own dream was straightforward and Freudian. The prayer rug, so he thought, symbolized that for which he had sought for years in vain and for which he was to continue to search for most of the rest of his life: an integration of his libido, a sublimation, for intellectual and spiritual purposes, of his sexual drives. For what does a prayer rug look like? Its central feature is a form rather like that of an erect penis. But this tremendous energy, transformed into a work of art, is *contained* within strong and beautiful borders. Wittgenstein's own situation was not that depicted by the rug-mandala, that goal for which he searched. Rather, at that time his own spiritual progress was checked and thwarted by the loose, ugly, *uncontained* serpents which haunted both his waking and his dreaming hours.

The dream also commented on the ironic contrast between the public and private Wittgenstein. Already in 1919, long before the publication of his *Tractatus Logico-Philosophicus*, Ludwig Wittgenstein was considered by many to be the finest philosophic talent of his generation; and today many still consider him the greatest philosopher of his time.

---

[2]Unless otherwise indicated, my information is based on conversations and other communications with friends of Wittgenstein, as explained in the Introduction and the Acknowledgements. My information is corroborated by Wittgenstein's own diaries, as explained in the "Afterword, 1985".

He was, so his teacher and friend Bertrand Russell wrote, "perhaps the most perfect example I have ever known of genius as traditionally conceived, passionate, profound, intense, and dominating. He had a kind of purity which I have never known equalled except by G. E. Moore".[3] Yet this pure and intense genius who himself wrote that he would like to die in a moment of brilliance[4] was also a homosexual given to bouts of extravagant and almost uncontrollable promiscuity.

Throughout his life, but especially during and following the First World War, Wittgenstein was tormented by intense guilt and suffering over his sexual desires and activities. Like thousands of his contemporaries, Wittgenstein had become convinced that the sort of high spiritual and intellectual creativity that he craved was virtually incompatible with sexual activity. It is often remarked that Wittgenstein admired the work of Otto Weininger but rarely explained that Weininger's fame stemmed from his extraordinary misogyny, his sustained and impassioned argument that women are inevitably inferior to men.[5] Although Weininger rather reluctantly concedes that women are human, he argues vehemently that they lack souls and are incapable of genius. Worse, physical contact with women despiritualizes men.

---

[3]Bertrand Russell, *Autobiography* (London: George Allen and Unwin, 1968), vol. II, p. 136. Leonard Woolf contests Russell's description in the final volume of his own memoirs, speaking of Wittgenstein's aggressively cruel streak. See Leonard Woolf, *The Journey Not the Arrival Matters* (London: Hogarth Press, 1969), p. 48.

[4]Paul Engelmann, *Letters from Ludwig Wittgenstein, with a Memoir* (Oxford: Basil Blackwell, 1967), p. 57.

[5]Weininger committed suicide not long after his book was published; and the claim has been made by Roland Jaccard, editor of the French edition of *Geschlecht und Charakter*, that there is evidence that Wittgenstein attended Weininger's funeral. Wittgenstein would have been only fourteen years old at the time (1903); and if this report is true he may well have read *Sex and Character* shortly after its publication. See the back cover of *Sexe et caractère* (Lausanne, 1975), and Alan Janik, "Wittgenstein and Weininger", in *Wittgenstein and His Impact on Contemporary Thought: Proceedings of the Second International Wittgenstein Symposium* (Vienna: Hölder-Pichler-Tempsky, 1978), pp. 25 and 29.

Thus Weininger advocated absolute sexual abstinence as a precondition of spiritual development and genius. Those today who tend to dismiss Weininger as a crank must remember, if they are to understand the subterranean currents of Central European thought before and after the First World War, that many of Weininger's contemporaries took him dead seriously: between 1903 and 1923, *Geschlecht und Charakter (Sex and Character)* went through twenty-five editions, and by 1923 the book had been translated into some eight tongues. Sigmund Freud, who had read Weininger's book in manuscript,[6] incorporated similar views about the clash between sexual activity and high spirituality in his own theory of sublimation, and is said to have abandoned sexual activity for this reason—as also did Gandhi.[7] Wittgenstein's English contemporary, J. D. Unwin, pushed such an outlook a step further in his own best-selling book *Sex and Culture*, in which, after examining some eighty societies, he came to the conclusion—one that he claimed harmonized with Freudian teaching—that anthropological evidence established sexual promiscuity and cultural achievement to be inversely proportional. Yet another of Wittgenstein's heroes, Leo Tolstoy, eventually, though reluctantly, also came to advocate celibacy.[8]

I have mentioned only comparatively well-known names, and names of thinkers who—with the possible exception of Gandhi—influenced Wittgenstein.[9] Another quite obscure

---

[6]Vincent Brome, *Freud and His Early Circle* (New York: William Morrow and Company, Inc., 1968), p. 9.

[7]See Sigmund Freud, *Civilization and Its Discontents*, or *Two Short Accounts of Psycho-Analysis* (Penguin Books, 1962), and many passages in Freud's writings. See also Ernest Jones, *The Life and Work of Sigmund Freud* (New York: Basic Books, 1953-57); and Erik H. Erikson, *Gandhi's Truth* (New York: W. W. Norton and Company, Inc., 1969).

[8]Leo Tolstoy, "What I believe", in vol. II of *The Works of Leo Tolstoy* (London: Oxford University Press, 1933), pp. 526-27; but more especially in his *Kreutzer Sonata* and in the *Afterword* thereto.

[9]As is well known, Wittgenstein was especially fond of the work of the Indian poet Rabindranath Tagore. Thus it is by no means impossible that Wittgenstein also knew of Gandhi's teaching. Tagore did know and write about Gandhi, and Gandhi too had been much inspired by Tolstoy.

writer also needs mentioning here, for possibly he had the profoundest effect of all: Dr. Ludwig Hänsel, with whom Wittgenstein struck up a friendship during their internment at Monte Cassino. An Austrian like himself, Hänsel was then already a schoolteacher by profession, and later became professor at a Gymnasium in Vienna. A puritanical Roman Catholic of talents far inferior to those of Wittgenstein, Hänsel nonetheless played a role akin to spiritual adviser and father confessor to Wittgenstein throughout his life. Although Hänsel had some philosophical pretensions (Wittgenstein had met him at a course in logic which Hänsel was conducting in the POW camp), his primary concern was with education, and a subject that deeply concerned him there was the sexual purity of boys. Some years later he published *Die Jugend und die leibliche Liebe (Youth and Carnal Love)*, a polemical tract against masturbation (contrary to nature and damaging to body and soul), against homosexuality, and against Freud, who "unfortunately had no understanding of morals and religion".[10] Evidently, although he had no illusions about Hänsel's talents, Wittgenstein came to rely on him for an odd sort of moral support. His encounter with Hänsel also played a significant role in leading Wittgenstein himself to become a schoolteacher on his release from the prisoner-of-war camp.[11]

---

[10]Ludwig Hänsel, *Die Jugend und die leibliche Liebe: Sexualpädagogische Betrachtungen* (Innsbruck-Vienna-Munich: Tryolia Verlag, 1938), bearing the imprimatur of the Viennese archdiocese of 8 January 1938.

[11]It must be a matter of speculation whether, as Freudian theory would suggest, Wittgenstein's striving for abstinence, and his actual practice of it for long periods, is connected with the agoraphobia and acrophobia from which he suffered. F. R. Leavis testified to Wittgenstein's agoraphobia in "Memories of Wittgenstein", in Rush Rhees, *Ludwig Wittgenstein: Personal Recollection* (Totowa, N.J.: Rowman & Littlefield, 1981), p. 73; M. O'C. Drury reports Wittgenstein's acrophobia in "Conversations with Wittgenstein", in Rhees, ibid., p. 115. See Sigmund Freud, "The Justification for Detaching from Neurasthenia a Particular Syndrome: The Anxiety-Neurosis", in his *Collected Papers* (New York: Basic Books, 1959), vol. I, pp. 76-106; and "Obsessions and Phobias", pp. 128-137.

II

What Wittgenstein called his "second dream" came to him some two years later, possibly in early December 1920, in Trattenbach. A rather more complicated dream, it goes as follows:

> I was a priest. In the front hall of my house there was an altar; to the right of the altar a stairway led off. It was a grand stairway carpeted in red, rather like that at the Alleegasse.[12] At the foot of the altar, and partly covering it, was an oriental carpet. And certain other religious objects and regalia were placed on and beside the altar. One of these was a rod of precious metal.
>
> But a theft occurred. A thief entered from the left and stole the rod. This had to be reported to the police, who sent a representative who wanted a description of the rod. For instance, of what sort of metal was it made? I could not say; I could not even say whether it was of silver or of gold. The police officer questioned whether the rod had ever existed in the first place. I then began to examine the other parts and fittings of the altar and noticed that the carpet was a prayer rug. My eyes began to focus on the border of the rug. The border was lighter in colour than the beautiful center. In a curious way it seemed to be faded. It was, nonetheless, still strong and firm.

Wittgenstein was never confident about how to interpret this dream, but he regarded it as most important: it is one source of his conviction that he had been "called",[13] and of

---

[12]The reference is to the Palais Wittgenstein, home of Wittgenstein's parents and family, purchased in 1890 by his father. It was located on Alleegasse, a street that was later renamed the Argentinierstraße. Seriously bombed during the Second World War, the building has since been demolished.

[13]See Ludwig Hänsel, "Ludwig Wittgenstein (1889-1951)", in *Wissenschaft und Weltbild, Monatschrift für alle Gebiete der Forschung*, vol. VIII, October 4, 1951, pp. 315-23, especially p. 322: "One night, during the time when he was a teacher, he had the feeling that he had been called but had refused."

his recurring notion that he ought perhaps to become a monk. Shortly after experiencing this dream he acquired a walking stick, which he carried constantly for many years.

Both of Wittgenstein's dreams are beautiful; both are deeply religious; in both dreams—in the first dream at the beginning, in the second dream at the end—attention comes to rest on the prayer rug, with its contained and spiritualized phallus. In the second dream Wittgenstein himself is serving at the sacrificial altar, which occupies a central place between the stairs at the right and an undefined *sinister* place at the left, wherein and wherefrom such things as thefts can originate. Wittgenstein, who by the time he had this dream had read a lot of Freud, made the association just mentioned between right and left, and identified the stairs as symbols indicating an upward path toward spiritual growth. The rod seemed at once obvious and bewildering. It was in an obvious sense a phallic object, and one rich in associations with serpents. For example, in Exodus (Chapters 4 and 7) the rods of Moses and Aaron, when cast on the ground, became serpents; and Aaron's rod devours the serpent-rods of the Egyptian magicians. A double reference to Aaron's rod is possible here: in the seventeenth chapter of the Biblical book of Numbers, Aaron, the first high priest of the Israelites, and his descendants in perpetuity are set apart from the rest of Israel for the priesthood following an incident when Aaron's rod, placed beside rods representing each of the tribes of Israel, quickly buds, blossoms, and bears almonds. Aaron's rod then became one of the most sacred religious objects of the wandering Israelites and was placed in the Ark of the Covenant along with the pot of manna and the tables of the Law. Wittgenstein discussed the connections I have just mentioned, but they appear to have come to him as suggestions for interpretation from some other party, possibly from Hänsel, who, unlike Wittgenstein, was well acquainted with the Old Testament. It puzzled Wittgenstein to think that *if* such an interpretation were to be attached to the dream, it would be *his* dream. An object made of precious metal more likely to be stolen would, at least in the Christian ritual, be the grail or chalice, long associated in myth and legend with the female. Possibly Wittgenstein's homosexuality would account for the absence from his dream's altar of the chalice and the substitution of a more archaic, more masculine symbol of the rod. Wittgenstein found this idea a speculative dead end.[14]

An interpretation which struck him as more likely, and which occurred to him spontaneously, was to regard the rod as both a phallic symbol and a *pestle*, as in the mortar and pestle of chemists and alchemists. For some sort of transformation, including a possible transmutation of substance, seems to be indicated in the dream. At first, attention is focused on the rod of precious metal; it disappears, the preciousness of its metal is doubted—in effect, precious metal is transformed into base metal; and then the rod's very existence is questioned. Only then is attention transferred to the prayer rug, wherein the rod reappears in spiritualized form.

As for the thief and the policeman, two other figures in the dream, Wittgenstein made associations of a fairly routine sort. The theft of the rod from the altar he associated with the Promethean theft of fire from the gods; the police, with the voice of conscience or parental authority. But he was never able to weave the various components of the dream into a coherent whole. And it would be foolhardy to make any such attempt over sixty years after the dream occurred, and more than thirty years after Wittgenstein's death.

What does strike one is the connection between this dream and the first dream. The prayer rug recurs. But in the second dream the rod-serpent, which had been so active and forbidding in the first dream, is snatched away, and it is even suggested that it is illusory, a kind of *maya*. The prayer rug, on the other hand, no longer furnishes a room but rather

---

[14]The altar itself, however, can, especially in the Indian traditions, be interpreted as a feminine symbol. Thus Heinrich Zimmer writes: "The fiery lingam is a form of the Axis Mundi, and can be equated with the shaft of light or lightning . . . that penetrates and fertilises the yoni, the altar, the Earth, the mother of the Fire . . . ." See Heinrich Zimmer, *Myths and Symbols in Indian Art and Civilization* (New York: Harper and Row, 1962), p. 128.

31

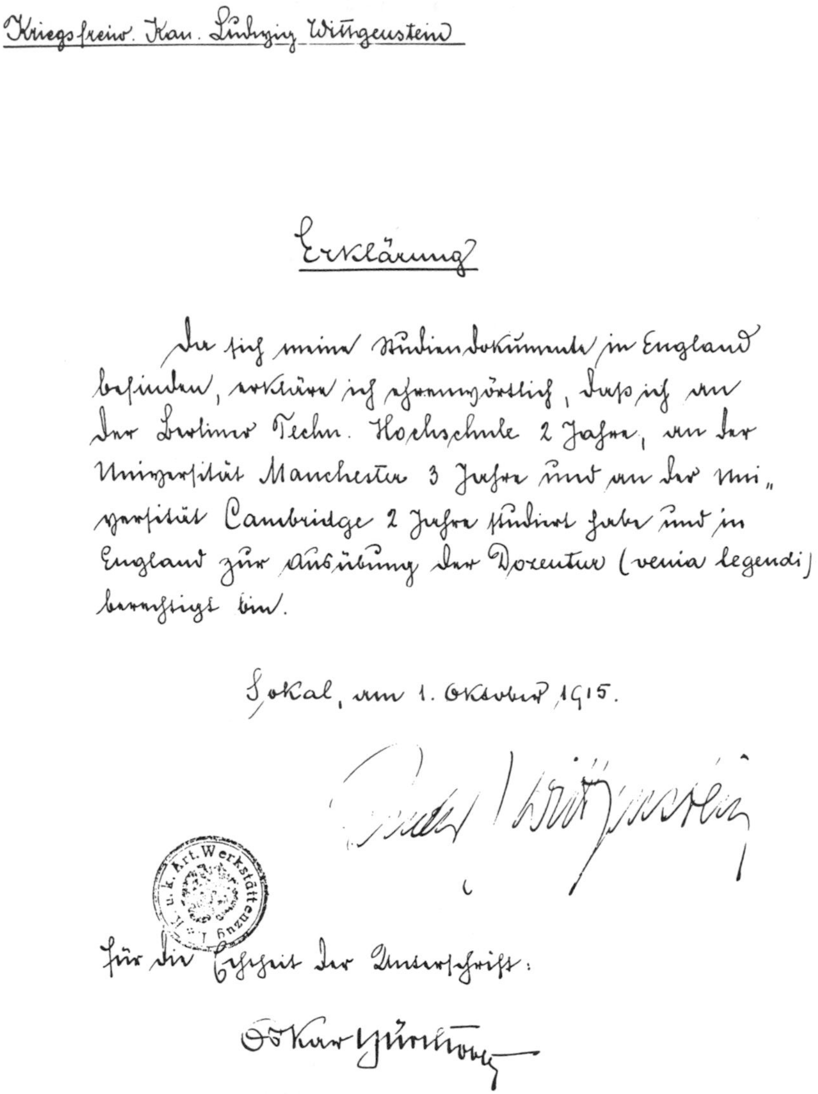

Kriegsfreiw. Kan. Ludwig Wittgenstein

Erklärung

Da sich meine Studiendokumente in England befinden, erkläre ich ehrenwörtlich, daß ich an der Berliner Techn. Hochschule 2 Jahre, an der Universität Manchester 3 Jahre und an der Universität Cambridge 2 Jahre studiert habe und in England zur Ausübung der Dozentur (venia legendi) berechtigt bin.

Sokal, am 1. Oktober 1915.

Ludwig Wittgenstein

k. u. k. Art. Werkstättenzug

Für die Echtheit der Unterschrift:

Oskar Gürth

This declaration, signed by Wittgenstein, was written on 1 October 1915 by his commanding officer, Oskar Gürth. It testifies that Wittgenstein's education qualifies him for a lectureship in a British University, and was put forward as part of an application for promotion. (Kriegsarchiv, Vienna)

adorns an altar of sacrifice, and it may be closely examined by the tortured philosopher-priest who serves at that altar. Yet the prayer rug is strangely unnoticed by this priest until *after* the disappearance of the phallic rod. It was as if the integrated spiritualized phallus became accessible to him only after the disappearance—the theft or even self-castration—of the rod.

The dream is fascinating, and could be examined at great length. What is important here is that Wittgenstein regarded it as a "good dream", pointing toward a resolution of his fundamental conflict, and that it came at a time when he was working out a self-protective pattern to shield him from his most extreme tendencies toward promiscuously homosexual behavior. Such action seemed to him to be urgently necessary, for the conflict which is so vividly portrayed in the first dream had come to a head in his life during the year preceding the second dream. Indeed, it virtually exploded within him in October 1919 and again in April 1920.

III

That October of 1919 had proved to be one of the cruelest months that Wittgenstein was to endure, cruel not only because of his intense hatred of the actions he performed during its passing weeks, but also because the pattern of behavior fixed during this interlude was to return repeatedly to torture him. It would have been hard for him in the best of times, but he was, in fact, at his lowest ebb physically and psychologically.

Wittgenstein had reached Neuwaldegg, the family summer home in Vienna, from Monte Cassino on Monday, 25 August 1919. The following day his military discharge was made official. It had been little more than a year that Wittgenstein had spent away from Vienna; early the preceding August, on military leave at Neuwaldegg, he had brought to completion the book which later came to be called the *Tractatus Logico-Philosophicus* and had submitted it to the publishers Jahoda and Siegel. In the few months following

Wittgenstein's departure from Vienna for the very last phase of the war, his and his family's situation had been transformed. On 13 August 1918, Wittgenstein's favorite uncle, Paul Wittgenstein, whom, together with Bertrand Russell, he had thanked in the preface to his newly completed manuscript, had died. By the 25th of October, 1918, Wittgenstein knew that Jahoda had rejected his manuscript; two days later Ludwig's brother Kurt shot himself when the troops under his command abandoned the field. On 3 November Wittgenstein himself had been taken prisoner at Trent by Italian troops; when he was captured he was riding on the gun carriage, whistling to himself the second movement of Beethoven's Seventh Symphony. The Austro-Hungarian Monarchy had tottered and fallen and had been dismembered; the Revolution had occurred; news had reached Wittgenstein that his Cambridge friend David Pinsent, whom he had loved deeply, had been killed in action the preceding May. After nine months in prison, a physically and mentally debilitated Ludwig Wittgenstein returned to Vienna to find himself the only son of Karl Wittgenstein who remained reasonably intact. He was greeted by his mother, widowed in January 1913; his eldest and favorite sister, Hermine, known as Mining; his sister Margarete Stonborough, whom he both loved and fought all his life; his sister Helene Salzer, whom he disliked; and his brother Paul, hailed at his debut in 1913 as one of the most promising pianists in Europe. Paul had lost his right arm on the Russian front early in the war and had been returned to Vienna where, with remarkable energy, he learned to play the piano prodigiously well with his left hand alone. Ironically, all that were really relatively intact in the family were the estates and the fortune; indeed, Wittgenstein returned to Vienna one of the richest men in Europe.

Before his death on 20 January 1913, Karl Wittgenstein, founder of the Austrian iron and steel industry, had transferred virtually all his liquid capital into American stocks and bonds, principally in the United States Steel Corporation. And thus the fortune, which was giving Ludwig alone an annual income of 300,000 Kronen (gold crowns) in 1914, prior to the start of the war,[15] had been vastly augmented by the prosperity of the nation whose forces had helped bring about his own country's defeat. As for the money that had been left in Austria during the war, for the most part Karl Wittgenstein's brother Ludwig, who had managed it, invested it in government bonds. But prior to the end of the war and the great inflation, he had sold most of the war bonds to buy real estate, one of the few things in Austria whose value was augmented by the inflation. Nor was the fortune to be dissipated in the years that followed. What was needed for the operating costs of the family was returned as required to Austria. But the bulk of the fortune was, for most of the interwar period, invested in Holland, relatively safe from the inflation that wiped out many rich families of Germany and Austria.

It takes little imagination to perceive how such a contradictory situation would have affected a man of the sensitivity of Ludwig Wittgenstein. Although his brother Paul and he would eventually become more famous than their father, there was little at that moment to suggest that they were other than a cripple and an exhausted veteran, the latter on the brink of suicide. Ludwig now talked of suicide incessantly, thereby—and with good reason—terrifying his sisters Mining and Margarete.

Kurt, it has been noted, took his life at the very end of the war. He was the third Wittgenstein brother to commit suicide. The eldest brother, Hans, a musical genius who had begun composing when four years old, had taken his life in Havana, Cuba, in April 1902, in his twenty-fourth year. The third son, Rudolf, killed himself in Berlin on 2 May 1904. Both Hans and Rudolf were known to be homosexual.[16]

---

[15]Stated in army records; the actual income, from various sources, was probably much larger. According to a very conservative estimate by Austrian National Bank authorities in Vienna, 300,000 Kronen (1914) would be equivalent in buying power for 1969 to 4,587,000 Austrian schillings, or approximately $185,000.00 If so, the capital on which the income was based could easily have been the 1969 equivalent of two million U.S. dollars. This would depend, of course, on how the income-producing money was invested and managed.

[16]Magnus Hirschfeld's *Jahrbuch für sexuelle Zwischenstufen* vol. VI,

In addition to these suicides within his immediate family, another suicide, apart from Weininger's, had affected Ludwig deeply: Ludwig Boltzmann, the great Austrian physicist with whom the adolescent Ludwig Wittgenstein had aspired to study, committed suicide in 1906, the year of Wittgenstein's graduation from secondary school.

In such a context there is no reason to suppose that Wittgenstein was less than serious in his own talk of suicide. He had, in fact, been thinking and talking of suicide for years under far less trying circumstances than those he faced in 1919. In 1912, when he was twenty-three, Ludwig confessed to David Pinsent that he had suffered from a terrible loneliness for some nine years, with thoughts of suicide constantly in his mind. That nine-year period to which Wittgenstein referred must have begun somewhere between 1902 and 1904, a time of enormous crisis and strain for all the members of his family, and perhaps especially for Ludwig, who, at fourteen years of age, may be presumed to have been undergoing the usual crises of puberty. In 1913, Wittgenstein had alarmed Bertrand Russell with talk of suicide. In

---

(1904), p. 724, reports Rudolf Wittgenstein's death as follows: "Yesterday evening, around 9:45, the twenty-three-year-old student of chemistry, Rudolf Wittgenstein, Uhlandstraße 170, Berlin, the son of a Viennese businessman, came into an inn in Brandenburgstraße and ordered two glasses of milk. After he had sat there a while, very disturbed, he had a bottle of Selters given to the piano player, and requested him to play his favorite song, 'I am lost'. As the musician played, the student took cyanide and collapsed onto his chair. The innkeeper brought in three doctors from the neighborhood, but it was too late, and the poisoned youth died under their hands. Wittgenstein left behind several farewell letters. To his parents he wrote that he had taken his life because a friend of his was dead, without whom he no longer wanted to remain in the world. On another page it was reported that the young man had committed suicide out of doubts about his perverted disposition." The preceding paragraph is quoted by the *Jahrbuch* from an unspecified Berlin newspaper, with the following commentary: "The unfortunate youth had some time earlier introduced himself in our [Scientific-Humanitarian] committee, but our influence did not reach far enough to turn him away from the fate of self-destruction." The Scientific-Humanitarian Committee, founded by Hirschfeld in 1897, was the German homosexual emancipation organization.

1920 Wittgenstein told his schoolteacher colleague Martin Scherleitner, in Trattenbach, that he had originally volunteered to serve in the First World War in order to find death, as a method of suicide; and the theme of suicide recurs repeatedly in Wittgenstein's wartime and postwar correspondence with his friend Paul Engelmann.

In these circumstances, Wittgenstein made two decisions on his arrival in Vienna. The first, which he had already formed during his internment,[17] and which had been urged on him by Hänsel, was to prepare for a career as an elementary schoolteacher. His family initially was repelled by the idea. Mining, for instance, at first found her brother's decision incomprehensible. "I told him", she wrote, "that imagining him with his philosophically trained mind as an elementary school teacher it was to me as if someone were to use a precision instrument to open crates". But Wittgenstein firmly replied to her: "You remind me of someone who is looking through a closed window and cannot explain to himself the strange movements of a passer-by. He doesn't know what kind of a storm is raging outside and that this person is perhaps only with great effort keeping himself on his feet."[18] Only then, Mining writes, did she understand his state of mind.

Once they understood the state he was in, both Mining and Margarete accepted school teaching as work therapy for their brother, and it was probably Margarete who had informed him on his return of the new teaching possibilities in the "School-Reform Movement" (to be discussed below) and who made arrangements for him through her friend

---

[17]Wittgenstein's fellow prisoner-of-war, Franz Parak, confirms that Wittgenstein had already decided, during his internment, to become a schoolteacher. See his "Ludwig Wittgensteins Verhältnis zum Christentum", in *Wittgenstein and His Impact on Contemporary Thought*, p. 91. See also Parak's book *Wittgenstein Prigionero a Cassino* (Rome: Armando Armando, 1978).

[18]Quoted in "Excerpts from chapters V and VI of the Family Recollections", written by Hermine Wittgenstein in the early 1940s. Printed in Bernhard Leitner, *The Architecture of Ludwig Wittgenstein: A Documentation* (Halifax: The Press of the Nova Scotia College of Art and Design, 1973).

Otto Glöckel, leader and administrative head of Austrian school reform—who had attained political power just a few months before, in the spring of 1919.

At any rate, Wittgenstein reported his decision to Engelmann on the second of September, just one week after his discharge from the army, and by 16 September he was enrolled in the Teachers Training College in the Kundmanngasse, one of the first such colleges operating under Glöckel's general direction, where he was permitted to enter in the fourth and final year.

Wittgenstein's second step was to divest himself of his fortune. His companion in the prisoner-of-war camp at Monte Cassino, Franz Parak, claims that Wittgenstein thought himself simply to be following the Gospel, which they had read together in prison, with its advice to the rich man (Matthew 19:21): "If thou wilt be perfect, go and sell what thou hast, and give to the poor, and thou shalt have treasure in heaven: and come and follow me."[19] Whatever its source, the idea was insisted on by Wittgenstein with almost insane passion. A member of his family reports that he caused enormous commotion by appearing suddenly at his bankers one morning to declare that he wanted nothing more to do with his money and that it must be disposed of forthwith. In accordance with his wishes, the entire liquid fortune was given to his brothers and sisters (with the exception of Margarete).[20] Rather elaborate steps had to be taken formally to distribute the money as Wittgenstein wished, with special measures being taken to ensure that none of the money at that time under temporary sequestration in America should ever come into Wittgenstein's hands. Despite the commotion—and despite the Gospel injunction—there was no thought of charity

---

[19]Parak, "Ludwig Wittgensteins Verhältnis zum Christentum", pp. 91-92.

[20]In the "Family Recollections", Mining writes: "He gave it all to us, his brothers and sisters, with the exception of our sister, Gretl, who at that time was still very wealthy, while we had forfeited much of our wealth." See also the republication of Mining's account in Rhees, ed., *Ludwig Wittgenstein: Personal Recollections*, p. 4.

in the transfer, and the decision seems to have been carefully reviewed by the family. Ludwig Wittgenstein was considered by his brother and sisters, and in particular by his Uncle Ludwig, to be in no condition to look after his inheritance in any case; there was the threat of suicide, with the possibility of further complications connected with death duty attached to a widely dispersed and partly sequestered fortune. So Uncle Ludwig approved the transfer to Mining, Helene, and Paul, with the implicit but strictly informal understanding that they should in effect hold it in trust for him. At first it was proposed that his money be held undivided, and held *formally* in trust by his siblings, so that he could recover it if he ever wished; but he rejected this plan, and the money was shared out.[21] The money was so held until the middle and late thirties when—with the approach of war and the possibility that the money would be confiscated by the Nazis in case Wittgenstein's siblings were ruled to be Jews under the Nuremberg laws—it was distributed among Wittgenstein's nephews and nieces.

These steps having been taken, Wittgenstein moved from the shelter of his family at Neuwaldegg on the outskirts of Vienna, and, also refusing to live at the Palais Wittgenstein, the town mansion near the city center, took up lodgings nearby, in rooms on Untere Viaduktgasse in Vienna's third district. These quarters, only ten minutes' walk from the Palais Wittgenstein on the Alleegasse, were apparently selected by Wittgenstein in large measure for their convenience to both home and school. Untere Viaduktgasse was

---

[21]The various participants in this plan had differing ideas about what was involved and expected. Thus Mining, in her recollections, wrote: "To this mentality of Ludwig's belonged a completely free and relaxed possibility of permitting his brothers and sisters to help him in any situation." (*Ibid.*, p. 4.) Yet Wittgenstein wrote to G. E. Moore on 18 June 1929, when the suggestion was made that the Wittgenstein family, rather than Trinity College, should subsidize his research: "Will you please accept my written declaration that: not only I have a number of wealthy relations, but also that they would give me money if I asked them to. BUT THAT I WILL NOT ASK THEM FOR A PENNY." See Ludwig Wittgenstein, *Letters to Russell, Keynes and Moore*, ed. G. H. von Wright (Oxford: Basil Blackwell, 1974), p. 154.

close not only to the family palace on the edge of the fourth district but also to his sister Margarete's flat on the Rennweg; and it was only six streets to the north of the Kundmanngasse, where stood the Teachers Training College which he was now attending, and where he was later to build a great house for his sister. By 25 September 1919, he was settled in Untere Viaduktgasse, and the month of October, described at the beginning of this section as his cruelest month, was about to begin—although in retrospect, it is just possible that the source of his suffering during October was also what prevented him from taking his life.

IV

Wittgenstein was now to find the third district, selected for its convenience, convenient in an unexpected way. By walking for ten minutes to the east, down Marxergasse and over the Sophienbrücke (now called the Rotundenbrücke), he could quickly reach the parkland meadows of the Prater, where rough young men were ready to cater to him sexually. Once he had discovered this place, Wittgenstein found to his horror that he could scarcely keep away from it. Several nights each week he would break away from his rooms and make the quick walk to the Prater, possessed, as he put it to friends, by a demon he could barely control. Wittgenstein found he much preferred the sort of rough blunt homosexual youth that he could find strolling the paths and alleys of the Prater to those ostensibly more refined young men who frequented the Sirk Ecke in the Kärntnerstraße and the neighboring bars at the edge of the inner city. And it was to this particular spot—still used for the same purpose at night, and still about as dangerous—that Wittgenstein was to hie almost as long as he lived in or visited Vienna. Similarly, in later years in England he was from time to time to flee the fashionable and intellectual young men who might have been ready to place themselves at his disposal, in favor of the company of tough boys in London pubs.[22]

---

[22]I do not claim, in this passage, that Wittgenstein was in the habit of

Happily, Wittgenstein now became the close friend of a heterosexual young automobile mechanic, Arvid Sjögren, who was later to marry into the Wittgenstein family. He had known Sjögren, whose father and maternal grandfather were both directors in the Wittgenstein steel enterprise, since childhood. By November, Wittgenstein had moved far from the third district into the large and pleasant home of Sjögren and his family in Hietzing, from which he had to ride the Stadtbahn to attend school and visit his family. By living closely and intimately with the Sjögrens, Wittgenstein began to experience a way of protecting himself from himself. But in April 1920 he was forced to break off his association with Sjögren temporarily, and literally to flee from the Sjögren household: Sjögren's mother had fallen in love with him! The story has the makings of a comic opera; but for Wittgenstein personally it was a tragic accident, for he returned, almost inevitably, to rooms in the third district, this time in the Rasumofskygasse, even closer to the Sophienbrücke and to the Prater. It was during this period that he engaged in perhaps the most promiscuous behavior of his life. On May 30, referring to his way of life, he wrote to his friend Paul Engelmann in Olmütz: "Things have gone utterly miserably for me lately. Of course only because of my own baseness and rottenness. I have continually thought about taking my own life, and now too this thought still haunts me. *I have sunk to the bottom.* May you never be in that position!"[23]

---

drinking or of consuming alcohol himself. Nonetheless, to dispute my claims concerning Wittgenstein and his homosexuality, and my accuracy generally, Rush Rhees contests this passage, remarking that he has "never known anyone who has seen Wittgenstein in a pub of any sort. He practically never took any kind of alcoholic drink. This was not a matter of principle. He just didn't. . . . He never objected if other people drank. But he did not drink himself", Rush Rhees, "Wittgenstein", *The Human World*, February 1974, p. 69. Contrast this with the testimony of Frances Partridge, *Love in Bloomsbury: Memories* (Boston: Little, Brown and Company, 1981), pp. 159-60. Writing of Wittgenstein, Partridge states: "He entered into a disastrous habit current in Cambridge at that time of mixing absolute alcohol from the labs with different flavours to make anything from port to crème de menthe."

[23]Engelmann, *Letters from Wittgenstein*, p. 32.

V

When one is terrified, as was Wittgenstein, of what one might do, one may attempt to construct an environment that will help to protect one from doing what one in a sense wants but must not do. Wittgenstein himself put the point in his notebooks, writing: "The way to solve the problem you see in life is to live in a way that will make what is problematic disappear. The fact that life is problematic shows that the shape of your life does not fit into life's mould. So you must change the way you live and, once your life does fit into the mould, what is problematic will disappear." Later he added: "Put a man in the wrong atmosphere and nothing will function as it should. He will seem unhealthy in every part. Put him back into his proper element and everything will blossom and look healthy."[24] Wittgenstein attempted to put his own advice into practice; and in the pattern of his construction is to be found some explanation for some of his odder actions.

Wittgenstein would seek milieux or situations satisfying two conditions: to be removed from the temptation of easy and casual sexual relationships with street youths, and such like; and to be surrounded by youths with whom he could enjoy platonic relationships that would "bring him to life". Thus a series of close friendships developed with good-looking young men of sweet and docile disposition, some insight, but no "cleverness", toward whom Wittgenstein could become emotionally very much attached. Such young men have been characterized as the "type" for whom Wittgenstein "fell" repeatedly, from his youth to the final decade of his life. It was in this way and in part to play this role that many young men, including some of his favored Cambridge friends and students, entered his life.[25] All were physically

---

[24]Ludwig Wittgenstein, *Culture and Value*, ed. G. H. von Wright (Chicago: University of Chicago Press, 1980), pp. 27e and 42e.

[25]With one of these Cambridge friends, Francis Skinner, his relationship did become sexual. (See the Afterword to this book.) One of Wittgenstein's students at Cambridge in the 1940s, Professor Georg Kreisel, reports that Wittgenstein often broached the subject of sex in conversations; but Kreisel

The Magic Carpet

attractive, "with nice faces", as Wittgenstein put it. All of them he could dominate easily, and he could relax in their company. And their companionship would distract and protect him from the loneliness that he hated,[26] the loneliness that would send him stalking into the night in search of sex. The other strategy that Wittgenstein used to protect himself from himself was simply to avoid "danger areas", such as Vienna, Manchester, and London, where casual and impersonal sex without any intellectual or spiritual dimension was easily come by: thus his monklike retreats to Norway, to the isolated villages of Semmering in lower Austria, and even to Cambridge.

Ludwig Wittgenstein's friendships, then, he used as moral encounters; within them he became creative, intimate, even playful. Sex was immoral; by and large it was not for friends.

And so Wittgenstein was to live. His life was lived in a kind of mourning, as it were, that he could not escape from sex entirely. For there recurred throughout his life episodes which he regarded as relapses, during which he would plunge into fleeting relationships with anonymous youths encountered in the dark and never met again. The second dream, the dream which he regarded as a token of his "call", haunted him after such episodes, and he condemned himself ruthlessly for his adventures. Not long after his second dream, on the second of January 1921, Wittgenstein wrote again to Englemann:

---

turned these aside because "it was certainly painful to me . . . to hear an old man talk of things that were intended only for us young chaps", and because "from what Wittgenstein said, I had the impression that he proceeded chiefly from his own fantasies, and not from manifold experience. For that reason the theme mentioned [sex] was particularly inappropriate". See Georg Kreisel, "Zu Wittgensteins Gesprächen und Vorlesungen über die Grundlagen der Mathematik", in *Wittgenstein and His Impact on Contemporary Thought*, pp. 79-81, esp. p. 81, note 7.

[26]For evidence of Wittgenstein's dislike and even fear of being alone, see Kurt Wuchterl and Adolf Hübner, *Wittgenstein* (Hamburg: Rowohlt, 1979), p. 91; and Wittgenstein, *Letters to Russell, Keynes and Moore*, p. 120.

I have been morally dead for more than a year . . . . I am one of those cases which perhaps are not all that rare today: I had a task, did not do it, and now the failure is wrecking my life. I ought to have done something positive with my life, to have become a star in the sky. Instead of which I remained stuck on earth, and now I am gradually fading out. My life has really become meaningless and so it consists only of futile episodes. The people around me do not notice this and would not understand; but I know that I have a fundamental deficiency. Be glad of it, if you don't understand what I am writing here.

As one reads this wistful, sad, and moving letter, one can almost see Wittgenstein gazing in through that forbidding window or standing before his altar, his eyes trained on the prayer-rug treasure that he was never quite to obtain. Yet we know today that what he wrote in his letter was hardly correct. Far from gradually fading out, his star was to soar during the next fifty years, and to transform philosophical activity. It is sometimes said that Wittgenstein lived his life on the edge of madness. It is just possible that those "futile episodes" which he occasionally permitted himself provided the sort of release that helped keep him sane and alive. Weininger, after all, did commit suicide.

2 ◆ The Proposition

I

During these years immediately following the war, the manuscript of Wittgenstein's *Tractatus Logico-Philosophicus* was being shuttled forlornly from publisher to publisher. The details of the many rejections, and the numerous misunderstandings and delays which kept it from being published in book form until 1922, have been carefully chronicled by Georg Henrik von Wright.[1] Wittgenstein had titled the manuscript "Der Satz", or "The Proposition", and it was not until shortly before publication that the book acquired the Latin title suggested by G. E. Moore.[2]

If one is to have any hope of seeing what connection the *Tractatus* might have with Wittgenstein's life, the first question to ask about it is this: Why was this book about propositions—statements of scientific fact—written in the first place, and what problem or set of problems was it meant to solve? Although it is easy to list answers to this question, few survive examination.

Some sections of the book, of a rather technical character, are obviously, and usually explicitly, meant to further, and in some cases to correct, the work of Gottlob Frege and Bertrand Russell in the foundations of mathematics and logic. Interesting and important as these sections of the book

---

[1]Georg Henrik von Wright, "Die Entstehung des Tractatus Logico-Philosophicus", in Ludwig Wittgenstein, *Briefe an Ludwig von Ficker (1914-20)* (Salzburg: Otto Müller, 1969), pp. 71-110.

[2]I received this information from some of Wittgenstein's former colleagues in Semmering, who saw his copy of the manuscript during his stint as a village schoolteacher.

may be, the book was not composed merely to answer such questions. We are concerned here with the main thrust of the book, not with its details.

Anthony Quinton has suggested[3] that the *Tractatus* sets out to answer a Kantian-style question, to wit: "How is language possible?" Yet not every question of the form: "How is *x* possible?" is Kantian in character. For a question of this sort to be Kantian, it would have to be set in the context of some theory or presupposition which made the existence of language seem impossible—or at least doubtful. Kant raised his question about the possibility of synthetic *a priori* knowledge, for instance, in the face of (1) the patent existence of knowledge of this sort (which for Kant included mathematics and part of Newtonian physics) and (2) a Humean theory of knowledge in terms of which such knowledge was impossible. According to a theory of knowledge then widely prevailing, such knowledge was impossible; yet it existed.[4] And thus the question.

No such question about language is present in Wittgenstein's *Tractatus*. One of the things he wants to determine is what conditions must obtain if a precisely meaningful language is to exist. But the presumption in the early writing is that these conditions do exist; the Kantian dilemma does not arise. To see a truly Kantian-style question about the possibility of language, one might by contrast turn to Noam Chomsky, who argues in *Language and Mind* (1968) that the learning theories of behavioristic psychology and empiricist philosophy, to which many contemporary linguists adhere, simply cannot account for the acquisition or learning of grammar and language. If empiricist assumptions about lan-

---

[3]Anthony Quinton, "Contemporary British Philosophy", in *A Critical History of Western Philosophy*, ed. D. J. O'Connor (Glencoe, Ill: The Free Press, 1964), p. 536. The same suggestion is made by Peter Hacker in "Nets of Language", *Encounter*, April 1971, p. 85; and a similar suggestion appears in Stephen Toulmin, "Ludwig Wittgenstein", *Encounter*, January 1969.

[4]See my discussion in *The Retreat to Commitment*, 2nd edition (La Salle, Ill: Open Court, 1984), p. 72.

guage acquisition are correct, then language is impossible. Chomsky sets out to escape this Kantian-style dilemma, just as Kant himself did, through a critique of contemporary empiricism. The question as to what extent other Kantian themes may be present in the *Tractatus* will be considered below. Meanwhile, it is clear that Wittgenstein was not, whatever he was doing, concerned with the question attributed to him by Quinton.

II

Another common answer about the nature of Wittgenstein's *Tractatus* is that he was attempting, like Kant, to draw a line of demarcation between science and nonscience. As far as it goes, the answer is correct: this line of demarcation corresponds to that between factual and nonfactual language. But the question then arises: why did Wittgenstein want to do that? It is easy to explain why some philosophers have wanted to draw such a line, but harder to state precisely what Wittgenstein's intention was. Most often, the demarcation between science and nonscience has been drawn for the purpose of evaluation and criticism. It has been assumed by many philosophers—perhaps most conspicuously in this century by the logical positivists of the Vienna School—that the way to demarcate good theories from bad theories, legitimate ideas from illegitimate ones, was to demarcate the scientific from the nonscientific. One could even write an acceptance and rejection rule in terms of the demarcation, to wit: "When in doubt about the merits of some particular idea, theory, proposal, or whatever, first determine if it is scientific. If it is, classify it as legitimate; if it is not; reject it."[5]

More than a suggestion of such an approach appears in the *Tractatus*: indeed, it is sufficiently strong to have led

---

[5]See my discussion in "Logical Strength and Demarcation", Appendix 2 of *The Retreat to Commitment*.

many interpreters of his thought to suppose that Wittgenstein's basic aim was to *condemn* as meaningless whatever could not be classified according to his criteria as factual or scientific. Yet other tendencies in the *Tractatus* prevent one from accepting this as its author's intention.

On the one hand, Wittgenstein himself states his aim as "to set a limit . . . . to the expression of thoughts". He writes: "The whole sense of the book might be summed up in the following words: what can be said at all can be said clearly, and what we cannot talk about we must pass over in silence." As he put it: "The correct method in philosophy would really be the following: to say nothing except what can be said, i.e., propositions of natural science,—i.e., something that has nothing to do with philosophy—and then, whenever someone else wanted to say something metaphysical, to demonstrate to him that he had failed to give a meaning to certain signs in his propositions" (6.53).

Not only is pre-Kantian speculative metaphysics excluded from the "sayable" and meaningful by Wittgenstein's criteria—a more detailed account of which will be sketched below—so are universal laws of nature, the "elucidatory" statements of the *Tractatus* itself, logic, ethics and aesthetics, philosophy, religion. Yet at most only speculative metaphysics is condemned outright. Logic, ethics and aesthetics, and religion, while described as "transcendental", are not condemned. And the philosophical statements of the *Tractatus* are taken to be elucidative in a most helpful way, despite their "meaninglessness".

While declaring that ethics is meaningless, Wittgenstein nonetheless reported to his friends Ludwig von Ficker and Paul Engelmann that the whole point of the book was ethical. As Wittgenstein explained to von Ficker,

> The book's point is an ethical one. I once meant to include in the preface a sentence which is not in fact there now but which I will write out for you here, because it will perhaps be a key to the work for you. What I meant to write, then, was this: My work consists of two parts: the one presented here plus all that I have *not* written. And it is precisely this second part that is

the important one. My book draws limits to the sphere of the ethical from the inside, as it were, and I am convinced that this is the ONLY *rigorous* way of drawing those limits. In short, I believe that where *many* others today are just *gassing*, I have managed in my book to put everything firmly into place by being silent about it. And for that reason, unless I am very much mistaken, the book will say a great deal that you yourself want to say. Only perhaps you won't see that it is said in the book. For now, I would recommend you read the *preface* and the *conclusion*, because they contain the most direct expression of the point of the book.[6]

III

It is, then, only in a rather odd sense of the word that the demarcation between science and nonscience, as it appears in the *Tractatus*, is a matter of evaluation. Nonscience is not *condemned*, but it is suggested that it is in bad taste—indeed, virtually immoral—even to *try* to talk about it. For that leads inevitably to gassing. The evaluation here, such as it is, is of an ascetic, aristocratic, elitist character. It is implied that those few who *can* understand Wittgenstein would know better than to—would have better taste than to—indulge in metaphysics or in moralizing, or, for that matter, in *anti*metaphysics. Wittgenstein does not suppose that his views will win wide support as, say, a useful measure for sorting out nonsense. Quite the contrary, in his Preface and in several letters he expressed doubt that anyone, even Russell and Frege, would understand him, let alone be capable of practicing his demarcation.

Just as fastidiously as he himself advocates silence, Wittgenstein avoids imposing his own silence on others. *Noblesse oblige*: a personal elitism is accompanied by a radical tolerance for those who either did not or could not live by a

---

[6]Wittgenstein, *Briefe an Ludwig von Ficker*, pp. 35-36. Quoted in English translation in Paul Engelmann, *Letters from Ludwig Wittgenstein, with a Memoir* (Oxford: Basil Blackwell, 1967), pp. 143-44.

similar code. These were not to be condemned; they were parts of forms of life in which one did not participate and about which one did not speak. There are, of course, dangers here: some silence is deep and some stems from having little or nothing to say. Wittgenstein provides no criterion to distinguish one kind of silence from the other.

Here the contrast between Wittgenstein and the members of the Vienna Circle with whom his ideas later became associated is particularly striking. For several prominent members of the Circle tended to think of it as a kind of embryonic political party embracing an ideology with potential mass appeal. Otto Neurath, in particular, who has been described as the "party secretary" of the Circle, certainly had ambitious political aims for the widespread dissemination of the ideology of logical positivism. Indeed, he went so far as to encourage the members of the group to drop the name "positivism" in favor of "physicalism". "Positivism" was objectionable to Marxists on several counts: for one thing, Lenin had denounced an earlier version of positivism as bourgeois; for another, the Austrian social democrat, Friedrich Adler, had used Ernst Mach's version of positivism to support his critique of Marx's materialism. Neurath, however, who had been an economist for the short-lived Spartacist Communist government in Munich at the end of the First World War, imagined that he could persuade Stalin to adopt a philosophy called "physicalism"—a word with connotations close to "materialism"—as the official doctrine of the Soviet Union. Neurath naïvely traveled to the Soviet Union on behalf of this cause, but he was not successful.[7]

On the other hand, one *can* find attitudes toward language reminiscent of Wittgenstein's among his contemporary Viennese, but not so much among the philosophers as among the Austrian writers and litterateurs.

---

[7]For further details of Neurath's work, see the biographical material in Marie Neurath and Robert S. Cohen, eds., *Otto Neurath: Empiricism and Sociology* (Dordrecht: D. Reidel, 1973).

IV

Perhaps the most appropriate example is that of Hugo von Hofmannsthal, one of several turn-of-the-century Austrian writers who voiced their loss of confidence in the power of speech. Hofmannsthal is often bracketed with Karl Kraus, Franz Kafka, and Fritz Mauthner; and in his way he shared with them the worry that speech was becoming a vehicle not of communication but of mendacity and pointlessness. Kafka had written, in rather obvious parables, of royal messengers who rush through the world with proclamations that no longer possess meaning. With tremendous energy Karl Kraus turned out his periodical *Die Fackel* almost single-handedly, scornfully attacking almost all of the other periodicals and newspapers of the land for their distortion of language and parading examples of their literary errors. Mauthner came to wonder whether language could survive as a means of responsible communication. Nonetheless, apart from their common conviction, surely correct, that language is subject to abuse and misuse, these writers are very dissimilar. Wittgenstein knew Kraus's work and admired his early publications; he was also acquainted with Mauthner's work and even quoted him in the *Tractatus*, although in disagreement. But their ideas are far apart.[8]

With Hofmannsthal, however, Wittgenstein did have more in common. From his first verse play, *Yesterday* (1891), to his classic comedy *The Difficult Man* (1921), Hofmannsthal elaborated on the themes of his famous *Letter to Lord Chandos*: not simply the inadequacy, but the *disgusting indecency* of talk—particularly talk about morality, about politics, about literature and aesthetics. Already in 1895, in reviewing a book on the actor Friedrich Mitterwurzer, Hofmannsthal wrote:

---

[8]Compare Gershon Weiler, *Mauthner's Critique of Language* (Cambridge: Cambridge University Press, 1970). The *later* ideas of Wittgenstein do bear some similarity to those of Mauthner.

People are tired of listening to talk. They feel a deep disgust with words. For words have pushed themselves in front of things. . . . We are in the grip of a horrible process in which thought is utterly stifled by concepts. Hardly anyone now is capable of being sure in his own mind about what he understands, what he does not understand, of saying what he feels and what he does not feel. This has awakened a desperate love for all those arts which are executed without speech. . . .[9]

Such aesthetic and ethical insistence on the indecent gassing of most speech recurs throughout Hofmannsthal's work, being most vividly expressed by the "Difficult Man" himself, the Count Hans Karl Bühl, who, when asked after his return from the war to deliver a speech in the Austrian House of Lords, demands: "Am I supposed to stand up and make a speech about peace among peoples and the unitedness of nations—I, a man whose sole conviction is that it's impossible to open one's mouth without causing the most ineradicable confusion? . . . Am I to let loose a flood of words every one of which will seem positively indecent to me?"[10]

Hofmannsthal and Wittgenstein were different personalities indeed, and it would be folly to exaggerate their similarities, even in their aesthetic preferences, let alone their philosophical views. But the fastidious reverence in which both Wittgenstein and Hofmannsthal held language— it is no accident that Hans Karl Bühl is a Count—helps illuminate Wittgenstein's oblique, indirect, evasive behavior toward the members of the Vienna Circle. Like Hofmannsthal's "Difficult Man", Wittgenstein was pursued and pressured by these more public men to join the philosophical arena, to attend their meetings, to proclaim his philosophy. He responded with *distance*, by evading philosophical discussion, by reading from Tagore and other poets to the members of the Circle who came to meetings and coffee houses expecting to hear him explain the *Tractatus*. Occasionally he

---

[9]Hugo von Hofmannsthal, *Selected Plays and Libretti*, ed. Michael Hamburger (New York: Pantheon Books, 1963), p. xvii.
[10]*Ibid.*, p. 820.

would be delightfully exasperating and just whistle to them from his extraordinary repertoire of classical music. With some members of the Circle—in particular Carnap and Neurath, whose antimetaphysical positivism struck him as vulgarian—Wittgenstein went to precautions more elaborate than those of the Count in *The Difficult Man* in order to avoid encounters. It was only with such people as Schlick and Waismann, "because of their high culture and refined tastes", that he would eventually, in the late twenties, discuss philosophy.[11] As Engelmann reports (page 118): "Wittgenstein found Schlick a distinguished and understanding partner in discussion, all the more so because he appreciated Schlick's highly cultured personality—something which Wittgenstein always found essential in his intellectual contacts with others."

V

The question may well be raised to what extent were the worries Wittgenstein and Hofmannsthal expressed about the capacity of language—in particular the language of morals, aesthetics, religion, and the emotions—well founded? To what extent were they, rather, an exaggerated response to a period of sloppy and overgrown misuse of language that accompanied the cataclysmic social changes of the German-speaking world during the latter part of the nineteenth century and the early part of this century?

No doubt the German language was undergoing a period of considerable change at this time. All languages and modes of communication, however, experience periods of change—sometimes of expansion, sometimes of compression. Wittgenstein and Hofmannsthal appear to have wanted compression and restraint. There is nothing new about that: in some

---

[11]For Wittgenstein's conversations with Schlick and Waismann, see Friedrich Waismann, *Wittgenstein and the Vienna Circle*, ed. Brian McGuinness (Oxford: Basil Blackwell, 1979).

of the most creative periods of Chinese painting, to take an example from another mode of expression, the crucial part of a picture was what had been left out. And one picture, of course, "is worth a thousand words".

Poetry is often likened to a process of compression, of conveying a great deal through leaving much more unsaid. Ezra Pound and Arthur Koestler, among others, have claimed that *Dichtung*, the German word for poetry, is related etymologically to *dichten*, which means "to compress". The etymology happens to be incorrect, but the idea behind it reflects a common assumption about language.

Nor was language the only mode of expression undergoing significant change during this time. Painters, architects and musicians were also, at the beginning of the century, radically re-examining their media. Influenced by the French, painters turned from representational painting to a variety of new modes of expression. As to architecture, the Bauhaus school in Germany and the work of Adolf Loos in Vienna, with its studied avoidance of ornamentation, had an important influence on Wittgenstein. Musicians, notably in Vienna, abandoned the diatonic system of scales and modulations: Arnold Schönberg is a conspicuous example.

Some historians and literary critics[12] have piled example on example to convey more an image than a thesis about this period, an image suggesting that the German language was, at the turn of the century, on the verge of collapse; that the various critiques of language produced then—whether by Mauthner, Wittgenstein, Kraus, or Hofmannsthal—were all responding, in a rather parallel way, to this crisis; and that, moreover, the route out of it lay more or less in the direction in which Wittgenstein and Hofmannsthal had pointed—in a recognition of some sort of "significant silence".

That those who have made such diagnoses and sugges-

---

[12]Among these historians and literary critics, George Steiner is probably the best known. See his *Language and Silence* (New York: Atheneum, 1970). See also Erich Heller, "L. Wittgenstein: Unphilosophical Notes", *Encounter*, September 1959, and *The Disinherited Mind* (New York: Meridian, 1959).

tions are correct is far from clear. Taking the lamentations of writers like Hofmannsthal rather literally and uncritically, they have stressed the crises of the German language without troubling much to investigate the development and refinement of the language that was also going on then, precisely in ethics, aesthetics, personal relationships, the emotions. Hofmannsthal was, after all, by no means the most distinguished poet of the period. An incomparably better poet, Rainer Maria Rilke, talked rather little about the crisis of language and, instead, went about composing magnificent verse in which language is both refined and enriched.

The case of psychoanalysis is also instructive. Tending as it does to concentrate on abnormal behavior, it reflects a general tendency in most languages to develop a more refined, precise, and differentiated terminology to deal with the abnormal, the deviant, the illegal, the "bad" than with what is normal, ordinary, legal, good. Words like "nice" and "good man" are indeed virtually meaningless in most contexts. In English, words like "guilt", "sin", "shame", and "vice" have no true positive counterparts, or at any rate are far more definite in their meanings than are their nearest positive counterparts, which more often indicate the absence of negative characteristics than anything definitely good. These negative terms continue to undergo modification and refinement as psychological theory develops: the distinction between guilt and shame coined by Helen Merrell Lynd and others is a good example.

The word "good", as used in the preceding sentence, illustrates the problem that the *pro*-words, such as "good", "merit", "virtue"—which are likewise opposed to "bad", "demerit", "defect"—may refer to nonmoral as well as to moral values. But "evil", particularly in its adjectival sense, carries a strong, almost exclusively moral meaning, to which one can oppose on the *pro* side the much less forceful "righteous" and "virtuous" or even "good", the latter being the most general *pro*-word. On the whole, then, with some exceptions, language tends to fuse *pro*-words, but to differentiate among various *con*-words. Thus the significance of moral evil is cast into higher relief.[13]

What I want to suggest in mentioning these matters is that much of what has been written about a linguistic crisis in the German-speaking countries is grossly overdramatized, making its case by oversimplification and an almost studied neglect of the sort of obvious counterexample that I have been citing: cases where language has been refined and improved rather than debased. If one focuses one's attention on particular writers, on certain philosophers such as Martin Heidegger, and on certain literary critics such as the ones mentioned and then embellishes one's account with some examples from the propaganda of two world wars, the rise of the popular press, and the street chatter of Vienna at a time when it was still the capital city of a multilingual empire, one crudely distorts the history of the German language.[14]

Paul Engelmann and others have claimed that Wittgenstein's attitude toward language was not only representative of the developments discussed here but was also typically Jewish. But contrast these two quotations, the first from a British historian, the second from a German Jewish philosopher. "Despite his repudiation of Judaism", writes Frank Field concerning Karl Kraus,

> his vision of language was, in the final analysis, *rooted in the specifically Judaic concept* of the revelation of the will of God through the word, the Word of power which brings what it says to pass.[15]

---

[13]Aurel Kolnai has made a special study of this phenomenon in his fine essay, "The Thematic Primacy of Moral Evil", *The Philosophical Quarterly*, January 1956.

[14]For a beautiful dissection of inflated language—the sort of language that is often associated with Heidegger, or with Adorno, Habermas, and their followers—see Karl Popper, "Reason or Revolution", in *Archives européennes de sociologie* XI, 1970, pp. 252-62; see also Popper's *Auf der Suche nach einer besseren Welt* (Munich: Piper Verlag, 1984), pp. 79-113.

[15]Quoted from Frank Field, *The Last Days of Mankind: Karl Kraus and His Vienna* (London: Macmillan, 1967). My italics.

On the other hand, Franz Rosenzweig writes:

> There is nothing in a deeper sense Jewish than a final mistrust
> in the power of the Word and an inner confidence in the power
> of silence.[16]

Which generalization about the Jewish concept of the power
of the Word is correct? *Neither*. Nor was there a catastrophic
collapse of the German language at the turn of the twentieth
century.

VI

So far, in order to try to make some sense of what Wittgenstein himself described as the main point of his *Tractatus*, I
have drawn attention to the so-called crisis that some persons suppose the German language to have undergone during the early part of this century, with particular attention
to those of Wittgenstein's Viennese contemporaries who
hailed, deplored and recorded this crisis, imaginary or real.
When put in this Viennese setting, the *Tractatus* does make
somewhat better sense.

Yet in one all-important respect Wittgenstein's work remains radically set apart from that of his Austrian contemporaries. Although Wittgenstein was to write beautifully in
the German language, even to be hailed as a creator of a new
style, he was by profession or avocation not a writer but a
mathematician and logician—so much so that, when he voiced
his own opinions on the limitations of language, he chose a
different medium. Although his medium gave his work a
power and scope that his literary contemporaries lacked, it
also lent his views a technical and esoteric air that distracted
attention from their practical inspiration and concern. I have

---

[16]Franz Rosenzweig, *Stern der Erlösung,* quoted in "Das Porträt: Ludwig Wittgenstein zur 80. Wiederkehr seines Geburtstages", Österreichische Rundfunk Studio Tirol, 1969.

in mind, of course, that Wittgenstein couched his own critique of language in the framework of Frege's logical theories and a variant of Russell's logical atomism.

Thus his message was to be misunderstood twice over. To his English readers, who had only a vague inkling, if any, of German linguistic crises, he was to appear as a brilliant critic of speculative philosophy—*but in the British tradition.* It had been German-inspired philosophizing in England against which G. E. Moore and Russell had directed their own analytical attack, and Wittgenstein, their student, was assumed to be working not only on the same lines but within the same limits. English readers missed Wittgenstein's wider role as a critic not only of the language of speculative philosophy but of the language of art and the emotions in the Viennese manner of Hofmannsthal. Nor did Wittgenstein fare better among his compatriots. To those Austrians and Germans who noticed him at all, he appeared as one quite foreign to the Viennese tradition of critique of language, as one who had assimilated the alien approach and techniques of British empiricism. The first among his fellow Austrians to take serious note of his philosophy were the philosopher-physicists and mathematicians of the Vienna Circle, a rather Anglophile group more interested in British empiricism and in Russell's new logic than in traditional Austrian and German philosophy. Only since Wittgenstein's death have Austrian and German litterateurs shown any interest in his work.

VII

When one turns from the question of the several motives behind Wittgenstein's composition of the *Tractatus* to attempt to comprehend the actual content of the work, it is necessary to explain something of the nature of logical paradoxes and the renewed research into the foundations of logic and mathematics which they occasioned during the first decades of the twentieth century.

Numerous logical paradoxes exist—those of Russell, J. Richard, and Kurt Grelling, for example, as well as the classical paradoxes—of which only a few illustrative examples need be given here. The best-known is commonly referred to as the Liar Paradox, where the perpetual liar reports: "I am now lying." If what he says is true, he is speaking falsely; and if what he says is false, he is speaking truly.

Another way to put this paradox, due to Jan Lukasiewicz and Alfred Tarski,[17] is thus:

> The boxed sentence is false.

If the sentence thus boxed is true, then it is false; if it is false, then it is true.

These are peculiar utterances, and it is hardly surprising that some philosophers and logicians, when confronted by them, have wanted to declare them somehow illegitimate, neither true nor false, but ungrammatical, improperly formed—meaningless. Russell took such an approach after his discovery in 1901 of the paradoxes that can be generated from certain long-accepted ways of constructing classes or sets. Russell with his theory of types (or categories), W. V. Quine with his method of stratification, as well as other logicians, tried to avoid paradoxes or antinomies by introducing certain grammatical and logical conventions prohibiting the construction of such antinomies. The aim was to show, through logical analysis, that wherever the required grammatical and logical precautions were not being taken, one's system was in danger of producing statements or formulae which were not *well formed*, which were meaningless. Even before Russell, it had been observed that many of the antinomies were produced by their self-referential or reflexive character, and the question had been posed—for example, by Lewis Carroll (the Reverend C. L. Dodgson)—whether such self-reference ought not to be prohibited.[18] Specific, conflict-

---

[17]Alfred Tarski, "The Concept of Truth in Formalized Languages", in Tarski, *Logic, Semantics, Metamathematics* (Oxford, 1956), pp. 157ff.

[18]See W. W. Bartley, III, "Lewis Carroll's Unpublished Work in Symbolic Logic", *Abstracts* of the 4th International Congress for Logic, Methodology and Philosophy of Science, Bucharest, 1971, p. 416; and W. W. Bartley, III, "Lewis Carroll's Lost Book on Logic", *The Scientific American*, July

ing techniques for dealing with self-reference have since been worked out by logicians, among them Russell, Ernst Zermelo, John von Neumann, and Quine.

In these circumstances it is in a certain sense laudable, even if the conclusion is incorrect, that some philosophers have supposed that techniques rather like those developed by Russell and others for isolating meaningless from meaningful, non-well-formed from well-formed, utterances could be extended *beyond* logic to the traditional problems of philosophy. It has been supposed that the ancient problems of metaphysics, like the *logical* paradoxes, could be made to disappear through the development of canons of meaningfulness and well-formed utterance; that indeed these hoary metaphysical theories had arisen in the first place only because of the absence of techniques of linguistic and logical analysis for ascertaining meaninglessness.

This project, ambitious and inspired, was doomed to failure. For it is a fact that the self-reference which is to be found in the logical antinomies is *simply absent* from most of the traditional problems of philosophy. The failure of the project was, however, not foreseen. The story of much twentieth-century philosophy, conspicuously that of Wittgenstein and his followers, is that of an attempt to dissolve traditional metaphysics through the systematic application of a false parallel: the assumption that philosophical problems were generated, and could be avoided, in a way parallel to that in which logical paradoxes were generated and resolved.

Thus Wittgenstein declared bluntly in the Preface to the *Tractatus*, "The book deals with the problems of philosophy, and shows ... that the reason why these problems are posed is that the logic of our language is misunderstood" (p. 3).

1972, pp. 38–46; "Lewis Carroll as logician", *The Times Literary Supplement*, 15 June 1973, pp. 665–66; and *Lewis Carroll's Symbolic Logic* (New York: Clarkson N. Potter, Inc., 1977), pp. 32–33, 350–61. See also my discussion in "On Alleged Paradoxes of Pancritical Rationalism", Appendix 4 of *The Retreat to Commitment*.

VIII

In providing a theory of demarcation between science and nonscience, Wittgenstein's *Tractatus* prescribes criteria that must be satisfied by any factual (not logical) utterances which are well-formed, and proscribes, in the several senses discussed above, utterances which do not satisfy these criteria. Factual propositions are well-formed scientific propositions. No other propositions exist, although there exist certain pseudopropositions—typically to be found in philosophy—which superficially look like propositions but which prove on analysis not to be well-formed. Wittgenstein himself does not use the expression "well-formed"; he speaks of propositions which are *meaningful* and pseudopropositions which are *meaningless*.

When confronted by a sentence whose meaningfulness may be questioned, something that may often happen since "language disguises thought" (4.002), the *Tractatus* specified what *must* be the case if it is in fact meaningful. Leaving aside pseudopropositions for the moment, we find specified in the *Tractatus* two separate and different sorts of *legitimate* meaningful propositions. These are atomic propositions and molecular propositions. A sentence which proves to be neither is in fact no proposition at all: it is meaningless.

Elementary, or atomic, propositions, into which all molecular propositions may be analyzed, are those propositions that derive their meaning from their direct relation to the world. Elementary propositions are themselves unanalyzable and logically independent one from the other. Very important, such an elementary proposition pictures a *possible* state of affairs in the world. If that state of affairs in fact obtains, the elementary proposition is true; if not, it is false.

So far, one might think oneself to be concerned entirely with the theory of language. In fact, an ontology, or theory of the nature and structure of reality, accompanies the linguistic theory. Wittgenstein sets out to answer the question: what has to be the case in order for there to be meaningful utterances? Part of his account of language emphasizes that the nature of the ultimate constituents of the world may be discovered by an examination of language, and the structure of language in turn is determined by the structure of reality. Wittgenstein does not restrict himself to some *particular* language here; rather, what is involved is the essential, if hidden, structure that has to be possessed by *any* language capable of meaningful expression.

In his view, the world is composed of *objects arranged as facts*. A true elementary proposition pictures such a fact, called an *atomic fact*, and such facts are, like the elementary propositions which picture them, independent one from the other. An elementary proposition may be meaningful without being true if it pictures a possible combination of objects (a state of affairs) which does not happen to obtain. Elementary propositions and the states of affairs that they picture have a common form.

Readers of the *Tractatus*—including, conspicuously, most of the logical positivists—have often supposed that elementary propositions report sense experiences. It is probably safe to assume that Wittgenstein did have, and must have had, *some* such idea in mind. But the *Tractatus* makes no declaration on this point. In his account of elementary propositions, atomic facts, and objects, Wittgenstein gives no examples; indeed, he does not even specify the *kind* of example that would qualify. It is not even stated *directly* that his objects must be *objects of human knowledge*, only that objects must exist in order for language to exist. The *Tractatus* is, then, a work in logic and ontology, not in the theory of knowledge. Ironically, Bertrand Russell is often blamed for having furthered the notion that the *Tractatus* is an epistemological work, although Russell himself, in his famous Introduction to it, wrote: "It is not contended by Wittgenstein that we can actually isolate the simple or have empirical knowledge of it. It is a logical necessity demanded by theory" (page xiii).

This interpretation of the bearing of the *Tractatus* on epistemology has been challenged. G. E. M. Anscombe, for instance, has argued that the *Tractatus* could not have involved a theory of sense data.[19] Unfortunately, just as this interpretation has been questioned, another serious misunderstanding has begun to emerge: namely, that the *Tractatus* is dominated by Kantian themes and is indeed more Kantian than empiricist in character, despite its outward dress and its most common interpretation in English and American philosophical circles. I have already alluded to this tendency above in my critical remarks about Quinton's interpretation of the goal of the *Tractatus*. Here it may be useful, in a corrective way, to note that one of the central components of the doctrine of the *Tractatus* is not only *non*-Kantian but *pre*-Kantian in spirit. I have in mind the doctrine that the nature of the world is to be discovered through the examination and analysis of language. Before Kant it was commonly assumed that some sort of harmony existed between the human mind and the external world so that the human mind could (in some accounts even unaided by the senses) apprehend the nature of reality. Should it fail to do so, this would often, in precritical philosophy, be attributed to some interference with the proper functioning of the human reason. When properly functioning, the human reason has access to the nature of reality.

Kant rejected this notion, conceiving the laws of rationality not as mirroring the structure of things in themselves, which was indeed *unknowable* to man, but as providing the "forms of human understanding". Insofar as man could know reality at all, he would have to know it in accordance with these forms of human understanding. But the study of the human mind would *not* reveal the nature of reality, the *Ding an sich*.

By contrast, the common pre-Kantian view had held that "the mind itself is, in effect, a mirror that reflects without distortion the indwelling structure of the external world".[20]

[19]G. E. M. Anscombe, *An Introduction to Wittgenstein's Tractatus* (London: Hutchinson University Library, 1959).
[20]Henry David Aiken, *The Age of Ideology* (New York: Mentor Books, 1956), p. 31.

Wittgenstein might have said: "Language itself is, in effect a mirror that—when well formed—reflects without distortion the indwelling structure of the external world." If one bears this aspect of Wittgenstein's thought in mind, it appears that the Kantian interpretation of the early Wittgenstein is wrong. To be sure, there are some traces of Kantian themes there, but they in no way predominate.[21] One can find a Kantian flavor in his remark, for instance, that just as one cannot imagine spatial objects outside space or temporal objects outside time, one could not imagine an object excluded from the possibility of combining with others.

My view, which I shall mention but not explain, since to explain it would require a treatise in itself, is this. It is *more* accurate, if also a bit misleading, to argue that the movement from the early Wittgenstein to the work of the later Wittgenstein is a movement from a precritical, pre-Kantian position to a post-Kantian, Hegelian-style position *without benefit of Kant.*

IX

Before turning from Wittgenstein's early work, as represented in the *Tractatus,* to the important period in his life during which he withdrew publicly from philosophy and reshaped his philosophical outlook, three other components of the doctrine of the *Tractatus* need to be mentioned briefly: Wittgenstein's theory of complex propositions; his idea of the logical, truth-functional scaffolding of language; and his famous doctrine of "showing".

So far, only that part of scientific meaningful discourse that is expressed in elementary propositions has been discussed. Most propositions with which one deals in ordinary

---

[21]As James Griffin has pointed out: "There is no possibility that 'the world' can be read as 'the world of my experience'; he [Wittgenstein] means, he says, reality." See James Griffin, *Wittgenstein's Logical Atomism* (Seattle: University of Washington paperbacks, 1964), p. 150.

life and in science, however, are, according to Wittgenstein's account, not elementary propositions but complex, molecular propositions which may be analyzed into *truth-functions* of elementary propositions, and which thus owe their own meaning, and their truth value, to the elementary propositions from which they are generated. To pursue an analysis in particular cases might be difficult, but *if* the compound proposition in question is truly meaningful, such a translation can be carried out: all meaningful languages have a uniform logical structure.

The phrases "truth-function" and "logical structure" need to be explained. To say that a complex proposition can be analyzed into a truth-function of elementary propositions is to claim that it can be analyzed into a set of elementary propositions *structurally linked* by means of certain logical terms. These logical terms, which include negation and conjunction, are themselves *nondescriptive*: they are rather like structural scaffolding on which propositions are arranged; they themselves stand for nothing in the world. Thus, if we were to suppose that the letters p and q, taken individually, stand for elementary propositions, then "p and q" would stand for a compound proposition in which the elementary components (p,q) are joined by the truth-functional connective of *conjunction* ("and"). Similarly, "neither p nor q" would be a compound proposition whose elementary propositional components are joined by the truth-functional connectives of *negation* and *conjunction*.

X

Wittgenstein repeatedly and unequivocally asserted that what could not be stated in a meaningful proposition could not be stated at all. He did allow, however, that certain things which could *not* be stated in propositions were nonetheless *manifest* in meaningful propositions, wherein they *showed* themselves. Thus, some of what cannot be *said* may be *shown*.

In correspondence with Russell, Engelmann, and others, Wittgenstein several times maintained that his "doctrine of showing" was the main point of the *Tractatus*. There is little doubt that Wittgenstein did regard the doctrine as important; nonetheless, it is an aspect of the book that has had insufficient attention, owing in part to the fact that Wittgenstein himself says so little about the matter and that what he does say is highly condensed and allusive.

The best attempt to make good sense of this difficult idea has, I believe, been made by James Griffin,[22] who rightly sets the doctrine in the context of Wittgenstein's logical theory and his developments and criticisms of the views concerning logic set forth by Frege and Russell. As Griffin puts it, Wittgenstein's doctrine is in part a development of the views concerning the definition of concepts set down in Frege's *Grundgesetze*, in part a reaction to Russell's theory of types, and in part the result of Wittgenstein's own reflection about the unique character of the propositions of logic. Thus logical controversy provides the *core* context in terms of which the theory must be understood. Wittgenstein does, however, extend the notion far beyond this core of logic in order to help convey his views on ethics, aesthetics, and religion.

Elaborating on his view that a proposition is a picture, Wittgenstein insists that a picture cannot depict its own pictorial form—in this case a form dictated by logic. For the logical, or formative, constants are not descriptive. Nonetheless, a pictorial proposition can *display* or *show* or *manifest* its logical structure (and the structure of the world which it pictures). Part of the import of this doctrine, if it were correct, would be to render Russell's theory of types both impossible and superfluous. By attempting to speak of such terms as "thing", "property", "fact", and "type", Russell's theory attempts to do what cannot be done even in its own terms and, in Wittgenstein's way of speaking, tries to say what cannot be said. To correct this, however, it is not necessary, so he believes, to revise the theory of types, but rather to understand, through the distinction between saying and showing, that such a theory, even if it were *per impossibile*

---

[22]Griffin, *Ibid.*

possible, is superfluous. Wittgenstein thought that to know the sense of a symbol, definitely and completely, is to know all its possible combinations; that is, *one would know its range of applicability and thus not need a theory of types,* since to know the range of applicability of a symbol is to know its type. And if one knows its range of applicability, one will run no risk of generating logical paradox by extending it beyond its range or type.

So: one need not attempt, impossibly, to *state* or to say what the range of applicability of a symbol is; this will be shown in the symbolism if that symbolism is fully and definitely understood. And thus the emphasis put by Wittgenstein in the *Tractatus* on precisely determinate, complete definition.

This notion, although difficult to explain nontechnically, is indisputably ingenious. Russell's own great respect for the *Tractatus* stemmed in large part from this portion of the book, even though Russell himself, in his Introduction, carefully records his disbelief in the solution, summarizing his appreciation of Wittgenstein in this way: "To have constructed a theory of logic which is not at any point obviously wrong is to have achieved a work of extraordinary difficulty and importance" (page xxii).

When Russell completed his Introduction, in May 1922, Wittgenstein's logical theory was indeed not obviously wrong. By the middle 1930s, however, his basic assumptions (as well as many of Russell's) had been completely undercut by the work of Kurt Gödel and Alonzo Church.[23] In paragraph 6.5 of the *Tractatus,* Wittgenstein had flatly declared: "The riddle does not exist. If a question can be framed at all, it is

---

[23]Wittgenstein lectured on Gödel in Cambridge in 1937–38. See Ludwig Wittgenstein, "Cause and Effect: Intuitive Awareness", *Philosophia,* vol. 6, nos. 3/4 (September-December 1976), esp. p. 429. See also Wittgenstein, *Remarks on the Foundations of Mathematics* (1937–44), ed. G. H. von Wright, Rush Rhees, and G. E. M. Anscombe (Oxford: Basil Blackwell, 1967), pp. 50–54, 174, 176–77; and A. W. Levi, "Wittgenstein as Dialectician", *The Journal of Philosophy,* vol. 61, no. 4 (February 13, 1964), pp. 127–39, esp. pp. 128, 132–36.

also *possible* to answer it." Gödel's results, published in 1931, show that every arithmetical system containing addition, multiplication, and prime numbers contains *undecidable* statements or equations. For instance, given any proof procedure whatever for elementary number theory, Gödel demonstrates that a statement of elementary number theory can be constructed which will be true if, and only if, it is not provable by the proof procedure given. Thus, either the statement is provable, in which case it is false and the proof procedure used discredited, or else the statement is true but not provable. But in that case the proof procedure is *incomplete*.[24] Gödel's work, in combination with further results achieved by Alonzo Church and S. C. Kleene, has produced the added result that every *disproof* technique, however intricate it may be, leaves the nonvalidity of some nonvalid theorems undiscoverable in principle.[25] Riddles exist.

Wittgenstein's logical theory, in particular his attempt to avoid difficulties in the theory of types through a distinction between what may be said and what shown, is no longer taken seriously by logicians, nor was it at any time very influential. His extension of the doctrine of showing from logic to ethics, aesthetics, and religion is not only very brief, taking up only about six pages of the *Tractatus*, but is also largely metaphorical, even though the metaphorical character of the extension is not declared and might well have been denied by him. Thus he indicates that value, *like logic*, pervades the world and may be conveyed or shown through the meaningful propositions that may be said, whereas to attempt to say what is valuable or right leads to nonsense.

Engelmann has provided us with one good, documented example of the sort of thing Wittgenstein was trying, even

---

[24]Kurt Gödel, "Über formal unentscheidbare Sätze der Principia Mathematica und verwandter Systeme", *Monatshefte für Mathematik und Physik*, vol. 38, 1931, pp. 173–98.

[25]S. C. Kleene, "Recursive Predicates and Quantifiers", *Transactions of the American Mathematical Society*, vol. 53, 1943, pp. 41–73; Alonzo Church, "A note on the Entscheidungsproblem", *Journal of Symbolic Logic*, vol. 1, 1936, pp. 40–41, 101–2.

if obscurely and unsuccessfully, to convey. During the war, Engelmann sent him a copy of Johann Ludwig Uhland's poem, "Count Eberhard's Hawthorn". Engelmann says of the poem: "Each one of Uhland's verses was simple—not ingenuous, but tersely informative. . . . But the poem as a whole gives in 28 lines the picture of a life."[26]

Uhland's poem goes as follows:

> Count Eberhard Rustle-Beard,
> From Württemberg's fair land,
> On holy errand steer'd
> To Palestina's strand.
>
> The while he slowly rode
> Along a woodland way;
> He cut from the hawthorn bush
> A little fresh green spray.
>
> Then in his iron helm
> The little sprig he plac'd;
> And bore it in the wars,
> And over the ocean waste.
>
> And when he reach'd his home,
> He plac'd it in the earth;
> Where little leaves and buds
> the gentle Spring call'd forth.
>
> He went each year to it,
> The Count so brave and true;
> And overjoy'd was he
> To witness how it grew.
>
> The Count was worn with age
> The sprig became a tree;
> 'Neath which the old man oft
> Would sit in reverie.

---

[26]Engelmann, *Letters from Wittgenstein*, pp. 84–85.

The branching arch so high,
Whose whisper is so bland,
Reminds him of the past
And Palestina's strand.
    (translated by Alexander Platt, 1848)

Wittgenstein wrote back: "The poem by Uhland is really magnificent. And this is how it is: if only you do not try to utter what is unutterable then *nothing* gets lost. But the unutterable will be—unutterably—*contained* in what has been uttered!"

XI

Helpful as such evidence is in better understanding Wittgenstein's application of his doctrine of showing to ethics, aesthetics, and religion, the best—and perhaps the only proper—way to explain the notion may be to recount some of the events of his own life during the 1920s, immediately before and after the publication of the *Tractatus*, when he was teaching elementary school in lower Austria. The next chapter attempts this task and, in so doing, tries to bridge the gap between the views of the *Tractatus* and those of the later *Philosophical Investigations*.

Wittgenstein was an ascetic. Such men are taken to be crazy, but one just oughtn't to measure them by ordinary standards.

—*Oskar Fuchs, Shoemaker of Trattenbach*[1]

At the present time, shoemakers, who make shoes to measure, deal more rationally with individuals than our teachers and schoolmasters in their application of moral principles.

—*Otto Weininger*[2]

3 ♦ Not Made to Measure

I

During the six years that Ludwig Wittgenstein spent teaching elementary school in lower Austria "the people were astonished at his doctrine: For he taught them as one having authority, and not as the scribes".

The passage just quoted is of course taken from the New Testament, and it would be possible to fit this segment of Wittgenstein's life into the framework of a morality play whose *leitmotivs* echo those of the Gospels. Almost all one would need for such a presentation is there: teaching the scribes in the temple; the call; the temptation; the life in the wilderness; the abandonment of the world and its comforts;

---

[1]The late Herr Fuchs made this remark to Frau Luise Hausmann, teacher of English in Kirchberg am Wechsel, and it is recorded in her manuscript, "Wittgenstein als Volksschullehrer", an abridged version of which is published in *Club Voltaire*, vol. IV (Hamburg: Rowohlt Verlag, 1970), pp. 391–96, as an appendix to my essay, "Die österreichische Schulreform als die Wiege der modernen Philosophie".

[2]Otto Weininger, *Sex and Character* (London: William Heinemann, 1906), p. 57.

the formation of a band of disciples; care for the poor, the meek, the peacemakers and the persecuted; the devotion to children; the working of miracles; and the healing of the sick. And there is also the antagonism of the elders, the betrayal, the trial, and rejection by the populace.

Yet we know both too little and too much about his life as a schoolmaster to cast the events of these years into such a mold. Moreover, although Wittgenstein had, as Bertrand Russell put it, "the pride of Lucifer", he also had a deep humility that any such comparison would have offended. Still, one might bear in mind several things: first, the experience to which the Gospels testify is, in one sense of the word, archetypal, and may thus be repeated without sacrilege in different ways in various times and circumstances; second, Wittgenstein had been overwhelmed by Tolstoy's version of the Gospels after reading it in Galicia in early 1915, and he had reread the Gospels countless times since then, so that, as his friends testify, he could recite large parts by heart; finally, an attempt to put something like the Sermon on the Mount, as rendered by Tolstoy, into practice is to show rather than say something. That Wittgenstein was, either consciously or unconsciously, for better or for worse, engaging in an imitation of Christ is a possibility that cannot lightly be dismissed when one attempts to comprehend his extraordinary life in Trattenbach, Puchberg, and Otterthal between 1920 and 1926. Since it is, however, only a possibility and one whose correctness would be impossible to establish or even seriously to test, it is in the spirit of Wittgenstein's philosophy to do no more than note it and for the rest to be silent, permitting the facts to speak for themselves.

There are other reasons, too, for caution in forcing any pattern, however appropriate, on these years in Wittgenstein's life. Aspects of his behavior, such as his sexual behavior or lack of it, might indeed conveniently and perhaps correctly be set into some pattern. The six years as a whole, however, lend themselves to no such treatment. Even if he was in his experiences in the villages attempting something like an imitation of Christ, he was not doing only that. For him to do that would at the same time be to essay an acting out of his own ethical position, as sketched in the *Tractatus* and in his *Notebooks*—itself an important experiment. Yet under no stretch of the imagination was Wittgenstein engaged only in ethical activity and practical philosophy during these years; he was, throughout the twenties, developing and revising some of the most technical aspects of his philosophy. Those who suppose that he dropped philosophy during this period only to be suddenly catapulted back into it again—through, for instance, attending a lecture by the Dutch mathematician L. E. J. Brouwer in March 1928—are misinformed.[3] Again, Wittgenstein was, in a manner he was not to repeat, a *participant*, acting throughout these six years in the Austrian school-reform program. Here too he did not simply follow; he innovated educationally in an individual way that was to influence his technical philosophy. All these activities worked together, and sometimes against one another, in a convoluted way.[4]

II

Both Wittgenstein's *Brown Book*, dictated in 1934–35, and the first part of his *Philosophical Investigations*, in which the core of his latter philosophy is brought to its most finished statement, criticize an account of how a child acquires language attributed by Wittgenstein to Saint Augustine and discernible in the writings of many philosophers. In 1926 Wittgenstein published a "Wordbook" for schoolchildren.[5]

----

[3]See Karl Menger's account of the impact of Brouwer's lecture on Wittgenstein in "Wittgenstein betreffende Seiten aus einem Buch über den Wiener Kreis", in *Wittgenstein, the Vienna Circle and Critical Rationalism: Proceedings of the 3rd International Wittgenstein Symposium* (Vienna: Hölder-Pichler-Tempsky, 1979), pp. 27–29.

[4]There is some disagreement among Wittgenstein's schoolteacher colleagues about the extent to which he was involved with school reform. Thus Rudolf Koder denies that Wittgenstein was involved at all; whereas Norbert Rosner and Franz Schiller maintain that he was involved.

[5]Ludwig Wittgenstein, *Wörterbuch für Volksschulen* (Vienna: Hölder-Pichler-Tempsky, 1926). Reprinted by the same publishers in 1977 with an Introduction in English and German by Adolf Hübner and Werner and Elisabeth Leinfellner, together with Wittgenstein's own Preface.

And in *Zettel* (412) he asks bluntly of himself:
"Am I doing child psychology?"

It comes, then, as no surprise to learn that one story he used to tell his elementary school pupils in Trattenbach as early as 1921 goes like this:

> Once upon a time there was an experiment. Two small children who had not yet learnt to speak were shut away with a woman who was unable to speak. The aim of the experiment was to determine whether they would learn some primitive language or invent a new language of their own. The experiment failed.

This story—or rather, the original version of which this can hardly be more than a partly remembered fragment—Wittgenstein recited to his nine- and ten-year-old schoolchildren during his first year of teaching. Some forty-eight years later, one of those students, now a farmer in Trattenbach, volunteered it to me as one of the things he had learned, and remembered, from Wittgenstein. In this brief tale are not simply anticipated, but embedded, some of the central concerns about language learning, primitive language, and private languages that were to preoccupy the "later Wittgenstein", who is commonly supposed to have emerged during the early thirties.

What is surprising is that Wittgenstein's six years as an elementary schoolteacher, during which he had sustained daily contact with children and was already engaged in the questions that dominate his later philosophy, were, for several decades after his death, cloaked in darkness. Philosophers appeared to suppose them unworthy of serious investigation. Accounts of Wittgenstein's life and work usually passed over them in a few sentences or a paragraph; rarely were even the correct dates and the right names and locations of the villagers given; what information was presented was usually drawn at first or second hand from the official reports which the school authorities in Neunkirchen drew up in response to written inquiries from the economist F. A. von Hayek (a second cousin to Wittgenstein, once removed) and others shortly after his death. These official reports, widely circulated among those interested in Wittgenstein, were prepared with little care and consist largely in uninterpreted and sometimes misleading anecdotes. One British scholar had visited the villages, but the villagers reported that he consulted only officials and schoolteachers and one former pupil of Wittgenstein's (now dead) who was known to possess a letter from him.[6] Engelmann had planned to discuss this part of Wittgenstein's life, but died before reaching that section of his Memoirs[7] and wrote only two very general reflective paragraphs on this matter. Others, while not making light of Wittgenstein's years as a schoolmaster, passed over them in hurried bewilderment, as if they constituted an eccentric act best not dwelt upon. Thus one American expositor of his thought wrote:

> A man of acknowledged genius, who, after knowing next to nothing about logic and philosophy, had made important contributions to both fields within a remarkably short period of time, a man who could not help having a brilliant future in one of the most sophisticated of all intellectual disciplines—this man turned his back on all that and devoted himself to the humble task of teaching young children in remote villages.[8]

However one cares to explain the neglect of Wittgenstein's schoolteaching experience, Wittgenstein himself was never much interested in academic careers. His decision to become a schoolmaster was closely related to the activities of his family immediately following the end of the First

---

[6]Since this was written, these villages have become much better known to philosophers. Since 1977, they have been the site of an annual international philosophical convention sponsored by the Austrian Ludwig Wittgenstein Society; and a Wittgenstein Documentation Center has been established at Kirchberg am Wechsel.

[7]See B. F. McGuinness in his Editor's Appendix to Paul Englemann, *Letters from Ludwig Wittgenstein, with a Memoir* (Oxford: Basil Blackwell, 1967), p. 145; and also Engelmann's own account, *ibid.*, pp. 114–15.

[8]George Pitcher, *The Philosophy of Wittgenstein* (Englewood Cliffs, N.J.: Prentice-Hall, 1964), p. 6.

World War. Confronted with the economically ruined strip of land now known as the Austrian Republic, the Wittgenstein family immediately engaged in wide-ranging social work. The family had a long tradition of public service, which most of its members treated, literally, as a duty. In creating the iron and steel industry of the Danube Monarchy (most of it situated in Bohemia and thus after 1918 in the new state of Czechoslovakia), Karl Wittgenstein had won a position in his country comparable to that of Andrew Carnegie in America and rather like that of the Krupp family in Germany; in fact, Carnegies, Krupps, Schwabs, and Wittgensteins were guests in one another's homes prior to the war. In prewar days, the Wittgensteins were prominent patrons of the arts. Gustav Mahler, Bruno Walter, Johannes Brahms, and Clara Schumann frequently visited the Palais Wittgenstein; Joseph Joachim and his quartet often played in its great salon.[9] Karl Wittgenstein also devoted himself passionately to the visual and plastic arts after his retirement from active business in the 1890s; he built the great Viennese exhibition hall, the Secession, and patronized many important contemporary painters. In 1914, over a year after his father's death, Ludwig made his own famous gift of 100,000 Kronen to Ludwig von Ficker to aid poets and writers, explaining to Ficker that he did so according to the custom of his class.[10]

In the immediate postwar years, however, social welfare more than the arts engaged the attention of Karl Wittgenstein's children. Herbert Hoover named Margarete Stonborough his personal representative for Austria in charge of work for the American Food Relief Commission, a role which put her in close touch with socialist and other political lead-

---

[9]See Bruno Walter, *Theme and Variations: An Autobiography* (London: Hamish Hamilton, 1947).

[10]The story of Wittgenstein's relationship with Ficker has now been recounted in great detail. See Ludwig Wittgenstein, *Briefe an Ludwig von Ficker* (Salzburg: Otto Müller, 1969). On Schwab and Karl Wittgenstein, see Robert Hessen: *Steel Titan* (New York: Oxford University Press, 1975), p. 136.

ers in Vienna including, conspicuously, Otto Glöckel, who, as administrative head of the school-reform program, was concerned directly with the economic redevelopment of the countryside through the education and re-education of the peasantry. Ludwig's eldest sister, Mining, opened a day school for poor Viennese boys near Grinzing, and eventually helped him with his own pupils in the countryside. In this context, Wittgenstein's decision to enter elementary school teaching—quite apart from any philosophical importance it may eventually have acquired—was hardly eccentric.

In any event, he was only one among hundreds of newly trained and often highly talented young schoolteachers, many of them returned veterans like himself, who poured out from Vienna into the Austrian countryside in September 1920. Among other talented young Austrians to enter the school-reform movement during the 1920s were Ludwig Erik Tesar, who, like Oskar Kokoschka, Adolf Loos, Rainer Maria Rilke, and Georg Trakl, had benefited from Wittgenstein's prewar bequest to Ficker, and at least two philosophers who were to become closely associated with the problems that preoccupied the members of the Vienna Circle: Karl Popper and Edgar Zilsel. The Vienna Circle itself, in its own manifesto, associated itself with the aims of the school-reform movement.[11]

III

What was the Austrian school-reform program? How and why did it arise? For what did it stand?

The unsatisfactory character of the prewar school systems of Germany and Austria has been dramatically conveyed by some of the most eminent German-speaking artists and writers. One need think only of Robert Musil's *Young*

---

[11]*Wissenschaftliche Weltauffassung: Der Wiener Kreis* (Vienna: Artur Wolf, 1929), p. 10. This has been republished in English as *The Scientific Conception of the World* (Dordrecht: D. Reidel, 1973).

Törless, Hermann Hesse's story "Beneath the Wheel", or the film *Mädchen in Uniform* to recall the themes and the mood of the protest against a repressive and counterproductive school system.

Nonetheless, the Austrians, under the Habsburgs, had enjoyed one of the more progressive school systems in Europe—progressive, of course, only by contrast to the systems of some other European countries, including England. In itself, it was anything but a paradigm of enlightened thinking: instruction, largely in the control of the Roman Catholic Church, was authoritarian and regimented. As Count Rottenhan, imperial adviser, had defined its aims, the purpose of the lower schools was "to make thoroughly pious, good, *tractable*, and industrious men of the labouring classes of the people". The constitution of the common schools issued by the Kaiser in 1805 was unequivocal: "The method of instruction", it decreed, "must endeavour first and foremost to train the memory; then, however, according to the pressure of the circumstances, the intellect and the heart. *The trivial schools will strictly refrain from any explanations other than those exactly prescribed in the 'school and method book' ...".*[12]

One might suppose that no educational philosophy other than expediency lay behind this approach. In fact, it was thoroughly dressed out in a philosophical psychology known as "associationism", a viewpoint that has some superficial points of similarity with Wittgenstein's early philosophy. Associationism as developed and presented in Austria derives chiefly from the view propounded by Johann Friedrich Herbart (1776–1841), whose followers filled most of the chairs of philosophy in Austria after the revolution of 1848.[13] This

---

[12]See Karl Strack, *Geschichte des deutschen Volksschulwesens* (Gütersloh: Bertelsmann, 1872), pp. 327–30, as quoted in Charles A. Gulick, *Austria from Habsburg to Hitler* (Berkeley and Los Angeles: The University of California Press, 1948), vol. I, p. 546. My italics.

[13]Heinrich Gomperz, "Philosophy in Austria During the Last Sixty Years", *The Personalist*, 1936, pp. 307–11. On Herbart's influence on Austrian philosophy, see also Barry Smith, "Wittgenstein and the Background of Austrian Philosophy", in *Wittgenstein and His Impact on Contemporary Thought: Proceedings of the Second International Wittgenstein Symposium* (Vienna: Hölder-Pichler-Tempsky, 1978).

view takes on subtle and complicated forms, but put crudely it considers the human mind to be neutral and passive, lacking innate faculties for producing ideas. The notion that the human mind is something like a passive storehouse suited admirably the conservative social goals of Habsburg educators. Teaching, for them, consisted in feeding students, by rote drill and association, those ideas which, so it had been decided, should dominate their lives. At no time, Herbart had argued, should a teacher engage in active debate with his students. As he explained in his *Outlines of Educational Doctrine*: "Cases may arise when the impetuosity of the pupil challenges the teacher to a kind of combat. Rather than accept such a challenge, he will usually find it sufficient at first to reprove calmly, to look on quietly, to wait until fatigue sets in."[14]

Against such a doctrine and the school system which embodied it, Otto Glöckel and his fellow reformers— building on a long tradition of school reform that had previously enjoyed little political power—mounted a fierce attack, insisting that the old "drilling schools" of the Habsburgs be replaced by a new kind of educational establishment, dubbed the "Arbeitsschule", or "Working School", in which the pupil would participate *actively* in his lessons. The word "Arbeit", or "work", referred in part to the new manual training and crafts that were introduced into the curriculum in order to acquaint middle-class children with some of the real difficulties and skills involved in manual labor. But more importantly, in the context of the German phrase "sich etwas erarbeiten", it referred to an active participation in lessons, aiming no longer simply at the passive rote learning and storage of facts of the drill schools, but at the development of capabilities. "Sich etwas erarbeiten" suggests in German acquiring knowledge by working or puzzling something out for oneself. What was wanted now was more independent and original thinking, activity, on the part of students—

---

[14]J. F. Herbart, *Outlines of Educational Doctrine* (Macmillan, 1904), p. 165.

activity, as opposed to the *fatigue* that Herbart thought would set in when a pupil dared to play an active part in his education.

The school reformers, most of whom were socialists (Social Democrats), viewed the change in orientation as politically necessary to free the future farming and working classes of the new republic from authoritarian attitudes toward learning and to fit them to participate as citizens of a democracy, actively weighing issues and deciding for themselves rather than passively accepting state decrees and church authority.

The program sounded admirable, in fact worked surprisingly well, and caught the attention of educators throughout the world. But in the semifeudal society that prevailed in much of German Austria after the First World War—outside of industrial cities such as Vienna and Graz—such an approach seemed less a program of educational reform, more a program for dissent and revolution. Ludwig Wittgenstein himself was less than enthusiastic in his support of the program; although he and his family got to know Glöckel himself fairly well, Wittgenstein often poked fun at the reform program's more vulgar slogans and projects. Yet hardly any better illustration can be found of the potentialities as well as the dangers of school reform from a political standpoint than Wittgenstein's own experiences with it in lower Austria. The majority of the villagers among whom he lived came to regard him and his new teaching methods as dangerously threatening to their way of life.

Wittgenstein's experiences provide a good, but by no means isolated, example of this reaction. It appears from the bitter reaction to the school-reform program which occurred in the late twenties and early thirties that even run-of-the-mill school reformers were able to evoke some such response when they attempted to put reforms into effect in the Austrian countryside. The peasant farmer forces eventually mounted a reaction to Glöckel throughout the land, first confining the reform to Vienna, and then, after the Dollfuss dictatorship of 1934 (the main support for which came from the countryside), abolishing it entirely.

Ironically, Karl Wittgenstein might have predicted such a response from the Austrian peasantry. Already in 1898, speaking of the importance of educating the industrial worker and the farmer, the elder Wittgenstein had written: "The uneducated peasant, who himself has learnt nothing, and does not have his son taught anything ... is the point of departure and the greatest support for all efforts, which, partly consciously and partly unconsciously, hinder all progress."[15] Karl Wittgenstein would hardly have suspected that his son Ludwig, then only nine years old, would eventually go into the countryside to try to educate the peasantry, armed not with his father's own dim view of them but with Tolstoy's romantic vision of the noble serf in mind.

IV

A man without expectations can hardly be disappointed; and there can be no doubt that a year in Trattenbach left Wittgenstein bitterly disappointed.

Although set in the mountains, Trattenbach is hardly one of Austria's more charming or pretty villages. Situated 2,500 feet above sea level and closed in between a steep range of mountains, reaching up to 5,000 feet, to the north and a small rivulet and further high mountains to the south, it is now an untidy, unkempt place with dreary buildings, and it must have been far drearier when Wittgenstein lived there. The climate is severe, and the steep mountains restrict the amount of sunshine reaching the villages except on those days when Trattenbach, which itself runs roughly from east to west, lies in the sun's direct path.

Yet Wittgenstein's first response to the place was almost enthusiastic. Within a week of his arrival he wrote to Bertrand Russell, then in Peking, to tell him of his new post and

---

[15]Karl Wittgenstein, "The Causes of the Development of Industry in America", Vienna, privately printed and published, in English, by its author, 1898, p. 23.

to report: "A short while ago I was *terribly depressed* and tired of living, but now I am slightly more hopeful."[16] Three weeks later a letter that was enthusiastic by Wittgenstein's standards went off to Engelmann: "I am working in a beautiful little nest called Trattenbach. . . . I am happy in my work at school, and I do need it badly, or else all the devils in Hell break loose inside. . . ."[17]

The about-face that Wittgenstein made during his first year in Trattenbach reminds one of several passages from one brief page of his *Tractatus*, written some years before he set foot in the village. There he had written:

> Ethics and aesthetics are one and the same. . . .
>
> If the good or bad exercise of the will does alter the world, it can alter only the limits of the world, not the facts—not what can be expressed by means of language.
>
> In short, the effect must be that it becomes an altogether different world. It must, so to speak, wax and wane as a whole.
>
> The world of the happy man is a different one from that of the unhappy man.[18]

It is hardly likely that Trattenbach or its people underwent any significant change—that the facts were altered—during Wittgenstein's first year there. But by the start of his second year in the village, Wittgenstein, deeply unhappy, found his "beautiful little nest" odious. Just a year after the letter to Russell quoted above, he wrote again to Russell, now returned to England, that he was "still at Trattenbach, surrounded, as ever, by odiousness and baseness. I know that human beings on the average are not worth much anywhere, but here they are much more good-for-nothing and irresponsible than elsewhere. I will perhaps stay on in Trat-

---

[16]Quoted in Bertrand Russell, *Autobiography* (London: Allen and Unwin, 1968), vol. II, pp. 166–67.

[17]Engelmann, *Letters from Wittgenstein*, p. 38–39.

[18]Ludwig Wittgenstein, *Tractatus Logico-Philosophicus*, new translation by D. F. Pears and B. F. McGuinness (London: Routledge and Kegan Paul, 1961), propositions 6.421, 6.43.

tenbach for the present year but probably not any longer, because I don't get on well here even with the other teachers (perhaps that won't be any better in another place). . . ".[19]

Russell objected that all men are wicked, and Trattenbachers no more than others.[20] Wittgenstein, who evidently did have some difficulty in expressing himself on this matter in language, took Russell's point, replying: "You are right: the Trattenbachers are not uniquely worse than the rest of the human race. But Trattenbach is a particularly insignificant place in Austria and the *Austrians* have sunk so miserably low since the war that it's too dismal to talk about."[21]

Wittgenstein's world had evidently waned as a whole. And it had waned during the course of his moral encounter with the Trattenbachers; in the exercise of his will upon them—and their will on him—the limits of his world had been altered.

Russell has described Wittgenstein's passionate, intense, dominating purity, while Leonard Woolf has commented on Wittgenstein's aggressively cruel streak. Russell and Woolf were able to discriminate and weigh such traits; to the villagers of Trattenbach, whose children and grandchildren, nephews and nieces, were being taught by Wittgenstein, honesty and cruelty often amounted to the same thing. Ruthless, impassioned honesty, particularly when unsolicited, can be cruelly sadistic.

A genius, Weininger writes, finds it tortuously difficult to lie. In Trattenbach and Otterthal, Wittgenstein came to avoid other adults as far as possible; but when he did encounter them, he did not lie, and they hated him for it. Many of the children, however, adored Wittgenstein. And they taught one another.

---

[19]Russell, *Autobiography*, vol. II, pp. 167–68.

[20]*Ibid.*, p. 139.

[21]*Ibid.*, pp. 169–70. Russell ignores Wittgenstein's actual reply, even though it was printed in his own book, and fantasizes the exchange. See p. 139, and compare pp. 169–70. Many factual misstatements concerning Wittgenstein appear in Russell's book.

V

What sort of people were these "good-for-nothing and irre-sponsible" Trattenbachers whose "wickedness" Russell had to defend? And how did they come so grievously to offend Wittgenstein?

It is hardly likely that Wittgenstein ever read E. M. For-ster's ironic remark, in *Howards End*, about the very poor who "are unthinkable, and only to be approached by the statistician or the poet". Had he read it, he would surely have rejected the remark, if not the irony, outright. Wittgen-stein had gone into the peasant countryside of lower Austria with a naïvely romantic notion of peasant simplicity and honesty, some of it derived from the democratic slogans of the new Austrian Republic, some from the school-reform program, some from his own experiences during the war, but most from reading Tolstoy's exaltation of "noble" peas-ant life. Wittgenstein's anticipation of peasant virtue was reinforced by his disgust with city life and his often voiced contempt for what he called the "half-educated" city folk corrupted by the popular press—against whom Wittgen-stein, like Karl Kraus, inveighed throughout the postwar period.

One need not exaggerate Wittgenstein's romanticism. But if the poor are not unthinkable, either in Wittgenstein's or in Forster's sense, it remains true that they are, at least as individuals, not really much thought about. In his first year in Trattenbach, charged with the responsibility for their future, Wittgenstein encountered individually, and thought about, poor central European peasants with an intensity not known to Tolstoy. Perhaps what most offended him was their obstinate failure to conform to anything approaching Tolstoy's portrait. Tolstoy, in his *Confession*, had reported how, on returning from abroad, he settled in the country and occupied himself with peasant schools, wherein he was able to avoid facing what he called the "falsity" of the cities. Wittgenstein, however, *did* encounter falsity and crude ven-iality among the peasantry. He learned that the poor were indeed, as Forster put it, "inferior to most rich people . . . not as courteous as the average rich man, nor as intelligent, nor as healthy, nor as lovable". If many things about Wittgenstein's sojourn in the countryside are unclear, it is all too clear that, with all the famous will power of his family working in him, he refused to accept what he clearly observed—indeed, what his father had already described; and despite his denunciations of these people and his early disillusionment with them, he threw his fantastic energy and imagination into a desperate six-year-long attempt to "get the peasantry out of the muck", to cite the phrase he used again and again when explaining his goals and educational views to friends and colleagues.

In the end, Wittgenstein's radical effort to reform the peasantry—even the few thousand that he encountered in three small villages—failed miserably. Not only did those he tried to help reject him, but they eventually ran him out of town. On the other hand, his effort may have succeeded in a way of which he never became aware. For Wittgenstein did have a profound effect on the peasant children whom he taught, and they on him. Moreover, one need not disagree with Forster to maintain that poor *children* are often superior in many ways to most rich *adults*: that they are more intelligent, healthier, more lovable, and in their own way more courteous, than rich adults—rich *adults*, not rich children. During his life Wittgenstein taught only two sorts of person: the privileged adults who were his students and colleagues at Cambridge and poor Austrian peasant children. His later philosophy suggests that he learned as much, and probably more, from those children than he learned from adults.

The some three dozen children with whom he had to deal directly in Trattenbach formed only a tiny fraction of the village's population. In 1920 some 800 persons lived there. By contrast to many Austrian mountain villages—including neighboring Otterthal, a farming community—Trattenbach was not homogeneous. A factory, a wool mill, had been established there, and some 200 inhabitants labored in it; most of the rest of the population, apart from a few village tradesmen such as the grocer and shoemaker, were engaged in farming.

In addition to reporting the size of the village and the distribution of its population, the statistician can confirm that it was indeed miserable: both farms and factories were in desperate shape right after the war. The Trattenbachers were undernourished; they were anxious and harassed by their condition; and democracy for them at first meant not independence but separation. Within the village a kind of class conflict already existed, separating workers and farmers—and their children—from one another. The reasons were not strictly economic: workers were sometimes better off than farmers, yet the farmers enjoyed a certain social status denied the workers. Projecting their internal troubles on the tiny mountain area surrounding them, the Trattenbachers proceeded to break away from their ancient economic and administrative unit: until 1923 Trattenbach had been united administratively with the neighboring communities of Kranichberg and Otterthal, but after some five years of bickering, Trattenbach, poorest of the three, managed to break away—and to remain poorest.

Besides the indigenous villagers a tiny outside élite lived or exerted its influence in Trattenbach: the village priest represented the presence and power of the Church; the village schoolmasters, including Wittgenstein, the presence of the State. Through the factory, outside economic interest was represented too. A certain Herr Mautner—of whom it is now remembered only that he was owner or part owner of the factory (now closed), that he was Jewish, that he had land and servants in the area, and that Ludwig Wittgenstein flatly refused to meet him despite repeated invitations—also resided in the village. Mautner does not enter into this story; but the village priest and schoolmasters, and their district superiors, do play an important role.

Among the latter, the most important was Wilhelm Kundt. He was not a Trattenbacher, but as District School Superintendent he figures importantly in any attempt to reconstruct school life in Neunkirchen, the large countryside school district in lower Austria which embraces all three of the elementary schools where Wittgenstein taught from 1920 to 1926. From what can be learned about Kundt, it can be established that Neunkirchen, unlike a large part of the countryside, was from the outset of the first Austrian Republic a district in which Glöckel's school reforms were being implemented. Kundt had come to Neunkirchen, full of the slogans of school reform, in 1919, a year before Wittgenstein arrived, and he remained superintendent there until 1933 when, during a period of drastic upheaval in Austria's educational programs, he was transferred to Mödling, near Vienna, and replaced after a few months by an opponent of school reform. Kundt is known to have achieved considerable success in implementing Glöckel's program in his district; as late as 1929, when the tide, in the Austrian countryside as a whole, had already turned strongly against the reform movement, visiting study commissions from such places as Carinthia turned in surprised reports about Kundt's success in reforming the schools of his district in line with Glöckel's principles.[22] Whether Kundt had had anything to do with bringing Wittgenstein to Neunkirchen is unknown, but for nearly six years he supported him, persuaded him to stay in the district, and attempted to soothe his relations with some of the villagers.

Already at Trattenbach before either Kundt or Wittgenstein arrived were two other schoolteachers, Georg Berger and Martin Scherleitner, both of whom had been assigned to Trattenbach in 1918. Both had missed formal training in school-reform principles, but Scherleitner, an energetic and intelligent man, picked up the new ideas and endorsed some of them strongly. The reform appears to have meant little if anything to Berger, a pathetically dull man. Three other teachers who came and went while Wittgenstein was there need not be mentioned here. Even Scherleitner was not

[22]Willibald Schneider, "100 Jahre Reichsvolksschulgesetz und Schulaufsicht im Schulbezirk Neunkirchen", in *Erziehung und Unterricht*, Vienna, May 1969, pp. 329–38.

stationed constantly at Trattenbach during this period, but went back and forth to Otterthal and other schools in the district. In effect, the school was run by Wittgenstein and Berger, and the latter in time became principal.

With Kundt and Scherleitner, Wittgenstein maintained good relations; Berger and another man who remained at Trattenbach only one term are those about whom Wittgenstein complained in his letter to Russell.

Wittgenstein's only genuine friendship in either Trattenbach or Otterthal, however, was with Father Alois Neururer, the parish priest. A petulant romantic like Wittgenstein, Neururer had arrived in Trattenbach in 1917. A rebel innovator, and a "long-haired socialist" to boot, Neururer was concerned less in providing the traditional comforts of religion than in effecting religious and moral awakening among the members of his flock. When one of the villagers, on his deathbed, refused the last rites of the Church and expressed his contempt for it, Neururer went about expressing his admiration for the man. When his conduct of the Mass was challenged (he often used German rather than Latin, and conducted Mass facing the congregation, liturgical practices which were approved for general use by the Roman Catholic Church only after Vatican Council II), Neururer calmly proclaimed to his parishioners that he could do anything that the Pope could do. From his pulpit, Neururer would abuse the people of the village mercilessly. When Arvid Sjögren came to visit Wittgenstein, as he did regularly, the two would gleefully go to church together—although neither was Roman Catholic—to listen to Neururer berate the Trattenbachers. Neururer was finally run out of Trattenbach in 1936.

In the early twenties Neururer and Wittgenstein found themselves allied in their efforts to reform the adult community of Trattenbach. Although kindred personalities in some respects, in an important way the two differed and complemented one another. Wittgenstein could rarely relax with adults outside his family, not even with those he knew well. Army records of him, while describing him as a "good comrade", also comment on his "shyness"; similarly, the adult Trattenbachers encountered only an aloof awkwardness from him that came across as gruffness. Toward the schoolchildren alone was Wittgenstein able to show affection and tenderness. Neururer, by contrast, although ineffectual with children, was able to show affectionate understanding as well as harsh discipline toward the adult villagers. So the Catholic priest deferred to Wittgenstein in teaching, even in religious instruction, whereas Wittgenstein used Neururer as his agent, in effect, in quite ordinary transactions with the townspeople.

To perform one of his most famous deeds in Trattenbach, his "miracle"—or rather, a miracle in the eyes of the villagers—Wittgenstein had to call on the good offices of both Berger and Neururer. I have in mind the well-known story of the time the steam engine in the wool factory stopped. Engineers called in from Vienna, at a loss to repair it, recommended, to the dismay of director and workers, that it be dismantled and returned to Vienna for repair. Since this would have meant a temporary closing of the factory, Wittgenstein asked Berger to secure permission from the factory foreman to let him examine the machine. After this request was reluctantly granted, Wittgenstein appeared at the factory, accompanied by Berger, examined the machine from all sides, and then requested the aid of four workmen. In accordance with Wittgenstein's directions, the workmen tapped the machine in rhythm and, to the astonishment of those present, it began to work. Wittgenstein refused the proffered payment but, when pressed, agreed to let the factory give Neururer woollen cloth to distribute to the village children. Here in one incident is displayed Wittgenstein's extraordinary competence, for which he was both admired and feared, and his intense fear of rejection. He did not have the courage to approach the factory foreman himself, but needed Berger to speak up for him; nor did he dare to distribute gifts to the villagers himself, having repeatedly been rebuffed by them. This work of charity, as well as numerous others, was undertaken by Neururer on Wittgenstein's behalf.

VI

Once, when questioned by a villager about his religion, Wittgenstein replied that although he was not a Christian, he was an "evangelist". The villager was bewildered, for Wittgenstein emphasized that he did not mean that he was a Protestant (or "Evangelical"). What Wittgenstein was trying to say cannot be determined with certainty, but it appears he intended to suggest that although his business had something to do with the saving of souls and the proclamation of a gospel, these need not take place in a formal Christian framework.

The gospel that he had to proclaim was one shown to the villagers by the form of life he adopted. His outward behavior seems to have been calculated to shock them into the awareness of different possibilities of life, to jolt them out of their prejudices, to confuse and bewilder them to a point where they, as well as their children, could learn what he had, if not to say, then to show.

The initial paradox was, of course, the presence of a man of his background in a place like Trattenbach. Wittgenstein himself was aware of and, at least at first, amused by his situation: when writing to Russell, he remarked that this was probably the first time the schoolmaster of Trattenbach had been in correspondence with the professor of philosophy in Peking. Had he wished to do so, Wittgenstein could probably have gone into Trattenbach and the other villages incognito: his family possessed enough influence in Vienna to make some such arrangement. However, he went out of his way to ensure that the villagers would know who he was, or at least that they would know of his family's wealth and influence, of his own education and aristocratic background, and of his academic achievement in England. He told his school colleagues and several villagers about the *Tractatus*: it had not yet been published, and when he first described it to them, he referred to it as a book called "Der Satz", or "The Proposition", adding that they would "not be able to understand one word of it". Shortly after his first arrival in Trattenbach, Wittgenstein was visited by

Hänsel (who came to see him—as did his friends Drobil, a sculptor, and Nähr, the Wittgenstein family photographer— approximately every second month throughout his sojourn in the villages). While taking lunch together in the inn, Wittgenstein and Hänsel talked about life in Vienna in voices that the villagers present, listening intently, easily overheard. One of Wittgenstein's remarks to Hänsel which is still remembered is this: "Ich hatte einst einen Diener, der hieß Konstantin" ("I once had a servant named Konstantin"). Later during Hänsel's visit, Wittgenstein and he cornered poor Georg Berger in the school office, and Wittgenstein demanded to know what the villagers had to say about him. Berger reports that he replied reluctantly, fearing Wittgenstein's temper: "The people take you to be a rich baron." Wittgenstein was satisfied with the answer, but remarked to Berger that although he had indeed been rich, he had given all his money away to his siblings "in order to do a good deed".

Having established his background, Wittgenstein set about showing his contempt, or at least lack of concern, for the things that villagers might expect money to buy. He lived in ostentatious poverty. Father Neururer had already irritated the villagers with his long hair and shabby clothes, but at least he maintained a house and housekeeper (his sister), whereas Wittgenstein lived in a tiny and primitive room. At first he had put up in a room in the building next to the inn, Zum braunen Hirschen, in Trattenbach; but one Friday evening not long after his arrival he stormed out in a rage at the loud and rather drunken singing of the villagers downstairs and demanded quarter that night with the Bergers. For a time after his departure from the inn, Wittgenstein slept in the school kitchen. Still later he moved into the tiny attic room over the grocery store. In Puchberg and Otterthal he was to live in even more primitive quarters.

In his dress, Wiggenstein rejected the traditional costume of the schoolmaster, hat, suit, tie and collar, in favor of a simple uniform: he wore a plain clean shirt with open collar; gray trousers; a pair of shoes for the warmer months, and boots in winter. For cold weather he wore a leather

wind jacket, but during his sojourn in Trattenbach he went
without a hat. Almost always he carried a walking stick and
was often seen on his solitary walks with an old briefcase or
a notebook tucked under his arm.

What struck the hungry villagers even more than Wittgenstein's living arrangements and dress was his diet. He
took his lunch with the family Traht, one of the poorest
families in the area, each afternoon. The Trahts were exceptionally simple and pious farmers, introduced to him by
Neururer, and they were the only villagers to whom Wittgenstein formed any emotional attachment. Each day he
made the half-hour hike up the mountain north of the village to their small house for his midday meal. Although
Wittgenstein could hardly have communicated with the
Trahts in a way that would have amounted to friendship, he
was greatly attracted to them and is said to have been particularly impressed by their religious piety. They were the only
villagers with whom he kept in contact after his departure
from Neunkirchen in 1926: he sent them postcards from
England, and twice during the 1930s, the last time in 1933,
Wittgenstein stole secretly back to Trattenbach, in Neururer's company, to visit old Frau Traht, who had become seriously ill.

However strongly attached to this family Wittgenstein
may have become, one can only speculate how poor the
lunch they served him must have been; for the other villagers, whose own food was inadequate, despised the Trahts
for their poverty. Wittgenstein's evening meal was no better.
It consisted of cocoa and oatmeal, which he prepared for
himself in his room. Sometimes he would fetch his milk
from the Trahts; sometimes one of his pupils fetched it for
him. Most of his best pupils took dinner with him at one time
or another, and each brought home the same horrified tale.
Wittgenstein used a sort of pressure cooker for heating cocoa
with oatmeal and other unspecified ingredients. He never
washed the pot, so that what remained became caked inside
it, got harder and harder, and grew ever larger, diminishing
the pot in volume. Finally the volume of the pot was so much
reduced that cocoa could be prepared for only one person
at a time.

VII

Wittgenstein's undisguised disregard for their material values unnerved the villagers of Trattenbach and Otterthal. But so much they might have tolerated; they had, after all, heard of eccentric millionaires as well as religious hermits, and they put up with Neururer until 1936. What alarmed and frightened them, as well as aroused their jealousy, was Wittgenstein's relationship with their children. The conflict between image and reality, or "cognitive dissonance", involved here must have been extreme. In the course of gossiping heatedly about him, the villagers gradually built up for themselves a picture of Wittgenstein as an unbelievably cruel teacher who constantly and mercilessly beat their children. Nonetheless, they were confronted with the brute fact that their children were more than willing to spend the entire day with this "monster", long after school hours, rather than to return home to their families. Eventually the villagers resorted to the courts in an unsuccessful attempt to *prove* that Wittgenstein did beat their children sadistically.

Only Neururer appears to have been entirely immune to the alarm, fright, and simple jealousy that Wittgenstein aroused. They got along very well indeed. They are said to have conversed and exchanged letters in Latin. And Wittgenstein read Dostoevsky's *Brothers Karamazov* aloud to Neururer over and over again.

Wittgenstein's colleague Berger, an inferior and unpopular teacher, was, however, as threatened as were the villagers by Wittgenstein's successes with the children, so much so that Berger in effect went native in order to protect himself, spending much of his time socializing and gossiping with the villagers and stirring up hard feelings against Wittgenstein. And he did what no Austrian schoolmaster need ever have done: he began social climbing in Trattenbach, of all places, playing favorites with the richer farm children and neglecting the children of the factory workers. After Wittgenstein's departure from the area he reversed procedures that the former had initiated, and in later years, still haunted by his encounter with Wittgenstein, he sought to erase the very name of Wittgenstein from the Trattenbach school records: in the large Trattenbach chronicle published in 1934 Wittgenstein's name is conspicuously missing from the otherwise accurate list of schoolmasters who had served there.[23] Only when he heard of Wittgenstein's posthumous fame did Berger acquire friendly memories of his former colleague.

VIII

To understand the intensity of the reaction of the Trattenbach and Otterthal villagers to Wittgenstein, a few examples of his way of dealing with his schoolchildren may be useful. To the adult villagers we know that for the most part he remained aloof; from time to time he would descend into their lives—by repairing the steam engine at the factory, for instance, or by prescribing a treatment for some illness, showing a farmer or a housewife how to mend some equipment, or sending a pair of shoes, by way of Neururer, to some poor village family. With the children he was another person entirely.

Some things that Wittgenstein could offer his pupils were of a tangible sort that any schoolmaster with some extra money could have given. He provided extra food out of his own or his sister Mining's pocket (fruit in particular and occasionally chocolate), and also routinely prescribed, but rarely issued, school equipment. He brought his own microscope to Trattenbach from Vienna, and in each of his schools he carefully put together, with the aid of the children, skeletons of small animals for use in the elementary zoology and nature-lore lessons. The skeleton of a cat that he assembled at Puchberg is still in use there. He also had the children help him construct models of steam engines, pulleys, and other mechanical instruments. The models that Wittgen-

---

[23]Franz Scheibenreif, *Orts- und Hauschronik von Trattenbach* (Gemeindeamt Trattenbach: Im Selbstverlag und Kommissions Verlag; Druck: K. Mühlberger, Neunkirchen, 1934).

stein and his pupils constructed were, one is told, rather better built than most of those made elsewhere at this time; but the act in itself was not unusual. During these years most village schoolmasters were being asked to construct such equipment, since school budgets could not afford professional equipment.[24]

The excursions on which Wittgenstein took his pupils— to the printing press in Gloggnitz, and to Vienna—fall more or less into the same category. Mining and her brother covered all expenses themselves, but another schoolmaster with extra cash might have done the same. Berger, who was at this time busily borrowing money from Wittgenstein—and returning it to him after inflation had reduced its value— could not afford these outings; but they were common in Austria at this time, particularly in the cities and larger towns where travel expense was less. Outings of some sort were prescribed by the reform program.

Wittgenstein would doubtless have made adventures of these activities whether a school-reform program had existed or not; nonetheless, some of his best-known feats, often treated as peculiar exploits, were directly in line with school-reform directives. Indeed, Wittgenstein wrote up his projects and school activities by reference to these principles in the reports he was required to submit regularly to Kundt.

Identifying catchwords were attached to the main school-reform principles, two of the most important of which were *"Selbsttätigkeit"*, meaning "self-activity", and *integrated instruction*. Some sense of Wittgenstein's way of implementing these principles emerges from the stories told about the composition of his Wordbook and about the excursions to Vienna on which he led his children.

"Self-activity" designated the attempt to encourage youngsters to figure things out for themselves actively instead of

---

[24]Wittgenstein had studied handcrafts ("Knabenhandarbeit") at the Teachers Training College in Vienna with Alexander Zinnecker. For an account of his approach see Zinnecker's book *Knabenhandarbeit: Handbuch der deutschen Lehrerbildung* (Munich and Berlin: R. Oldenbourg, 1931).

being force-fed information by the teacher in the style of the pre-reform drilling school. Prior to 1919, in accordance with drill-school methodology, rules of spelling and grammar had been dictated, written on the blackboard perhaps, and then memorized by rote. After the reform, drill was dropped in favor of an attempt to encourage the children to discover the rules of spelling and grammar for themselves. First they wrote essays freely without particular attention to spelling or grammar; only after they had acquired some fluency in written expression was grammar introduced to correct what had been written. To introduce grammar as well as correct spelling, students were asked to compile word lists. Wittgenstein's own *Wörterbuch für Volksschulen,* which was published as an officially approved school textbook in 1926, was meant to aid the active learning of both spelling and grammar. He had begun to compile it, with the aid of his students, as early as 1921. Each pupil was required to prepare at home, and to bind for himself, his own wordbook containing the words he had used in his own essays. The resulting booklets were 16 x 10 cm in size, and were comprised of three sections, covered in brown cardboard and sewn together with strong thread, to make a book of 64 sheets. Wittgenstein, in turn, compiled a corrected master list of words, which was available in his schoolroom as the students' "dictionary". If, in the course of writing further essays, doubts arose about spelling or certain sorts of usage, the pupils could check for themselves in the wordbook to which they themselves had contributed.

In explaining his decision to publish his own wordbook, Wittgenstein would produce examples of wordbooks then in general use and show, page by page, how poorly adapted these were for teaching either spelling or grammar. They were, for instance, littered with foreign words that were not only unknown to the children but that might make a wordbook appear an awesome tool to handle. Also, in these traditional wordbooks examples of usage tended to be literary and complicated, often far too difficult for the average child to comprehend. Wittgenstein's own wordbook is distinctive in that it consists entirely of words actually used by his own

The elementary school in Otterthal, as it appears today.

The house of Dr. Bevan, in Cambridge, where Wittgenstein died in 1951.

Ludwig Boltzmann, the Viennese physicist with whom Wittgenstein wished to study as a youth.

Karl Kraus.

Otto Glöckel, 1874-1935. Leader of the School Reform movement in Austria.

Adolf Loos.

Otto Weininger.

Drawing of Wittgenstein by David Levine.

*Below: Farmer Traht, Trattenbach,
whose family provided Wittgenstein
with lunch during his years in
Trattenbach.*

*Above: Karl Gruber and Johann
Scheibenbauer, elementary-school
students of Wittgenstein. Trattenbach,
summer 1969, in front of the grocery
store where Wittgenstein once lived.*

Wittgenstein in his boat, near his hut in Skjolden i Sogn, Norway.

Wittgenstein in the 1930s, after his return to Cambridge.

Wittgenstein at Cambridge in the late 1930s.

The garden at Hütteldorf, where Wittgenstein worked as a gardener during the summer of 1926.

The grocery store in Trattenbach. Wittgenstein lived in the middle attic room under the gable.

Karl Wittgenstein, father of Ludwig Wittgenstein.

The Secession, Friedrichstraße 12, Vienna. Sponsored by Karl Wittgenstein.

Looking out onto the terrace, from the interior of the house on the Kundmanngasse which Wittgenstein designed for his sister Margarete Stonborough.

Plan of the ground floor in the house at Kundmanngasse 19.

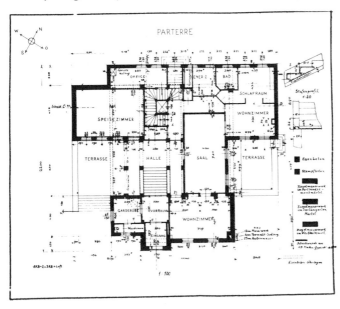

The house at Kundmanngasse 19.

Gustav Klimt's portrait of Margarete Stonborough.

Wittgenstein with his schoolchildren in Puchberg. Spring 1923.

Pencil drawing of Wittgenstein by Michael Drobil.

*Wittgenstein as an Austrian army officer, from his army
identity card, June 30, 1918.*

Wittgenstein's army identity card, verso.

The Palais Wittgenstein, Alleegasse, Vienna.

On the Hochreit, the Wittgenstein family summer home, summer of 1920. To Wittgenstein's right is his sister, Helene Salzer; to his left, his friend Arvid Sjögren. Seated across from Sjögren and Wittgenstein are Sjögren's brother and Helene Salzer's daughter. At the far end of the table is the painter Hänisch.

pupils in their essays *and* introduces words from the dialect as well as from High German. Wittgenstein deliberately took the unorthodox step of introducing dialect in order to teach grammatical usage. People who use dialect German quite often mix up dative and accusative constructions. Therefore, to bring home to them the difference between the two cases, Wittgenstein introduced simple examples where the distinction was clear even in dialect. His method is especially clear in his presentation of the dative and accusative of the third-person pronouns:

> *ihm*, "to him", a dative form, is introduced as follows: "In dialect, 'eam'. For example: 'I hob *eam* g'sogt.' " (The sentence that Wittgenstein presents here is a dialect rendering of the High German: "Ich habe ihm gesagt", or "I said to him".)

> *ihn*, "him", an accusative form, is introduced in this way: "In dialect, 'n' or 'm'. For example: 'I hob *m* g'sehn.' " (Here Wittgenstein's example exhibits the dialect rendering of the High German sentence: "Ich habe ihn gesehen", or "I saw him".)

> *ihnen*, "to them", a dative plural form, Wittgenstein introduces in a similar way: "In dialect: 'eana'. For example: 'I hob 's *eana* g'sogt.' " (Here the example is a dialect rendering of the High German sentence: "Ich habe es ihnen gesagt", or "I said it to them".)

Such a presentation is simple and straightforward, yet ingenious. Instead of campaigning against the use of dialect, Wittgenstein himself uses dialect in order to teach grammar!

Wittgenstein used similar step-by-step procedures and illustrations from the dialect to teach other distinctions; for example, that between the definite article *das*, 'the', and the conjunction *daß*, 'that'.

Here, as in mathematics, Wittgenstein argued that the child should learn the principle of a thing through an *interesting*, though possibly difficult, specific case; even if other standard examples were easier to learn, there was no point in cluttering up the mind of the child with them unless he understood and could apply the principle behind them. Thus one went from the unusual to the ordinary rather than—as many teachers had hitherto supposed—from the ordinary to the unusual. When Robert Dottrens, of the Institut Jean-Jacques Rousseau in Geneva, wrote of the school-reform program, "Like the instruction in the native tongue and in writing, the teaching of arithmetic is completely changed. ... *The meaning of the operations is discovered while their technique is being acquired*",[25] he touched on the nerve of Wittgenstein's later comment in *Zettel* (412) that he was "making a connexion between the concept of teaching and the concept of meaning".[26]

In putting together his wordbook, Wittgenstein implemented not only the school-reform principle of "self-activity" but also the reform aim that had been dubbed "integrated instruction". The second slogan designates two closely connected goals: the teacher is encouraged to relate the teaching process to the student's local environment and customs; and he is given the latitude to determine how and when the students will turn from one subject to another during the school day, and how they will integrate or connect one to another—no reading or spelling period as such, for example, is set aside. Although general goals were indicated, the interest of the children was supposed to determine how the day would be divided. Here, as in the presentation of the idea of self-activity, one finds a rather explicit criticism of prewar associationist educational psychologies, in which it had been taken for granted that everything could, and should, be broken down into "unit ideas", which meant in practice that the teaching of different subjects was rigidly compartmentalized. In the case of Wittgenstein's *Wörterbuch*, the self-activity of the students in compiling their own dictionaries, which alerted them to an awareness of the ambiguities of their own usage, was integrated with the local environ-

---

[25]Robert Dottrens, *The New Education in Austria* (New York: The John Day Co., 1930), p. 58, my italics.

[26]Ludwig Wittgenstein, *Zettel*, 2nd. edition (Oxford: Basil Blackwell, 1981), item 412.

ment through the use of dialect.

Prior to its being authorized by the Ministry of Education, Wittgenstein's wordbook was sent for examination and review to an expert, Eduard Buxbaum, district school inspector in Waidhofen an der Thaya. In his report, Buxbaum invoked the school reform's "work-principle" *(Arbeitsprinzip)* in defence of such wordbooks, writing: "The work-principle has made the use of a wordbook in the upper classes of the Volk and Bürger schools into the most topical question."[27] Buxbaum went on, however, to cite several faults in Wittgenstein's work, particularly in his Preface, and also objected to a certain onesidedness in the choice of the words. Allowing that the dictionary would be a "somewhat useful educational tool" once its shortcomings were corrected, Buxbaum nonetheless judged that "In its present form it could hardly be designated as worthy of recommendation to a school authority".[28] Buxbaum's report did not prevent the wordlist itself from being printed, but Wittgenstein's Preface was omitted.

One could cite numerous additional anecdotes and examples to illustrate Wittgenstein's style of combining the various principles of the school-reform program. The excursions to Vienna mentioned above provide an appropriate final example. On these jaunts the children usually spent two nights in Vienna, where Mining put them up at her school in Grinzing. But the integration began the moment the children assembled for departure in Trattenbach. As they hiked through the woods to catch the train from Gloggnitz, Wittgenstein required them to identify the local plants and stones, samples of which they had already studied in class. While they wandered through the streets of Vienna he threw a barrage of questions and information at them, calling their attention to machines, architectural styles, or other things they had already learned about at school. For instance, at the Techni-

---

[27]Quoted in Adolf Hübner's introduction to the new 1977 edition of the wordbook, p. XI.
[28]*Ibid.*

cal Museum the children had to explain the models of steam engines, block-and-tackle, pulleys, and other mechanisms by reference to what they had studied in class. In Trattenbach, Wittgenstein had taught his pupils the laws of the lever; now he asked them to apply those laws to specific examples. When they reached St. Stephen's Cathedral, they identified the reliefs and the different styles of architecture, such as gothic and baroque, which they had already drawn in school. As they walked through the city, or into the Palace of Schönbrunn, Wittgenstein pointed out the different kinds of columns—Corinthian, Ionian, Doric—and asked for identification. Only at the very end of the trip did the intensive questioning abate. The return train did not reach Gloggnitz until after nightfall, and the children had to make the twelve-mile hike with Wittgenstein through the dark forest. Sensing that some of them were frightened, Wittgenstein quietly went from one to another, asking: "Are you afraid? Well, then, you must think only about God." The non-Christian "Evangelist", who began and ended each school day with the Pater Noster, did not attack the religion of his villagers any more than he attacked their dialect.

IX

In Austria as a whole, the reform in the elementary schools was often criticized by those in the upper schools and Gymnasia for emphasizing activity at the expense of content. Wittgenstein, however, achieved stunning results in mathematics, teaching ten- and eleven-year-old boys advanced algebra and geometry. About a third of his male pupils learned to handle mathematical theory and tasks that were usually not taught at all in elementary school, but introduced only in Gymnasium. In defence of his ambitions, which went far beyond the school-reform program, Wittgenstein explained to his colleague Norbert Rosner in Puchberg that "one could never begin algebra early enough". He also took his students far beyond ordinary elementary-school standards in the study of history, and in literature he and his students read together not only folk and fairy tales, but also the type of poem that a student would usually not encounter before the equivalent of the American junior high or high school.

One might suppose, from such an emphasis on content and achievement, that this teacher—to get his peasant students "out of the muck"—would have liked them to forsake country life. Wittgenstein did from time to time, with little success, encourage a few of his pupils to continue their studies beyond elementary school, but he did not encourage them to leave the land. Rather, it appears that he sought to awaken them to the life of the spirit, to the activity of thinking for themselves. Perhaps most of all, he tried to infuse in them a devotion to honesty. Rather than breaking them away from the village and practical tasks, he attempted to transform their attitudes toward the kind of life they led, to turn them into peasants who would want their children to educate themselves.

To convey some sense of his aims, his flexibility in dealing with different students and family situations, and also to give an idea of the opposition he encountered from parents, it is worth touching briefly on his efforts with three of his best students: Emmerich Koderhold, Karl Gruber, and Oskar Fuchs.

Emmerich Koderhold, who later, after the Second World War, served for fourteen years as mayor of Trattenbach, is the prosperous farmer son of a prosperous farmer. An intelligent and warmly extroverted man, he still remembers—and can sing for hours—the student and other songs, some of them in Latin, that Wittgenstein taught his classes; and he can still recite poems from Mörike, Keller, and Schiller that Wittgenstein expected his students to memorize. His talent was obvious to Wittgenstein, who, during his second year in Trattenbach, which was Koderhold's final school year, called on Koderhold's father to tell him that his son had the ability to do advanced study, that he ought to do so, and that he was willing to help make arrangements in Vienna. His father would have none of it and explained politely to Wittgenstein that he needed a successor to carry on his farm. "Of course you do", answered Wittgenstein "but he'll even carry the manure better if he studies". Wittgenstein finally talked Koderhold's father into permitting his boy to visit a Gymnasium in Vienna; but Wittgenstein could not go along, Koderhold was lodged with an old woman, appears to have been lonely, and didn't get enough to eat. After a few days he returned home—to the considerable relief of his father—with no great opinion of student life in Vienna; and eventually he did take over the farm. Yet the man is clearly no ordinary peasant farmer or, to use Karl Wittgenstein's words, a "hindrance to progress". He is an educated farmer, Gymnasium education or not. He speaks High German as well as the village dialect and maintains a lively interest in world affairs as well as in Trattenbach and Austrian politics.

Karl Gruber, Wittgenstein's favorite and most talented student, impresses in a different way. He came from a poor family of six children, several of whom attended Wittgenstein's classes. Like his teacher, Karl was introverted and reflective as well as talented, and Wittgenstein became intensely fond of him. He did not object to Karl's helping less able students to do their homework in order to earn bread for himself and his brothers and sisters. A year older than the others, Karl proceeded to continue studying with Wittgenstein privately after formally finishing school in 1921. Each day, from four o'clock in the afternoon until seven in the evening, Wittgenstein conducted him through lessons in advanced Latin, Greek, and mathematics. Usually the two took dinner together in Wittgenstein's room above the grocery. Wittgenstein obviously enjoyed the boy's companionship, and throughout that year only Ludwig Hänsel's bimonthly visits to Trattenbach interrupted Karl's daily lessons. Even then the boy was not forgotten. Hänsel, who was by this time a Gymnasium professor in Vienna, acted as Karl's external examiner, quizzing him in history, geography, Latin, and other subjects that he needed to qualify for entrance to Gymnasium in Vienna.

Eventually Wittgenstein concluded that he must adopt Karl to ensure that he would get a proper education in the capital, an education for which his parents, unlike Koderhold's, could never have paid. Karl was willing to be adopted,

Land: Österreich unter der Enns.   Nummer des Klassenkataloges: *20*

Schulbezirk: *Neunkirchen*

Drei Klaffige allgemeine Volksschule in *Trattenbach*

Entlassungszeugnis.

Gruber: Karl, geboren am *9 Juni 1907*
zu *Trattenbach* in *N.Ö.* röm. kath. Religion,
hat die allgemeine Volksschule vom *1. Mai 1913* bis *9 Juni 1921*
und zuletzt die *vierte* Klaffe der obenbezeichneten Schule befucht und am
Schluffe des schulpflichtigen Alters nachstehende Noten erhalten:

Betragen: *lobenswert*

Fleiß: *ausdauernd*

Lehrgegenstände	Fortgang	Unterschriften
Religion	sehr gut	
Lesen	sehr gut	
Schreiben	sehr gut	
Unterrichtssprache	sehr gut	
Rechnen in Verbindung mit geometrischer Formenlehre	sehr gut	
Naturgeschichte und Naturlehre	sehr gut	
Geographie und Geschichte		
Zeichnen	sehr gut	
Gesang	sehr gut	
Turnen	sehr gut	
Weibliche Handarbeiten		
Äußere Form der schriftlichen Arbeiten	gefällig	

Da diefe Schüler den Anforderungen des Reichsvolksschulgefetzes
entfprochen hat, fo wird derfelbe demnach *laut § 27 R.V.J.*
aus der Schule entlaffen.

Trattenbach, am *9 Juni* 19*21*

Ludwig Wittgenstein

Leiter der Schule.   Klaffenlehrer.

The report card of Wittgenstein's favorite pupil in Trattenbach,
Karl Gruber (Karl Gruber, Vienna)

103

and Wittgenstein called on his family to propose an arrangement under which he would supervise Karl's further studies in Vienna and bear all costs. Frau Gruber was willing to entertain the proposal, but the father bluntly told Wittgenstein that further education for his son was out of the question, that he had probably already had too much, and that a boy of his age ought to be working for his own money. After Wittgenstein had left the house, the elder Gruber declared him a "crazy fellow" ("ein verrückter Kerl") to whom he could hardly entrust his son.

So Karl Gruber did go to work, and when Wittgenstein left Trattenbach for Puchberg at the end of that year his lessons ended. Yet he eventually did break away from his family and go to Vienna, unlike most of his school fellows, who remained either in Trattenbach or in one of the other villages of Neunkirchen. After finding a job for himself in Vienna, Karl tried to contact Wittgenstein, only to learn that he had left Vienna for Cambridge. He contemplated writing to him, but decided against it. In due course he married and became a post office official in Vienna. Lacking credentials, he never attained the kind of success for which his intelligence suited him, but managed nonetheless to provide an adequate and sometimes comfortable city life for himself and his family. Today he reflects wistfully that, had Wittgenstein succeeded in adopting him, he too might have become a university professor of philosophy. Any such turn of events might well have distressed Wittgenstein, who urged even some of his most talented Cambridge students to avoid professional philosophy.

Still, Wittgenstein left his mark here. Gruber impresses by his difference from Wittgenstein's other village students. Even Koderhold refers to Gruber's intelligence with reverential awe. And when Gruber returns to visit Trattenbach, his old colleagues and friends greet him with a kind of reserved respect that they do not pay to one another. Nor has he forgotten his teacher: he treasures his mementos of his school days with Wittgenstein, and he alone among Wittgenstein's old pupils was aware of the general course of Wittgenstein's career.

The third student in whom Wittgenstein took a deep interest, Oskar Fuchs, died before this study was begun. For information on him and his relationship to Wittgenstein one has to rely chiefly on two sources: a brief manuscript account of Wittgenstein's activities in Neunkirchen prepared in 1964 by Frau Luise Hausmann, a high school English teacher in Kirchberg-am-Wechsel, and a marvelous letter from Wittgenstein to Fuchs which, one hopes, Wittgenstein's executors will one day publish.[29] Although Fuchs, as one of Wittgenstein's brightest pupils, also received private instruction from him, Wittgenstein apparently did not encourage him to continue with formal studies. Fuchs recalled to Frau Hausmann that Wittgenstein expressed his delight when Fuchs announced that he wanted to become a shoemaker like his father. "A man has to have something ordinary to do", Wittgenstein commented, "in order to be able to let off steam". Why Wittgenstein reacted differently to Fuchs, one cannot determine. Perhaps he was less talented than the others, certainly his home life was happier, and possibly Wittgenstein, who was deeply hurt when the Gruber family rejected his overtures, may have been unwilling to chance being rejected once again. He had in any case already been rebuffed by the Fuchs family. Wittgenstein had wanted to take Fuchs to Vienna with him at Christmas-time to see a play at the Burgtheater, but was evasively refused, Fuch's mother having opposed the idea of his going off with "the weird fellow". It is also possible that Wittgenstein surmised that any attempt on his part to sponsor Fuchs would, if successful, have a crushing effect on Karl Gruber, who had keenly wanted to get away from home to study in Vienna.

In any event, Wittgenstein and Fuchs kept in touch. A year and a half after Wittgenstein's departure from Tratten-

---

[29]A photograph of part of this letter has been published in Kurt Wuchterl and Adolf Hübner, *Wittgenstein* (Hamburg: Rowohlt, 1979), p. 97. See also now Michael Neldo and Michele Ranchetti: *Wittgenstein: Sein Leben in Bildern und Texten* (Frankfurt, Suhrkamp Verlag, 1983), pp. 184-185.

bach, the two were exchanging letters between Puchberg and Trattenbach, Wittgenstein was sending Fuchs books, and Fuchs, who was studying geology in his spare time, was mailing him samples of stones found in Trattenbach.

Emmerich Koderhold, Karl Gruber, and Oskar Fuchs formed the nucleus of a small band of pupils who met with Wittgenstein after school hours or in the evening when possible. The total group was not large, consisting chiefly of his brightest students and a few "whose faces he liked". These boys often remained with Wittgenstein until eight o'clock in the evening. The subject of their discussions varied. Sometimes the daily school lesson would be continued. At other times entirely new subjects would be introduced. Wittgenstein took them off to the woods to collect stones and plants, which they would label carefully. Or, after dark, Wittgenstein taught them the constellations and a bit of elementary astronomy. It was due to these late sessions that Wittgenstein encountered the most serious resistance from the parents.

One fact about the villages shows clearly through these brief sketches: children were an important part of the local labor pool. Most families depended on hours of help from their children, around the house, in the barns, on the farm. Karl Gruber's father was by no means satisfied with the bread his son could earn helping other students do their homework; he wanted him to get a job. Emmerich Koderhold, like Oskar Fuchs, was being groomed to take over his father's business or occupation. With these economic facts of village life Wittgenstein was actively interfering; in building up his cadre of disciples, he was stealing the time—and the affection—of his pupils from their families.

Nor, despite complaints, would Wittgenstein desist from his after-hours instruction. In Puchberg and Otterthal, as in Trattenbach, he followed the same pattern with successive groups. In more prosperous Puchberg he encountered comparatively little resistance, but in Otterthal, where the children's evening work on the farms was important indeed, Wittgenstein finally faced quite fierce, active, and vicious opposition.

X

The ground for his eventual undoing in Otterthal in 1926 had unwittingly been laid four years earlier in Trattenbach, when another of Wittgenstein's favored students, Karl Gruber's brother Konrad, had played a trick on his teacher that was to make his "practice of corporal punishment" the talk of the town. During a geography lesson Wittgenstein had once slapped Konrad for poor performance. Surreptitiously Konrad put his pencil into his nose until it bled. The sight of blood caused some commotion; Konrad was permitted to leave the room to stop the bleeding, but in fact, according to his own account some forty-five years later, he managed to extend the bleeding for the remainder of the lesson. The story about how Wittgenstein had given Konrad a bloody nose quickly spread throughout the town. By this time Konrad was too deeply involved to admit what he had done; some of the other children, however, learned what had really happened and tried similar tricks themselves. For example, when told to stand in the corner as a punishment, a pupil would stand for five minutes or so and then pretend to swoon and fall to the floor. So it came to be said in Trattenbach and Otterthal that Wittgenstein's rough discipline caused children to bleed and to faint.

What are the facts? It is not entirely clear, since there are a number of conflicting accounts.

Those of his pupils who are alive now avow that Wittgenstein certainly did cane his boys[30] and box their ears when they misbehaved and that he slapped their cheeks for minor offenses. Such behaviour was absolutely contrary to the principles of school reform.[31] Other reports, moreover, suggest

---

[30]He may also have administered some sort of corporal punishment to a little girl. Fania Pascal reports that Wittgenstein confessed to her in 1937 that he hit and hurt a little girl and, when she ran to the headmaster to complain, denied that he had done so. See Pascal's "Wittgenstein: A Personal Memoir", in Rush Rhees, ed., *Ludwig Wittgenstein: Personal Recollections* (Totowa, N.J.: Rowman & Littlefield, 1981), p. 51.

[31]Glöckel himself described teachers who used corporal punishment as degenerate and disturbed creatures in need of psychiatric help. See his *Selbstbiographie sein Lebenswerk: die Wiener Schulreform* (Zürich: Verlag

that Wittgenstein was at this time in a very high-strung nervous state. He would frequently break out in a sweat while teaching, would repeatedly rub his chin and pull his hair, and bite into his crumpled handkerchief.[32]

On the other hand, according to these same students, Wittgenstein used his rod not one whit more than did the other teachers and differed from them only in that he used it fairly, consistently, and predictably. His punishment was neither arbitrary nor whimsical, and he never took a student by surprise. Although many educators would oppose, just as did the school reformers in Austria, any sort of corporal punishment, they usually agree that the worst possible system of rewards and punishments, whether corporal or otherwise, is one that is vacillating, where the child is left in a state of anxiety-producing uncertainty about the consequences of his actions. Wittgenstein did not vacillate: he was firm, consistent, and made thoroughly clear to his pupils what sorts of behavior would result in punishment. One sort of behavior that was invariably punished was dishonesty; and one way to escape punishment was to confess honestly when Wittgenstein demanded an explanation. For instance, one day in class he inquired how many pupils knew the months of the year. A number of children raised their hands, and Wittgenstein asked each one in turn. As it happened, very few were in fact able to recite the months, whereupon Wittgenstein became very angry. Turning to Konrad Gruber, one of those who had raised his hands but had not known, Wittgenstein demanded an explanation. Konrad replied, "Because I was ashamed not to know". For his candid answer Konrad escaped punishment. The same was true of the others: those who could provide explanations for their dishonesty were spared; those who could not were punished.

A comparable episode took place at Carnival Time during Wittgenstein's second year in Trattenbach. Farmer Traht sent some doughnuts to Wittgenstein, which, as usual, were

---

Genossenschaftsdruckerei, 1939), pp. 22, 43; and *Die österreichische Schulreform* (Vienna: Verlag der Weiner Volksbuchhandlung, 1923), pp. 4–5.
[32]See Wuchterl and Hübner's account in their *Wittgenstein*, pp. 93–4.

fetched by one of the pupils. On the way to Wittgenstein's room the boy ate two of the doughnuts himself. The following day in class, Wittgenstein asked him, "How many of my doughnuts did you eat?" The boy turned crimson, flabbergasted that Wittgenstein should have found out what he had done, but he replied, "I ate two of them". When Wittgenstein heard his reply, he thanked the boy for his truthfulness, did not punish him, but instead explained that Farmer Traht had enclosed a slip of paper, unnoticed by the student, with the number "13", a baker's dozen, written on it.

But Konrad Gruber, with his self-induced bloody nose, and the other children who had "fainted", had unwittingly laid the groundwork for a lie. The man who had so captivated the children of Trattenbach and Otterthal that they would spend long hours after class with him, risking punishment for bad behavior rather than returning to their families, was now to be formally charged with sadistic punishment of his pupils.

The crisis flared up in April 1926. According to some of the villagers, a genuine "conspiracy" against Wittgenstein had formed by this time. The leader, or at any rate, the chief agitator, was a man named Piribauer, who is said to have spent months "waiting in ambush" for an opportunity to "get Wittgenstein into trouble". His opportunity came at last when Wittgenstein slapped on the cheeks or beat the ears of a child whose foster mother dwelt in Piribauer's house. The child is supposed to have been carried swooning into the school office. Some of Wittgenstein's old students who had themselves faked fainting have suggested that this boy too was faking. The same boy, however, fainted on numerous later occurrences, after Wittgenstein had left the district and without any external provocation; and two years later he died of leukaemia.

Whatever the exact circumstances may have been, legal proceedings were brought against Wittgenstein. When he was confronted, he commented quietly, "If you intend to rise up against me, that doesn't matter to me, provided only that you are agreed among yourselves. I am ready for you", whereupon he abruptly left town, never to teach elementary school again.

The Kirchberg doctor who was called in to treat the boy filed a report in accordance with his duty. A hearing in Gloggnitz followed, interrupted by a compulsory psychiatric examination to determine Wittgenstein's mental responsibility. Wittgenstein was acquitted, but firmly refused to consider continuing to teach school; his voluntary resignation is dated April 28. He had by now had enough of Tolstoy's noble serfs; and by this time even Kundt, who had cautioned Wittgenstein about the hostility of the Otterthalers, and who even at this late date tried to talk Wittgenstein out of his decision to resign, seems to have accepted the fact that it would be pointless for him to continue teaching in that district.

XI

If taken strictly in isolation, these closing events in Wittgenstein's career as a schoolmaster might appear odd but, apart from their having happened to Wittgenstein, of little importance. But against the background of the school-reform program and Austrian politics, they are far more significant.

If a complaint about rough discipline was permitted to get as far as it did—namely, to force Wittgenstein to stand trial—there must have been more than a question of discipline behind it. For even allowing for Wittgenstein's not entirely deserved reputation as a strict disciplinarian, one has to remember that corporal punishment was quite common at this time. School discipline of the roughest sort had been common in the Habsburg domains and was still widely prevalent in the twenties and thirties, although it had by that time become a subject for debate among school reformers themselves. Thus it is on the face of it unlikely that Wittgenstein's colleagues would not have supported him against a parent's complaint, even if the charge were true.

A rather more complicated explanation of the whole incident occurs. A disciplinary complaint appears to have been the pretext for a more deep-seated objection. The "conspiracy"[33] against Wittgenstein, the details of which we are no longer likely to learn, was led by some of the villagers, like Piribauer, some of the district clerics (but not Neururer), and some of Wittgenstein's colleagues. And it was political as well as personal in nature: it came at a highly charged time throughout Austria, in the spring of 1926, when the school-reform program suffered a setback in the country-side from which it never recovered. Once the conservative farmer forces in Otterthal sensed the national strength of the movement against the school reformers, they lost no time in using the first pretext they could find to send packing back to Vienna a man who must have threatened and offended them on many levels. Wittgenstein was, despite his ascetic life, still thought to be rich; he was also assumed to be a socialist; he was known not to be a Roman Catholic; he was a proponent of progressive education, was the author of a positivist tract, was known by the villagers to be homosexual (how, one does not know), was considered by the women of the village to be misogynistic; and, what must have been hardest to bear, he was an extremely successful teacher for all that, so much so that he had weaned the most talented children in town away from their homes.

The persecution of Wittgenstein in Otterthal was in any case no isolated incident. The compromises effected among the Austrian political parties as a result of the disturbances of 1926 meant in practice that wherever Social Democrats remained dominant, as in Vienna, Glöckel's basic program could be maintained. In the countryside, however, the Catholic party of Christian Socialists obtained firm control in most districts. After his loss of national office, Glöckel became administrative president of the Vienna School Council and remained in that capacity until 1934, when the Dollfuss

---

[33]Adolf Hübner disagrees with the reports of some of the villagers and flatly denies that there was any conspiracy against Wittgenstein, claiming, rather, that the charges were all the work of one "psychopathic peasant". See his "Bartley Refuted", *Schriftenreihe der Österreichischen Ludwig-Wittgenstein-Gesellschaft*, 1978. See also the Afterword to the present book, footnote 11.

dictatorship—whose main support came from the country—
ended school reform entirely, arrested many of its leaders,
including Glöckel, and forced its chief publications, the journals *Die Quelle* and *Schulreform* (to which Wittgenstein had
for a time subscribed), to cease publication. During the cen-
sorship that followed, these journals were even locked up in
the National Library and were thus made inaccessible to the
general reader. Educational reform was thought to be dangerous indeed.

Even Wittgenstein's friend Hänsel, who had at first been
a glowingly enthusiastic supporter of the reform program,
later—for political, social, and religious reasons—turned
against it bitterly. Eventually he even published a polemical
tract against school reform: *Der neuen Schule entgegen.*

XII

Lest my remarks about the relation between Wittgenstein
and the school-reform movement be misunderstood, I must
say something about intellectual "influence" and the sort
that I believe was present here.

Some persons think of influence in absolute terms, as if
to be influenced by someone is slavishly to accept his entire
view of the world.[34] This kind of influence does occur, and

---

[34]See Eugene E. Hargrove, "Wittgenstein, Bartley, and the Glöckel
School Reform", *Journal of the History of Philosophy* 18 (October 1980), pp.
453–61. Hargrove's main claim in this article—mixed in with false statements and faulty reasoning—is that my argument is not sufficient to establish Wittgenstein's connection to the school-reform movement. I could not
agree more: I have written a book against this sort of "sufficient" reason:
The Retreat to Commitment, second, enlarged edition (La Salle: Open Court,
1984). My argument is conjectural and aims to make more sense of Wittgenstein's life in the 'twenties than alternative accounts, and to connect it to
his later work, in which problems of child psychology and learning theory
figure prominently. My conjecture survives close scrutiny—provided it is
not first reduced to absurdity by interpreting words like "was influenced
by" to mean "was totally subjugated by". See also Hargrove's introduction
and notes to Luise Hausmann's "Wittgenstein in Austria", *Encounter*, April
1982, and my reply to him, "Remembering Wittgenstein", in *Encounter*,
September-October 1982, pp. 111–12.

is the source of that dogmatic "followership" which is the bane of scholarly and scientific endeavor and of much personal interaction as well. Anyone who is himself such a follower may suppose that any case of influence must resemble his own, and may hence suppose that, in saying that Wittgenstein was influenced by Glöckel, Bühler, and the school reformers, I was suggesting that he had become a blind follower of their ideas and practices.

Few serious, self-critical, and original thinkers are importantly influenced in this way; and I have never supposed that Wittgenstein was a slavish follower of the school-reform movement. Quite the contrary. As Wittgenstein himself declared on such matters: "It's a good thing I don't allow myself to be influenced! . . . It is humiliating to have to appear like an empty tube which is simply inflated by a mind."[35]

But there is another kind of influence which consists in the critical and passionate confrontation with a point of view, in the course of which one absorbs the point of view— i.e., one is able to understand and think in terms of it, and seriously tries it out; withdraws from it whatever is of value— whether theoretical, practical, or in conception of problems; and rejects what is false or useless, and whatever, for any reason, one is incapable of absorbing. In the process one may tremendously clarify and enrich the original idea. Wittgenstein was influenced by Frege in this positive way; Russell and Wittgenstein influenced one another in this way; and in my view Wittgenstein was in this sense only influenced by his schoolteaching experience and by the reform movement and the philosophical psychology in which it was couched. The school reform was an encounter in Wittgenstein's life which made an important difference to his thought.

Wittgenstein himself believed, and modestly stated, that he was subject to influence of this sort. In his notebooks, he writes of taking a line of thinking over from someone else, and—seizing on it with enthusiasm—proceeding to clarify

---

[35]Ludwig Wittgenstein, *Culture and Value* (Chicago: University of Chicago Press, 1980), pp. 1 and 11.

it. He spoke of this sort of work as "making a drawing of the flower or blade of grass that has grown in the soil of another's mind and putting it into a comprehensive picture".[36] He even claimed, with a modesty that few commentators would accept, that his originality was "an originality belonging to the soil rather than to the seed. (Perhaps I have no seed of my own.) Sow a seed in my soil and it will grow differently than it would in any other soil". He went on to compare his own originality to that of Freud, which he found similar in this regard.[37]

XIII

The story just told has focused on Trattenbach and Otterthal, where Wittgenstein taught from 1920 to 1922 and 1924 to 1926 respectively. This has meant neglecting Puchberg am Schneeberg, where he taught during the two intervening years. Wittgenstein's experience there was rather different from that at the other two villages. At Puchberg he was *comparatively* happy.

Puchberg is now, and was even during the twenties, a fairly prosperous resort town. It is also larger, with a population of over three thousand, being rather more town than village. And it is lovelier by far. It brought Wittgenstein a friend—not another Neururer, a possessed crusader like himself, but a modest yet talented young music teacher, the pianist Rudolf Koder. Koder, who with his wife and family later moved to Vienna, became a lifelong friend of Wittgenstein's and a welcome guest of the family as well.

Then too, by the time Wittgenstein was settled in Puchberg the *Tractatus* had finally been published and was getting considerable philosophical attention in England. F. P. Ramsey made his pilgrimages to Wittgenstein in Puchberg. Wittgenstein also hit it off with the local priest and—despite the

---

[36]Wittgenstein, *Culture and Value*, p. 19.
[37]*Ibid.*, p. 36.

forebodings that he related to Russell—had more or less cordial relations with his colleagues. With one of them, the mathematics teacher Norbert Rosner, he enjoyed something approaching friendship: Wittgenstein endeavored, at Rosner's request, to re-educate him in mathematics. He did not, by Rosner's own account, appear to have had much success, but Rosner was nonetheless eager to learn, and their relations remained amicable. The school principal in Puchberg also admired Wittgenstein immensely, remarking of him: "This man is already able to do everything that I myself should like to be able to do."

The tranquillity need not be overestimated. Quite the contrary, Wittgenstein behaved in Puchberg as he had in Otterthal and Trattenbach. He was strict with the children, performed educational feats with them that were as impressive, built experimental models and constructed skeletons, and treated the children of Puchberg to an excursion to Vienna.

In Puchberg too, Wittgenstein played town eccentric. Following a spat with his landlady he had to move, and this time he managed to find an unbelievably tiny room only eighteen feet square where, so it is said, he would practise his clarinet under the covers after ten o'clock at night. He practised music with Rudolf Koder daily and took long walks with him. But when Arvid Sjögren would arrive for a visit, as he did regularly, the villagers came to attention and watched in quiet amusement. Sjögren, who was unmusical, would lie down on a bench or on the floor and fall fast asleep while Wittgenstein and Koder practised. When Wittgenstein eventually located someone who was musical to join their sessions, he found him in the most unlikely place. A local coal miner, named Postl, joined Wittgenstein and Koder to form a musical trio. Later Wittgenstein saw to it that his family in Vienna hired Postl as a retainer, and the man spent the remainder of his working years in the service of the Stonboroughs.

The difference between Puchberg and the other villages appears to have been simple enough. The townspeople of Puchberg were more prosperous and ambitious; and they were, through their resort and tourist trade, more familiar with the ways of city folk. They valued Wittgenstein for the success he enjoyed with their children and were not so dependent economically on them. Thus Wittgenstein's after-hours sessions with his pupils in Puchberg brought only a few minor complaints. In distance, Puchberg was close to Otterthal; in time, nearer to Vienna.

XIV

The months following Wittgenstein's departure from Otterthal marked a period of deep transition in his life. On June 3, some six weeks after his departure from Otterthal, his mother died. The remainder of that summer he spent in retreat in a monastery of the Barmherzige Brüder in Hütteldorf, a suburb of Vienna. Although Wittgenstein worked as a gardener, as he had done once before, he entertained seriously the idea of becoming a monk. The monastery no longer exists, and its buildings now serve as a home for destitute mothers and their children; yet some of the old retainers still remain, and a few remember Wittgenstein as "a very good and highly industrious gardner—and a left-winger".

When the summer of 1926 had passed and Wittgenstein returned to Vienna, he drew closer to his family than he had been for some years, and entered into a project for his sister Margarete Stonborough which eventually led him out of his shell and into an adult world from which he would venture back to philosophy. Margarete had undertaken to build a large mansion on a great piece of land, nearly a city block in area, in the Kundmanngasse. Once part of the grounds of the Palais Rasumofsky, the land lay directly across the street from the Teachers Training College that Wittgenstein had attended during 1919–20.

Wittgenstein came to play a dominant role in the construction of the house, and is often named, together with his friend Paul Engelmann, as co-architect.

Initially, Wittgenstein had regarded such a step—becoming an architect—as a step backwards. As he had confided to Josef Putré, a fellow teacher in Otterthal: "I considered at one time the idea of becoming an architect or pharmacist, but came to the conclusion that I would not find what I was looking for in these professions. In these and other such professions, a person becomes in principle nothing more than a small-time businessman. I want to die as a respectable citizen. It seems to me that this can best be achieved in the seclusion of a place like Trattenbach, where as a teacher and educator of youth I can engage in what seems to me to be respectable work together with a simple style of life."[38]

The step was, however, to prove a decisive advance. Hitherto the role of neither Wittgenstein nor Englemann in designing this house has been very clear, the less so since Engelmann himself gave most of the credit for the house to Wittgenstein. The facts appear to be these: The basic plan of the house was drawn up by Engelmann, and his original sketchbooks, corresponding closely to the final plan and drawn up at a time when Wittgenstein was still teaching school in the villages, have been preserved. In exterior appearance the house is highly derivative of the work of Engelmann's teacher, the great Viennese architect Adolf Loos, as a comparison with some of Loos's other work, such as the Steiner House in Vienna, which had been built as early as 1910, easily shows.[39] The most striking individual feature, the use of tall floor-to-ceiling windows in much of the house, was introduced by Margarete herself, who had used a similar device successfully some five years earlier when reconstructing her country villa at Gmunden.

Wittgenstein's contribution to the house was, first, to introduce certain engineering features—part of the electri-

---

[38]From Josef Putré, "Meine Errinerungen", quoted in Hargrove, "Wittgenstein, Bartley . . . ", p. 457.

[39]See Bannister Fletcher, *A History of Architecture*, 17th ed. (New York: Scribners, 1961), pp. 1072ff. See also Heinrich Kulka, *Adolf Loos* (Vienna: Löcker, 1979), illustrations 39–41; and Ludwig Münz and Gustav Künstler, *Der Architekt Adolf Loos* (Vienna and Munich: Anton Schroll, 1964).

cal system and the heating system. He also supervised the workmen in the most meticulously careful and exacting way during the construction of the building. His own original contribution was the design of the interior of the house. Of this it has been written: "The interior ... is unique in the history of twentieth-century architecture. Everything is rethought. Nothing in it has been directly transplanted, neither from any building convention nor from any professional avant-garde."[40] Wittgenstein himself, however, had reservations about it. Years later he wrote: "Within all great art there is a WILD animal: *tamed*. ... The house I built for Gretl is the product of a decidedly sensitive ear and *good* manners, an expression of great *understanding* (of a culture, etc.). But *primordial* life, wild life striving to erupt into the open—that is lacking. And so you could say it isn't *healthy*."[41]

However this may be, the building of the house was clearly healthy for Wittgenstein. The activity connected with it drew him back into a cosmopolitan and educated society of adults. And during this period he began his meetings with Schlick, Waismann, and other members of the Vienna Circle, and began to discuss philosophy again. Thus his time as an architect prepared him psychologically, if in no other way, for his eventual decision to return to philosophy—and to Cambridge—in January 1929.

---

[40]Bernhard Leitner, *The Architecture of Ludwig Wittgenstein: A Documentation* (Halifax: The Press of the Nova Scotia College of Art and Design, 1973), p. 11.

[41]Wittgenstein, *Culture and Value*, pp. 37e-38e.

One wonders what philosophy would have been like in Britain and the United States had it not been for the accident of Wittgenstein, for he might not have been on the scene at all. . . . I mean that he became known to the world of philosophy through the very special circumstances of making a strong impression on Bertrand Russell and being accepted into the world of philosophy through the bold initiative of Cambridge. Nature is wasteful, and if one wants to get something exceptionally good one must take great risks about having a great deal that is simply wild. I am sure that both Russell and Cambridge were right to adopt such a policy; and Cambridge is probably the only university in the world that would have touched Wittgenstein at any price. Had it not been for Cambridge and had it not been for Russell—and some people would hold that he made an error of judgement—almost certainly nothing more would have been heard of Wittgenstein.

—*J. O. Wisdom*[1]

4 ♦ The Language Game

I

During Wittgenstein's prewar days in Cambridge, his genius and the importance of his work were undisputed. Some nine years prior to the publication of the *Tractatus*, Russell and Moore had been ecstatic in their praise of him. Russell, as he testifies in *My Philosophical Development*,[2] radically revised his own doctrines in the light of Wittgenstein's criti-

---

[1]J. O. Wisdom, "Esotericism", *Philosophy*, October 1959, pp. 348–49.
[2]Bertrand Russell, *My Philosophical Development* (New York: Simon and Schuster, 1959).

cisms, and told Wittgenstein's mother that he expected the next great advance in philosophy to come from her son. Prior to 1922, many of the best minds of England were prepared to go to great lengths to put Wittgenstein in the best circumstances to continue his philosophical development. Thus John Maynard Keynes's intervention to secure Wittgenstein's release from prison-camp in Monte Cassino (which, once secured, Wittgenstein refused), Russell's visits to The Hague and to Innsbruck for talks with him, and the pilgrimages of Ramsey and other young English students to Puchberg.

During the 1920s there was an occasional hint that things were not the same between Wittgenstein and his old teachers. Russell and Wittgenstein, for example, both departed from their meeting in Innsbruck in 1922 irritated and disgusted with one another. But not before Wittgenstein's return to Cambridge in January 1929 did the full extent of the change, both in Wittgenstein's way of thinking and in his relationships with his former teachers, begin to surface. The initial encounters, in particular that with Moore, whom he had not seen since April 1914 when Moore had visited him in Norway, were largely satisfactory. It was found that Wittgenstein's prewar residence in Cambridge could be credited toward the Ph.D., and Wittgenstein presented the *Tractatus* as his dissertation, with Ramsey named as his supervisor and Moore as examiner. Owing to Ramsey's illness and early death, Moore and Russell came to act as oral examiners. The whimsically cordial mood of that meeting in June of 1929 is conveyed in the report that Moore is said to have written about Wittgenstein's "thesis":

> It is my personal opinion that Mr Wittgenstein's thesis is a work of genius; but, be that as it may, it is certainly well up to the standard required for the Cambridge degree of Doctor of Philosophy.

As it turned out, the next great change in philosophy *did* stem largely from Wittgenstein's influence. But it was not the influence of the *Tractatus*, but of the "new" or "later"

Wittgenstein that accounted for this. Nor was that change anything like what Russell had anticipated. Writing of Wittgenstein's "treachery to his own greatness", Russell recorded: "I admired Wittgenstein's *Tractatus* but not his later work, which seemed to me to involve an abnegation of his own best talent. ... Its positive doctrines seem to me trivial and its negative doctrines unfounded. I have not found in Wittgenstein's *Philosophical Investigations* anything that seemed to me interesting and I do not understand why a whole school finds important wisdom in its pages."[3]

Even more vitriolic than Russell was C. D. Broad, the Knightbridge Professor of Moral Philosophy, himself a highly distinguished philosopher of science, who later, in his own intellectual autobiography, reported:

> The one duty which I wittingly neglected was to attend the weekly meetings of the Moral Sciences Club. ... I was not prepared to spend hours every week in a thick atmosphere of cigarette-smoke, while Wittgenstein punctually went through his hoops, and the faithful as punctually "wondered with a foolish face of praise".[4]

Wittgenstein himself, reflecting on his philosophical work, scribbled down this musical passage into his notebooks:

---

[3]*Ibid.*, pp. 214–16.
[4]*The Philosophy of C. D. Broad*, ed. P. A. Schilpp (New York: Tudor, 1959), p. 61.

He then wrote: "That must be the end of a theme which I cannot place. It came into my head today as I was thinking about my philosophical work and saying to myself: 'I destroy, I destroy, I destroy—' ."[5]

The Cambridge authorities did not, despite rumblings of disapproval, and despite the difficulties that Wittgenstein himself gave them, fail to support him. In June of 1929 the Council of Trinity College awarded him a research grant; and on October 16 of that year, the University Faculty Board of Moral Sciences invited him to give a course of lectures. By December 1930 Wittgenstein had been elected a Research Fellow of Trinity College. The growing reserve about his work, however, perhaps best expressed itself in the exchange between Moore and Russell concerning Wittgenstein's appointment to the Trinity Fellowship.

In early March of 1930 Moore wrote to Russell, on behalf of the Council of Trinity College, asking him to prepare a report on the research Wittgenstein had been doing during the course of that academic year and to meet with Wittgenstein to discuss it. "There seems", Moore wrote, "no other way of ensuring him [Wittgenstein] a sufficient income to continue his work, unless the Council do make him a grant; and I am afraid there is very little chance that they will do so, unless they can get favourable reports from experts in the subject". Russell replied cautiously to the effect that although he did not see how he could refuse to report on Wittgenstein's work, it would involve a great deal of time: later, after a weekend discussion with Wittgenstein, Russell wrote again to Moore to ask for a delay of a month or so in making his report, "since my impressions at the moment are rather vague, and he intends while in Austria to make a synopsis of his work which would make it much easier for me to report adequately". After a further session with Wittgenstein at the beginning of May and a study of his manuscript, Russell reported to Moore: "His theories are certainly

[5]Ludwig Wittgenstein, *Culture and Value*, ed. G. H. von Wright (Chicago: University of Chicago Press, 1980) , p. 21.

important and certainly very original. Whether they are true, I do not know; I devoutly hope they are not, as they make mathematics and logic almost incredibly difficult. . . . I am quite sure that Wittgenstein ought to be given an opportunity to pursue his work." Two days later Moore wrote back that Russell's report as it stood would not do, and requested a more formal report for the Council's permanent records, in which Russell should emphasize his high opinion of the importance of Wittgenstein's *new* work. Russell reluctantly complied, and Wittgenstein was in due course elected a Fellow of Trinity. One need not read between the lines of this correspondence to observe that not only Russell but also the Council of Trinity College were unconvinced of the real merit of Wittgenstein's latest work.[6]

II

This doubt lingers on in many minds today, more than fifty years after Wittgenstein set down the *Philosophische Bemerkungen* (the work that Russell read for Trinity College) and the *Philosophische Grammatik*, the first works written more or less in the manner of his later philosophy. Although Wittgenstein's work was for many years more influential in the English-speaking countries than that of any other philosopher, it was also the most sharply criticized.

While some quite obscure passages appear in the *Tractatus*, it was nonetheless a systematic work the gist of whose aims and content might be summarized. With almost all of Wittgenstein's later work, even *Philosophical Investigations*, the most finished statement of his later ideas, the situation is otherwise. The intent and aim of the work, other than the part that is purely polemical, are less than clear; and the work is written in a style that hardly lends itself to summary

---

[6]The correspondence in question, together with Russell's formal report to Trinity College, is printed in *The Autobiography of Bertrand Russell* (London: George Allen and Unwin, 1968), vol II.

form, since some of the chief points are exhibited or insinuated rather than being stated. The difficulty in coming to grips with this later work explains the existence of such a large secondary literature of books, articles, and anthologies devoted to its clarification and explanation as well as to its criticism. In preparing this essay, I read much of this secondary literature while re-reading Wittgenstein's own work. My experience was, so I understand, similar to that of many others: I was often unable to locate in his own writings theses widely attributed to him by commentators. A connected problem is that the commentaries contain widely varying interpretations of his later thought, as well as widely varying conceptions of where its emphasis falls and its importance lies.

Thus I begin my account of Wittgenstein's later work with a reminder of the difference between his own philosophy, itself highly controversial, and any number of positions, differing to a greater or lesser extent, which may be dubbed part of "*Wittgensteinian* philosophy", in that they emphasize the influence of Wittgenstein's work on their own work; address themselves to problems, formulations, and examples drawn from his work; and are frequently composed by philosophers who either studied with Wittgenstein or else were in close contact with those who did, whether as students or colleagues.

To write about Wittgensteinian philosophy would be to undertake to write a history of a large portion of a philosophical era in Britain and North America, dating at least since the early thirties, when Wittgenstein's later ideas began to be disseminated through his teaching at Cambridge and through reports of this teaching by way of lecture notes and books and articles inspired by him. This essay has no such aim: I aspire to do no more than give a brief report of his own work.

For there now was *work*. In the 1920s, Wittgenstein had been a wreck, physically and emotionally. Ramsey, and many others, including Wittgenstein himself, reported how exhausted he was, how close to collapse, how he was barely able to work. In the thirties, however, a dramatic change occurred.

People once again began to talk of his vitality and his great ability to work. And there was no doubt that he was now happier. On his return to Cambridge he had made a friend, Francis Skinner, a young mathematician twenty-three years younger than himself. Skinner and Wittgenstein lived and worked together in Cambridge, and were constant companions until Skinner's early death in 1941.[7]

III

The earliest expression of Wittgenstein's later views is usually dated to the late twenties. Some of the changes in his outlook emerged during his conversations with Schlick and Waismann in 1928, and Wittgenstein himself reports that his conversations with Ramsey and Piero Sraffa in Cambridge in 1929 forced a radical change in his thinking. From 1929 to 1933 he recorded in two large manuscripts, now published posthumously as *Philosophical Remarks* and *Philosophical Grammar*, some of the main shifts in his position. By the early 1930s, if the notes of Wittgenstein's lectures which Moore published after Wittgenstein's death are accurate, many of the leitmotivs of his later work and the details of his rejection of his earlier work had already been displayed. These received a more polished preliminary statement in English in *The Blue Book* and *The Brown Book*, two typescripts named after the colors of the covers in which they were bound, which Wittgenstein dictated during 1933–35, and which are direct forerunners of *Philosophical Investigations*. Several other works have also been published posthumously. Never intended for publication by Wittgenstein, these works, such as *Zettel* and *Remarks on the Foundations of Mathematics*, have been collated by his executors in the

---

[7]See Fania Pascal, "Wittgenstein: A Personal Memoir", in Rush Rhees, ed., *Ludwig Wittgenstein: Personal Recollections* (Totawa, N.J.: Rowman & Littlefield, 1981), pp. 26–62, and my brief discussion of Skinner in the Afterword to this book, "On Wittgenstein and Homosexuality".

form of remarks. These unfinished, and sometimes very rough, treatments of various problems are nonetheless useful in illustrating Wittgenstein's application of his new method of philosophizing to a wide range of examples.

Just how and precisely when Wittgenstein changed his philosophical approach provides a historical puzzle that probably cannot be solved. It is quite possible that he himself did not become aware of the extent to which his philosophical outlook had shifted until the late twenties. But there is evidence that the change began earlier, long before his contact with the members of the Vienna Circle and his return to Cambridge. I have already mentioned the anecdote that Wittgenstein told his student in Trattenbach in 1921 about an experiment aimed to determine whether three persons who had learned no language would, if shut away from the world, learn or invent a primitive language for themselves, an anecdote whose themes anticipate some of his later concerns with private languages and with the conditions of language acquisition.

This example, as well as the character of some of Wittgenstein's earliest conversations with Schlick and Waismann, suggests that he had already departed from the *Tractatus* by the late twenties and, moreover, had a fairly definite idea of what was wrong with it and in what direction a more satisfactory way of philosophizing would lead. What triggered the change? There are of course *legends* about the metamorphosis; for example, Wittgenstein is said to have attributed the change to his realization that he could not "analyze" a Neopolitan gesture made by Sraffa. But even if the ancedote is genuine, it explains the change in Wittgenstein's outlook about as much—and as little— as the story about the apple explains Newton's theory of gravitation.

My own conjecture is that the themes of the Austrian school-reform movement, which were deeply opposed to Wittgenstein's early work, gradually—and perhaps quite contrary to his intentions or expectations—eroded his earlier beliefs and insinuated themselves in their place. If any individual thinker can be said to have influenced Wittgenstein

during the course of this change, it must have been Karl
Bühler (1879-1963), Professor of Philosophy at the University of Vienna and chief theoretician of the school-reform
movement.[8]

IV

An implicit child psychology had undergirded Glöckel's reforms: to wit, a theory of the child as an active social being
whose mind was far more than an empty bucket to be filled
with appropriate information. In their attack on the Drill-
schule and Lernschule, the reformers were quite explicitly
anti-Herbartian, antiassociationist, and antiatomist in learning theory and psychology. The alternative learning theory
and educational philosophy that were taught at the University of Vienna, at the Pedagogical Institute in Vienna, and at
the various teacher training colleges were dominated by the
views of Bühler, who—together with his wife Charlotte, herself an eminent child psychologist—had been lured to Vienna in 1922 by Glöckel and his colleagues.[9] In 1923, only a

---

[8]See my "Theory of Language and Philosophy of Science as Instruments of Educational Reform: Wittgenstein and Popper as Austrian Schoolteachers", in *Methodological and Historical Essays in the Natural and Social
Sciences, Boston Studies in the Philosophy of Science*, vol. XIV (Dordrecht:
D. Reidel; 1974). Since I arrived at my conclusion that Bühler and Wittgenstein must have been connected, several other scholars have reached similar conclusions. See, for example: Stephen Toulmin, "Ludwig Wittgenstein",
Encounter 1969, and "Ludwig Wittgenstein, Karl Bühler and Psycholin-
guistics", mimeographed, 1968. See also Bernard Kaplan, "Comments on
S. Toulmin's 'Wittgenstein, Bühler and the Psychology of Language' ", mimeographed, 1969. See also my review of S. Toulmin and A. Janik, *Wittgenstein's Vienna*, in *Philosophy of the Social Sciences*, March 1975. Doctoral
students at a number of American universities are at present preparing
theses on the connections between Bühler and Wittgenstein; and a session
of the Wittgenstein Symposium in Kirchberg in 1984 was devoted to
Bühler's thought.
    [9]For an account of Bühler's life and a bibliography, see *Karl
Bühler: Die Uhren der Lebewesen und Fragmente aus dem Nachlass*, ed.
Gustav Lebzeltern (Vienna: Hermann Böhlaus Nachf., Kommissionsverlag
der Österreichischen Akademie der Wissenschaften, 1969). See also Robert
E. Innis, *Karl Bühler: Semiotic Foundations of Language Theory* (New York:
Plenum Press, 1982).

few months after the Bühlers arrived in Vienna, Glöckel declared formally what had long been assumed: "The entire School Reform is, essentially, built on the results of psychological research into the mind of the child."[10] Bühler's work, particularly his *Geistige Entwicklung des Kindes* (1918), an abridged version of which later appeared in English as *The Mental Development of the Child* (1930), influenced the school-reform movement from the outset and was introduced almost at once as a textbook in pedagogy in the new teacher training colleges.

Bühlerian child psychology is a critical version of Gestalt psychology, difficult to classify precisely but perhaps closer to the thought of the Swiss psychologist Jean Piaget, whom Bühler greatly influenced, than to that of the well-known leaders of the Gestalt school: Max Wertheimer, Kurt Koffka, Wolfgang Köhler, Kurt Lewin.

Bühler himself began his career in Würzburg, Germany, where in 1906 he became assistant to Oswald Külpe, the critical realist famed for his attacks on Ernst Mach's positivism. Building on Külpe's work, Bühler began to develop a theory called "imageless thought", and extended and refined his views as he moved from Würzburg, along with Külpe, first to Bonn and then to Munich. The idea of imageless thought, as presented by Külpe and Bühler, stressed that in the intentional act of representing, the particular image or model used, if any, need bear no "imaginal" resemblance to that which it represented. Abstract words, it was claimed, are used conventionally, and neither can nor need be reduced to atoms or elements, including sense impressions. Such a view was, like those put forward by the Gestalt psychologists, radically opposed to positivism and to any number of related philosophical and psychological doctrines, such as associationism, reductionism, behaviorism, and logical atomism.

Like the Gestaltists, Bühler sought to show that theory

[10]Otto Glöckel, *Die Österreichische Schulreform* (Vienna: Wiener Volks-buchhandlung, 1923), p. 11.

making—organization—was a basic function of the human mind independent of associations of sense impressions or other "atoms of thought". The organizing and theorizing activity of the mind enjoyed a kind of priority which determined the kinds of wholes with which one would deal as "elements" in thinking. Like Köhler, whose work is better known in the English-speaking countries, Bühler insisted that his arguments against psychological atomism also defeat epistemological and philosophical atomism.

By the end of the war, Bühler had made important contributions to the theory of language and to child psychology. These subjects dominate the discussion of his *Geistige Entwicklung* and of three other important works that he published after his move to Vienna: *Die Krise der Psychologie* (1926), *Ausdruckstheorie* (1933), and *Sprachtheorie* (1934). Within Austria, and particularly in Vienna, it would be hard to overestimate the extent of his influence, nor was it confined to the Austrian Republic. As Robert Dottrens, of the Institut Jean-Jacques Rousseau in Geneva, reported:

> At the conclusion of a tour through Czecho-Slovakia, Germany, Belgium, England and France, I do not hesitate to say that Vienna is ahead of all the other cities of Europe from the point of view of educational progress. . . . It is to Vienna, the pedagogical Mecca . . . that the new pilgrims of the modern school must go to find the realization of their dreams and hopes.[11]

During his sixteen years in Vienna, Bühler attracted many such pilgrims—students and associates who later attained distinction in their own right, among them Paul Lazarsfeld, Egon Brunswik, Else Frenkel-Brunswik, Konrad Lorenz, Karl Popper, Lotte Schenk-Danzinger, Albert Wellek, Edward Tolman. Although his name appears in no list of Bühler's students, it appears that among the most eminent of those who learned from Bühler was Wittgenstein.

---

[11]Robert Dottrens, *The New Education in Austria* (New York: John Day, 1930), pp. ix and 202. Similar testimony may be found in Richard Meister, "Teacher Training in Austria", *Harvard Educational Review* 8 (January 1938), pp. 112-21.

V

Wittgenstein undoubtedly read, and was impressed by, the writings of the Gestalt psychologists. Several examples in *Philosophical Investigations* are taken from the work of Koffka, and Wittgenstein attributes his famous "duck-rabbit" example (a figure that can be seen as a duck or as a rabbit) to Joseph Jastrow—although in fact it had been part of the parlor magician's repertoire for several hundred years. Wittgenstein does not mention Bühler by name; he had taken an intense personal dislike to the man's "self-important professorial manners" and from time to time Wittgenstein would denounce Bühler as a charlatan. Karl and Charlotte Bühler had, nonetheless, been present at the well-known first encounter between Wittgenstein and Moritz Schlick, as the guests of Wittgenstein's sister Margarete Stonborough[12]; they had been invited at the suggestion of Wittgenstein's nephew, who was studying with Bühler at the University of Vienna. Wittgenstein's personal reaction to Bühler, far from precluding some positive intellectual influence, indicates that he took much more than passing interest in the man.

In the passage from *Zettel* (412) quoted earlier, Wittgenstein asks himself whether what he is doing is child psychology. *Zettel, The Blue and Brown Books*, and *Philosophical Investigations* must be read in a number of different ways; but two necessary ways are as polemics against the atomism represented by the *Tractatus* or by Russell or Herbart and as attempts to develop the outlines of a child psychology of language. How, after all, does the *Investigations* open except as a critique of Saint Augustine's account of how a child learns a language? Much of the first part of the *Investigations* focuses on the question of how children learn their native tongues.

References to Bühler and other Gestalt psychologists,

---

[12]See Paul Engelmann, *Letters from Paul Wittgenstein, with a Memoir* (Oxford: Basil Blackwell, 1967), p. 118; see also the remarks of Brian F. McGuinness, the editor of Friedrich Waismann, *Wittgenstein and the Vienna Circle* (Oxford: Basil Blackwell, 1967), p.15*n*.

therefore, crop up from time to time in my discussion of Wittgenstein's later philosophy, for there are striking similarities between some of Bühler's leading ideas and those of the later Wittgenstein. Among these are: (1) their opposition to psychological and logical atomism; (2) in the place of atomism, a contextualism or configurationism; (3) a radical linguistic conventionalism built up in opposition to essentialist doctrines; (4) the idea of "imageless thought".

To suggest that Bühler influenced Wittgenstein is in no way to belittle Wittgenstein's own contribution. Quite the contrary, the importance of Wittgenstein's own work can be stoutly maintained. What I do wish is to shift the very English context in which Wittgenstein is usually read and to bring another, less familiar background of his thought to light. Nor do I suggest that the views of Wittgenstein and Bühler are identical. But one needs comparable theories at one's disposal before the important job of differentiation can be carried out. Both Wittgenstein and the Gestalt psychologists would have to agree that not only are shapes or figures similar or different depending on their ground or context, but *people and their ideas are also similar or different in relationship to a background*. When the missing background of the "very different" philosophies of Wittgenstein and the Gestaltists is provided, their similarities on basic issues emerge.

VI

The *Tractatus* had recognized only one meaningful function of language: that of picturing the world. If this function was not always apparent in ordinary usage, it could nonetheless be exhibited through logical analysis of the complex into its simple atoms.

The philosophy that Wittgenstein was advocating by 1930, shortly after his return to Cambridge, differs so markedly from his earlier work that it appears that the undermining of his earlier work, begun during his schoolteaching career and furthered by his exposure to Bühler and the Gestalt psychologists, was by then far advanced. Yet the development of his "later thought" continued until the very end of his life. Never did it reach the systematic shape of the *Tractatus*, and Wittgenstein confessed his deep dissatisfaction with the result. In his *Philosophical Investigations* (1953), published two years after his death, he records these misgivings, comparing his new work to an "album" of philosophical remarks. These remarks could, he noted, be seen rightly "only by contrast with and against the background of" his old way of thinking as expressed in the *Tractatus*, a book that, he now declared, contained "grave mistakes" (P.I., page x). "My thinking, like everyone's", he wrote, "has sticking to it the shrivelled remains of my earlier (withered) ideas".[13]

The *Investigations* is, thus, in part a polemical attack on the ideas of his younger self. But it also develops new arguments concerning logic, meaning, thinking and understanding, language, the nature of philosophy, intended both to replace and to supplement those displaced by his criticism of the doctrines of the *Tractatus*.

That Wittgenstein should eventually have come to reject logical atomism is hardly surprising. A battery of arguments against atomism had been developed during the nineteenth century, following Kant, by both philosophers and psychologists. Although some were new, many were ancient, the novelty being the systematizing of a quite powerful war machine against atomism or, as it was often called, "elementarism". What is striking about Wittgenstein's rejection of atomism is that he rarely relied on arguments taken from this readily available canon, but developed and deployed different ones. The question is what these new arguments are, and whether they are as effective as the old, let alone superior to them.

Just as traditional atomism had tended to maintain that legitimate theory must be derivable from sense observation reports, so traditional arguments against atomism had maintained that sense observation reports untainted by theory

---

[13]Wittgenstein, *Culture and Value*, p. 23.

were impossible: i.e., that all observation was theory-impreg-
nated. Moreover, these arguments continued, even if pure
observation reports could, *per impossibile*, exist, these would
not be sufficient to generate all legitimate theory.

In his notes on Wittgenstein's lectures, Moore reports
that, very soon after they began, Wittgenstein announced
that his opinions had changed most with respect to elementary propositions. After pointing out that he had produced
no examples of elementary propositions in the *Tractatus*, he
commented that it was indeed senseless to talk of a final
analysis into elementary propositions. From Moore's report
alone, one might conclude that Wittgenstein was headed in
the direction of a traditional critique of atomism that would
show that no examples of atomic propositions had been
produced because in fact no such propositions were, either
psychologically or logically, possible.

It soon became evident, however, that Wittgenstein's as-
sault on atomism was to be quite unconventional. In *The
Blue and Brown Books*, as well as in *Philosophical Investigations*, he did not concern himself much with the impossibility or insufficiency of atomic propositions; rather, his argument
is that they are *not needed for meaningful communication*.
Yet it is not clear that many philosophers had ever claimed
that meaningful communication alone required analysis into
atomic propositions, or even the possibility of such analysis.
The need stressed by earlier proponents of atomism had
been that of sorting out legitimate from illegitimate claims.
To answer this need, one resorted, when in doubt, to analysis. Earlier proponents of atomism might well have conced-
ed, had they been asked, that analysis was not ordinarily
needed for meaningful communication and that for the sort
of meaning required for meaningful communication an analysis of *usage* would usually suffice.

Nonetheless, Wittgenstein's attack appears to be quite
definite about its aims and assumptions. He notes that in the
Tractatus (e.g., 3.251) he had assumed that every proposition
has a perfectly determinate or definite sense, and he re-
hearses the reasoning that led him to that conclusion as
follows:

We are under the illusion that what is peculiar, profound, essential, in our investigation, resides in its trying to grasp the incomparable essence of language. ... The sense of a sentence—one would like to say—may, of course, leave this or that open, but the sentence must nevertheless have *a* definite sense. An indefinite sense—that would really not be a sense *at all.*—This is like: An indefinite boundary is not really a boundary at all. Here one thinks perhaps: if I say "I have locked the man up fast in the room—there is only one door left open"—then I simply haven't locked him in at all; his being locked in is a sham. One would be inclined to say here: "You haven't done anything at all". An enclosure with a hole in it is as good as *none*—But is that true? (P.I., pars. 97, 99)

Wittgenstein answers his question firmly in the negative, rejecting the view, which he traces to Frege, that a "blurred concept" is no concept at all. "Frege", Wittgenstein remarks, "compares a concept to an area and says that an area with vague boundaries cannot be called an area at all. This presumably means that we cannot do anything with it. —But is it senseless to say: 'Stand roughly there'?" (P.I., par. 71.)

The bulk of the examples Wittgenstein marshalled against the view that a sentence must have a definite sense are of the sort cited. He argued, with such homely examples, that the degree of precision required in particular cases is relative to the context and that one does not necessarily improve one's communication by heightening the degree of precision, or the extent of analysis, of a proposition.

In the course of attacking, by means of examples taken from ordinary discourse, the *a priori* requirement that each proposition have a definite sense, he comes to stress the importance in philosophy of detailed examination of ordinary language. It turns out that in language, as used, many propositions are vague, inexact, indefinite, but nonetheless quite adequately serve our purposes without demanding further analysis. His broomstick argument provides a justly famous example of the style as well as content and method of his later work:

When I say, "My broom is in the corner",—is this really a statement about the broomstick and the brush? Well, it could at any rate be replaced by a statement giving the position of the stick and the position of the brush. And this statement is surely a further analyzed form of the first one.—But why do I call it "further analysed"?—Well, if the broom is there, that surely means that the stick and brush must be there, and in a particular relation to one another; and this was as it were hidden in the sense of the first sentence, and is *expressed* in the analysed sentence. Then does someone who says that the broom is in the corner really mean: the broomstick is there, and so is the brush, and the broomstick is fixed in the brush?—If we were to ask anyone if he meant this he would probably say that he had not thought specially of the broomstick or specially of the brush at all. And that would be the *right* answer, for he meant to speak neither of the stick nor of the brush in particular. Suppose that, instead of saying, "Bring me the broom", you said "Bring me the broomstick and the brush which is fixed to it".—Isn't the answer, "Do you want the broom? Why do you put it so oddly?"—Is he going to understand the further analysed sentence better?—This sentence, one might say, achieves the same as the ordinary one, but in a more round-about way. [P.I., par. 60]

As an alternative to the idea that one must be able to give an exact definition or analysis of one's terms, Wittgenstein advances the notion of "family resemblances".[14] Instead of producing something common or essential, he remarks, he wants to show that the phenomena he is discussing have no single thing in common which makes one use the same word for all, but are, rather, *related* to one another in a variety of different ways. To explain his meaning, he invites his readers to consider *games*:

I mean board-games, card-games, ball-games, Olympic games, and so on. What is common to them all?—Don't say, "There *must* be something common, or they would not be called

---

[14]Wittgenstein was using this notion already in 1931. See his *Culture and Value*, p. 14.

'games',"—but *look and see* whether there is anything common to all.—For if you look at them you will not see something that is common to *all*, but similarities, relationships, and a whole series of them at that. To repeat: don't think, but look! Look for example at board-games, with their multifarious relationships. Now pass to card-games; here you find many correspondences with the first group, but many common features drop out, and others appear. When we pass next to ball-games, much that is common is retained, but much is lost.— Are they all "amusing"? Compare chess with noughts and crosses. Or is there always winning and losing, or competition between players? Think of patience [solitaire]. In all ball games there is winning and losing; but when a child throws his ball at the wall and catches it again, this feature has disappeared. ... And we can go through the many, many other groups of games in the same way; can see how similarities crop up and disappear.

And the result of this examination is: we see a complicated network of similarities overlapping and criss-crossing: sometimes overall similarities, sometimes similarities of detail.

I can think of no better expression to characterize these similarities than "family resemblances"; for the various resemblances between members of a family: build, features, colour of eyes, gait, temperament, etc. etc. overlap and criss-cross in the same way.—And I shall say: "games" form a family. [P.I., pars. 66–67]

The example is delightful, just as the idea of family resemblances is ingeniously applied as an alternative to essentialist-oriented analysis. Yet, unless it can be shown that atomism depended greatly on the claim that *meaningful communication* requires analysis into atomic propositions, Wittgenstein's entire discussion of essentialism and attack on analysis, even if correct both in theme and in detail, is beside the point. It was this combination of brilliance and apparent irrelevance that so angered Russell and Broad.

It might also be wondered if Wittgenstein's arguments against the philosophical program of defining—or analyzing—terms are indeed correct. To decide this issue, it is not necessary to quarrel with his claim that one may very often, and probably usually, communicate with vague and inexact language. Nor need one challenge his suggestion that to push the demand for exactness too far—to become *over-exact*—is to run the risk of being silly. Nor need it be questioned whether his individual arguments showing the impossibility of giving a precise definition to certain terms such as "game" and "family resemblance" are sound. One may agree with him on all these points without granting that the necessary and sufficient conditions required in definitions can never be given—or that they are never needed. In fact, there do appear to be important cases where necessary and sufficient conditions, unique defining criteria, both can, and need to be, given. One example quite appropriate to Wittgenstein's discussion is that of *family relationships*. One may give exact definitions of words like "sibling", "mother", "father", "aunt", "guardian". And one may need to do so—in legal disputes, for instance. There are, then, some *contexts* where definitions and essences are quite in order.

This point leads to another of Wittgenstein's main arguments against atomism: the contextualism or configurationism of his later philosophy. In the *Investigations* he argues that it is senseless to talk of a one-to-one correspondence between the simples of language and those of reality (even assuming that either sort of simple existed). He reasons that simplicity is not a matter of absolutes, but is context-dependent: one might, he notes, break down the visual image of a flower into all the different colors of which it is composed—although even that, as he failed to remark, would presuppose a highly sophisticated theory of color absolutes. Even were this possible, the question of which properties are more simple, he reasons, makes little sense. Multicoloredness is one kind of complexity; being composed of straight lines is another. Since, in Wittgenstein's view, we use the words "composite" and "simple" in a great many different ways, and ways that are also differently related, questions that presuppose *absolute* complexity and simplicity *apart from context* are not answerable and ought not to be asked. On this point Wittgenstein's line of reasoning is, again, quite close to that of Bühler and the Gestalt psychologists. Külpe, for instance, had contrived a famous experiment with cards (which resembles Wittgenstein's example of colored boxes in *Investigations* 48) in order to combat Mach's claim that the mental processes could be reduced to sensations. Külpe presented his subjects with cards containing non-sense syllables of various colors and arrangements. Some subjects were asked to report on the *color*, others on the *pattern*, others on the numbers of the items seen. In every case, the subject abstracted those features that he had been instructed to report and made no mention of—and in many cases could not remember—other features of the card that could equally well have been taken as simples. Here again the answers depended on the question asked, on the context. Whereas for the associationist, organization or theory arises from previous association, for Külpe, Bühler, and other Gestaltists—and for Wittgenstein in his later work—association depends on organization or theory.

VII

In the *Tractatus* Wittgenstein had marked off legitimate scientific propositions from all other utterances. Even if he paid little honor to scientific propositions, which leave "the problems of life ... completely untouched" (*Tractatus* 6.52) and show "how little is achieved" (*Tractatus*, page 5), they had pride of place in his philosophy. So when he discovered that the position of the *Tractatus* was impossible, he made a quite radical *volte-face*. In the *Investigations* there is no longer any prideful place: scientific propositions connect with many other kinds, with many other language-games, no one of which enjoys the power of judging or criticizing any other, and each of which gains its meaning from the use to which it is put within some established area of discourse. If science was not authoritative, nothing was authoritative; if no atomic scientific propositions mirrored the world, then the world was not mirrored by language at all. From his discovery that *his* theory of criticism, as developed in the *Tractatus*, could not work, Wittgenstein concluded that any philosophical theory of criticism was impossible. To criticize, to justify, to explain, these were no longer proper philosophical aims: all that remained to the philosopher was to *describe* the many different sorts of language-games and the "forms of life" in which they were embedded. Such description was in itself *subject-neutral*: while attempting to bring out—to describe—the logics or grammars of various kinds of discourse, it could not *in principle* presume to elevate one of these above another. Even the basic laws of logic, which logicians were having some measure of success at articulating, were now to be regarded as *conventions*, as highly systematic schemes for ordering statements which, far from "making manifest" the logical structure of the world, were man-created schemes of classification, *in no way more basic* than other language-games, which were also man-created. A sophisticated anthropocentric relativism, a kind of comparative anthropology of linguistic systems whose meaning was determined by their usage, replaced the objective realism of the *Tractatus*.

One thing, however, had evidently not changed: namely, Wittgenstein's conviction that the solution of the *Tractatus* was "definitive and unassailable": it had stated how analysis into simples would *have to* proceed if there was to be any such analysis. If *his* account did not work, *no* such account could work!

Wittgenstein's later radical subjectivism is—despite occasional claims to the contrary—no more Kantian than was his earlier realism. Nonetheless, there are in the later Wittgenstein echoes of some Kantian themes: to the extent that the categories, logics, grammars, frameworks of different language-games are seen as records of the natural history of man's interaction with his environment, rather than as reflections of the structure of the world, there is a *touch* of Kantianism there. Human language, embedded in human conduct, is taken as the starting point for an investigation that no longer assumes that the exploration of human language gives access to reality, but rather proposes that human language, as a *projection* of the mind rather than a picture of the world, in a sense *creates* reality. Yet here too the differences with Kant are basic. For Kant the structure of the world was unknowable and the categories of the understanding unchanging; for the early Wittgenstein the structure of the world was knowable; for the later Wittgenstein the categories of the understanding—of language—were in constant flux.

VIII

In the *Philosophical Investigations*, then, the claim that one single language of science exists is dropped, and introduced in its stead is the view that language consists of a multitude of different, often interacting, language-games, each with its own "grammar" or rules of use. The word "grammar", as used here and by Wittgenstein, does not refer to the school grammar of subject and predicate, noun, verb, adjective and other "parts of speech", a system of classification which Wittgenstein viewed as highly misleading. Very likely he chose quite deliberately to use this old word in a new way, for just as school grammar was tied closely to the theory of Aristotelian logic, rendered obsolete by the work of Frege, Russell and Whitehead, Wittgenstein, and others, just so was his new sense of grammar as "depth grammar" or "the underlying logic of a language" linked to the new logic. In fact, Wittgenstein uses the word "grammar" in at least two senses, neither of which corresponds to school grammar. The first, surface grammar, concerns the way in which a word is used in the construction of a particular utterance; the second, depth grammar, relies more on the *point* of the language-game or form of life in which that word plays some part.[15]

---

[15]Wittgenstein's depth grammar does not, contrary to what is occasionally suggested, correspond to the deep grammar that Chomsky expounds in his linguistic theory.

IX

It is not necessary for the later Wittgenstein that all, or even any, of the languages that concern the philosopher have the particular grammar of being reducible to atomic propositions, nor is philosophical bewilderment or puzzlement any longer attributed to the use of utterances that are not analyzable into atomic propositions.

His concern, however, is still to eliminate philosophical puzzlement, and his whole view of the nature of philosophy hinges on his understanding of this concern. His program for eliminating philosophical puzzlement, which he regarded as "a battle against the bewitchment of our intelligence by means of language" (P.I. 109), depends on the explanation he provides for the *origin* of this puzzlement. In the *Philosophical Investigations*, philosophical perplexity is traced to several main sources of error. One is to be "held captive" by a picture—of time, say, as a stream. A second is to confuse surface and depth grammar. A more important error is a third: becoming confused about the complex interaction of different language-games, applying the rules of one language-game erroneously to another, mixing different grammars. When this occurs, an important utterance may quite inadvertently be jerked out of its proper context. "A wheel that can be turned though nothing else moves with it, is not part of the mechanism" (P.I. 271).

The sort of error that Wittgenstein sees as the source of philosophical perplexity is very much like that often described by contemporary analytic philosophers as a "category mistake", although Wittgenstein himself does not use this terminology.[16] To avoid category mistakes it becomes necessary to undertake the detailed study of ordinary language, the study of language in context in all its interactions with life, behavior, nature. Wittgenstein writes (P.I. 7): "I shall also call the whole, consisting of language and the

---

[16]But compare Friedrich Waismann's semi-official exposition of Wittgenstein's later thought in *The Principles of Linguistic Philosophy* (London: Macmillan, 1965), p. 104.

actions into which it is woven, the 'language game'."

Through detailed "purely descriptive" studies of "what has to be accepted, the given . . .", Wittgenstein tries to explain how one learns the "proper use" within a socially fixed "language-game" or form of life of various expressions; in learning this proper use, one learns the rules of the game in which the expressions occur. Language will then trespass its limits, or "go on holiday" as he puts it, when particular sorts of expressions are used outside their proper domain or range of application. Thus philosophical critique becomes the activity of showing how language may stray from its proper place and then bringing it back to its correct context. "One of the most important methods I use", Wittgenstein explained, "is to imagine a historical development for our ideas different from what actually occurred. If we do this we see the problem from a completely new angle".[17]

The *Tractatus*, taken as a whole, is thus regarded as itself one grand category-mistake, in this case that of supposing that different language-games must satisfy the criteria of one supremely authoritative language-game—namely, science. Wittgenstein presents in the *Investigations,* and in other later writings, numerous examples of such "grammatical" errors. Many of these have to do with what he regards as our tendency to impose on our *mental* concepts tasks and rules appropriate at best to our physical concepts, and often not even to them. A tendency to mix mental with physical concepts goes far, he suggests, to explain why philosophers spend so much time arguing about the existence of "Mental Substance" and dividing themselves into Monists and Dualists. These old disagreements, Wittgenstein suggests, are not disagreements about matters of fact, as they appeared to be to most of those who engaged in them, but are, rather, rooted in such mistakes as misapplying the grammar of mental concepts to the grammar of physical concepts and vice versa, and taking words out of their proper grammatical context.

Wittgenstein is led by this route to devote a large part of

---

[17]Wittgenstein, *Culture and Value,* p. 37.

the *Investigations* to mental concepts, to the study of words such as "thinking", "feeling", "meaning", "understanding", "intending". Here he develops an idea of "imageless thought" closely resembling that of Külpe and Bühler. "There is a lack of clarity", he writes,

> about the role of imaginability in our investigation. Namely, about the extent to which it insures that a proposition makes sense. It is no more essential to the understanding of a proposition that one should imagine anything in connexion with it, than that one should make a sketch from it. Instead of "imaginability" one can also say here: representability by a particular method of representation. And such a representation may indeed safely point a way to further use of a sentence. On the other hand a picture may obtrude itself upon us and be of no use at all. [P.I. 395, 396, 397]

Wittgenstein talks in a similar way, at once developing his notion of imageless thinking and repudiating the very different presuppositions of the *Tractatus*, in his *Lectures and Conversations* (page 30), where he denies that when a Frenchman says "Il pleut" and an Englishman says "It is raining", something happens in both minds which is the real sense of "It is raining". Wittgenstein explains: "We imagine something like imagery, which is the international language.[18] Whereas in fact: (1) Thinking (or imagery) is not an accompaniment of the words as they are spoken or heard. (2) The sense in the thought 'It's raining' is not even the words *with* the accompaniment of some sort of imagery."[19]

Against the picture theory of the *Tractatus*, Wittgenstein

---

[18]This is obviously a not very veiled criticism of Otto Neurath, who had produced, as his own contribution to the school-reform program, what he dubbed the "Viennese method", which advocated the use of pictures rather than words in order to avoid verbal misunderstandings and to contribute to the creation of an international "universal language".

[19]Professor J. N. Findlay, in his recollections of Wittgenstein at Cambridge, reports Wittgenstein's discussing "imageless thought", using Bühler's own words. See J. N. Findlay: "My Encounters with Wittgenstein", *Philosophical Forum*, vol IV, no. 2, 1972-73, p. 175.

notes that even if we were to assume that we *did* have mental images, these would still have to be interpreted and thus would be incapable, even if available, of providing an immediate and infallible point of contact between thought and reality. Thus not only is the language of the physical not reducible to the language of the mental; the latter could not in any case give us access to the ultimate constituents of reality, any more than logic gives us access to the ultimate structure of reality.

X

A new explanation of error—and Wittgenstein's later thought ranks as such—has often, in the history of philosophy, led to a research program whose aim is to create conditions under which such errors will no longer arise. So it was to be with Wittgenstein. He himself never claimed that all specifically identifiable disciplines and activities in which people engaged were separate language-games each with its own sets of rules (or grammar); it is evident that he thought things more complicated than that. Many of his followers, however, made just this mistake, supposing that each individual activity—law, history, science, logic, ethics, politics, religion—has its own special grammar or logic; that mixing the grammar of one of these with that of another leads to philosophical error; and that it is the *new* job of the philosopher—his new research program under the Wittgensteinian dispensation—to describe in detail these separate logics or grammars. In this spirit two generations of British and American philosophers came to write books with titles such as *The Vocabulary of Politics, The Language of Morals, The Logic of Moral Discourse, The Logic of Historical Explanation, The Language of Literary Criticism, The Language of Fiction, The Uses of Argument, The Logic of the Social Sciences, The Logic of the Sciences, The Province of Logic, The Language of Education, The Logic of Religious Language, Faith and Logic, Christian Discourse, The Language of Christian Belief, The Logic of Colour Words,* and so on *ad nauseam.* Any philosopher, whether well-seasoned in his subject or a budding Ph.D., was thus provided with a simple "research formula" whereby a book or learned paper could be produced: "Take one of the phrases: 'The logic of *x*', 'The language of *x*', or 'The grammar of *x*', substitute for *x* some activity or discipline such as were named above; write a treatise on the topic so created." The facile ease with which such programs could be executed goes far to explain the immense success of such Wittgensteinian philosophizing—as witness to which I should mention that each of the titles cited has decorated a book or monograph actually published. Had Russell appreciated this aspect of the *Investigations*, he would have better understood, although he would still have been dismayed, that "a whole school finds important wisdom in its pages".

Still, Wittgenstein himself did not endorse, or engage in, this sort of activity. Indeed, the actual sorting out of categories, language-games, grammatical rules, or whatever one might wish to call them, is—even granting that it is useful—by no means easy, as Wittgenstein well knew, and as can be shown by a few examples. Cases often cited in illustration of mistakes in philosophical grammar are: the confusion of a class with its elements, a university (such as Oxford, Cambridge, London, Durham, Yale, or Santa Cruz) with the colleges that comprise it, or a company of soldiers with the soldiers who form it. By what criteria does one distinguish such categories? Often it is suggested that two subject terms are of different categories, with different applicable grammars, whenever different kinds of predicates are appropriate to them. For instance, one would say: "The soldiers are fat" but not "The company is fat", or "The colleges are cozy" but not "The University is cozy". Similarly, it is suggested that two subject terms are of the same category whenever the same predicates may be attached to them: "being well fed", for instance, applied both to soldiers and sailors in the American forces. It is easy, however, to show that this particular way of distinguishing language-games or categories often breaks down: both a person and his body may be emaciated although the two subjects would on the face of it be thought to be of different categories. Again, whereas 2 and 0 would be regarded in many contexts as being of the same category, the first may be used as a divisor while the second cannot. Or take the difference between electromagnetic waves, light waves, sound waves, and water waves: a common-sense approach might to be to put the first in one category, the second and third in another category, and the last in yet another — whereas in physics the first two are put together and the last two are put together, owing in the first case to the theory that electromagnetic and light waves are identical and in the second to the theory that sound and water waves undulate in a material medium.[20]

The underlying problem here is, of course, that while it is indeed wrong to apply inappropriate criteria to a particular subject matter, we often cannot say in advance which criteria or which categories of criteria will be appropriate or inappropriate. This too will be a matter for exploration. It is, therefore, probably wrong to ask first of some criticism whether it is appropriate to its subject matter in that it, say, satisfies some such condition as "scientific character". It may be better to take the criticism seriously on its own grounds in order the better to *discover* what categories of objections one is prepared to accept against the subject matter in question. This may well come as a surprise.

Wittgenstein, as opposed to some of his followers, avoided such difficulties at least in theory: for he stoutly maintained, as part of his attack on essentialism, that no language or language-game (any more than *any* game) possessed essential defining criteria.

XI

At the heart of the account just given of the later philosophy

---

[20]Several examples in this paragraph are borrowed from J. O. Wisdom's very interesting discussion in "Esotericism", *Philosophy*, October 1959, p. 346ff. See also J. J. C. Smart, "A Note on Categories", *British Journal for the Philosophy of Science*, 1953.

of Wittgenstein lies one of the basic issues of philosophy and one of the most troublesome aspects of Wittgenstein's later thinking. I have in mind the issue of the development, refinement, change, birth, and death of language-games, forms of life, grammars. Although those parts of his writings dealing with this issue are obscure, a consistent, if unsatisfactory, position is stated.[21]

The difficulty arises from three important contentions that do not fit together in any easy way. While insisting (1) that one language-game or grammar may not judge another, Wittgenstein also (2) allows (by contrast to Kant) that our language-games and grammatical categories and concepts may change, develop, evolve. Writing of the differences among kinds of sentences, Wittgenstein states: "This multiplicity is not something fixed, given once for all; but new types of language, new language-games, as we may say, come into existence, and others become obsolete and get forgotten. (We can get a *rough* picture of this from the changes in mathematics.)" (P.I. 23) Yet he goes on to say (3) that philosophy may not intervene in this change: "Philosophy may in no way interfere with the actual use of language. ... It leaves everything as it is" (P.I. 124), and "What has to be accepted, the given, is—so one could say—*forms of life*" (P.I., page 226).

The first and third claims are often, and understandably, taken to endorse an ideological conservatism, a peaceful coexistence of those forms of life already entrenched and recognized, a stance that in practice leaves no room for change. The second claim is often neither ignored or passed

---

[21]On these matters, see the much more extended argument in my *The Retreat to Commitment*, 2nd, revised edition (La Salle, Ill: Open Court, 1984); see also my "Non-Justificationism: Popper *versus* Wittgenstein", in *Epistemology and Philosophy of Science, Proceedings of the 7th International Wittgenstein Symposium* (Vienna: Hölder-Pichler-Tempsky, 1983), pp. 255–61; and my "Group Chairman's Remarks" and "On the Differences Between Popperian and Wittgensteinian Approaches", *Proceedings of the 11th International Conference on the Unity of the Sciences* (New York: ICF Press, 1982).

over as an insignificant token concession without import.

The problem is twofold. First, if conflicting language-games or forms of life are not themselves permitted to initiate grammatical change by sitting in judgment one on the other, then how *does* such change get started? And how is it to be evaluated? Wittgenstein provides no explanation. Second, if he is willing to countenance fundamental grammatical change, why does he forbid philosophy any role in effecting it? His account is at odds with the philosophical tradition, wherein it is widely assumed that perhaps the most important way to bring about fundamental categorical change occurs through rational intellectual criticism involving a clash between opposing categorical frameworks. Basic shifts in the grammars of the linguistic activities in which we engage have often in the past involved criticism of one set of categories, of one grammar, of one language-game, by another. This was true in the conceptual shifts that took place in the development of modern logic, of non-Euclidean geometry, and of Einstein's relativity theory, to mention only a few important conceptual or categorical shifts with which Wittgenstein was familiar. In line with the historical record, one of Wittgenstein's own most faithful disciples, Friedrich Waismann, in a book intended to be an introductory exposition of the principles of Wittgenstein's later philosophy, cites Einstein's analysis of simultaneity as an example of conceptual change and clarification in which philosophy aided scientific advance.[22]

The issues at stake here—the development and change of conceptual fameworks, the scope and limits of language-games and forms of life, decision making, rule following, the nature of philosophy—are treated throughout Wittgenstein's work. Perhaps they display themselves most illuminatingly and importantly, however, in his treatment of religion. He himself seems to have sensed this. Commenting on his later philosophy, Wittgenstein once remarked: "Its advantage is that if you believe, say, Spinoza or Kant, this

---

[22]Waismann, *Wittgenstein and the Vienna Circle*, pp. 11–14.

interferes with what you believe in religion; but if you believe me, nothing of the sort."[23] Nor have Wittgenstein's critics overlooked the significance of this part of his philosophy. Ernest Gellner's attack is representative in focusing on religion. "By destroying philosophy", he states, Wittgenstein "made room for faith . . . religious believers can find in Wittgensteinianism not merely a device for ruling out philosophic criticism, they can find in it a positive validation of their belief".[24] They not only *can* do so; they have done this. Several of Wittgenstein's closest students converted to Roman Catholicism; another was a postulant for the Anglican priesthood. And most contemporary philosophies of religion in England and America draw on Wittgensteinian arguments.

Gellner's remarks are exaggerated but not unwarranted. Wittgenstein (as opposed to some of his disciples) neither provided a "positive validation" for religious belief nor ruled out criticism of religious grammars or forms of life. What he *did* do was to state that the latter was not the job of a philosopher *qua* philosopher. In limiting the philosopher to the *description* of various categories or frameworks, Wittgenstein did indeed depart from that part of the philosophical tradition associated with such names as Plato, Spinoza, Hume, Kant, and—among Wittgenstein's contemporaries—Russell. All these thinkers stressed the need for the philosopher to undertake radical criticism of fundamental categories and even spoke at times as if this were his main role. Allowing that the tradition might be bad, one still fails to see the point of Wittgenstein's artificial construction of "the philosopher *qua* philosopher". For, while not denying either that forms of life embodying various religions pass in and out of existence or that they might be criticized, Wittgenstein forbade the philosopher to try to effect such changes *qua* philosopher. The distinction is silly: one does not don a

---

[23]Reported in W. D. Hudson, *Ludwig Wittgenstein* (Richmond: John Knox Press, 1968), p. 67. See also G. E. M. Anscombe, "What Wittgenstein Really Said", *The Tablet*, April 17, 1954.

[24]Ernest Gellner, "Reply to Mr MacIntyre", *Universities and Left Review*, Summer 1958.

certain sort of cap to make a philosophical utterance—nor does one doff it to undo one!

If Wittgenstein's approach to religion was not, then, that of a critic, it was hardly that of a defender either. To be sure, he himself prayed during the First World War; but he wished to disassociate this from belief in or defense of *doctrine*. He made it quite clear that he neither supported traditional religious doctrines nor in many cases even understood what they could mean. "Suppose", he suggested, "someone said, 'What do you believe, Wittgenstein? Are you a sceptic? Do you know whether you will survive death?' I would really, this is a fact, say, 'I can't say. I don't know,' because I haven't any clear idea what I'm saying when I'm saying, 'I don't cease to exist,' etc."[25] Again, he remarked that although he could understand the conception of God as it involved aware-ness of one's sin and guilt, he could not understand the conception of a Creator.[26]

In the *Investigations*, as in other of his writings, he quite self-consciously adopted toward religion and other forms of life which were puzzling to him the role of an anthropologist or "explorer into an unknown country with a language quite strange to you" (P.I. 206–8)[27] and posed the possibility that although the people in that country had evolved a language and engaged in "the usual human activities . . . when we try to learn their language we find it impossible" (P.I. 207). What he says of such a tribe might be remarked of any number of contemporary forms of Christianity: "There is

---

[25]Ludwig Wittgenstein: *Lectures and Conversations on Aesthetics, Psy-chology, and Religious Belief*, compiled from notes taken by Yorick Smythies, Rush Rhees, and James Taylor, ed. Cyril Barrett (Berkeley: University of California Press, 1967), p. 70.

[26]Norman Malcolm, *Ludwig Wittgenstein: A Memoir* (London: Oxford University Press, 1966), pp. 70–71.

[27]See his "Bemerkungen über Frazers *The Golden Bough*," *Syn-thèse*, 1967, pp. 233–53; Rush Rhees, ed., *Remarks on Frazer's* Golden Bough (Retford: Brynmill, 1979); and Wittgenstein, *Lectures and Conversations*. See also Norman Rudich and Manfred Stassen, "Wittgenstein's Implied Anthropology: Remarks on Wittgenstein's Notes on Frazer", *History and Theory*, 1971, pp. 84–89.

no regular connexion between what they say, the sounds they make, and their actions; but still the sounds are not superfluous."

Even where the language is understood, Wittgenstein allows for mutual incomprehension. "One human being can be a complete enigma to another", he observes, "We learn this when we come into a strange country with entirely strange traditions; and, what is more, even given a mastery of the country's language. We do not *understand* the people. (And not because of not knowing what they are saying to themselves.) We cannot find our feet with them." (P.I. ii, page 223). Of his close friends and students Smythies and Anscombe, both of whom had become Roman Catholics, he remarked to Malcolm: "I could not possibly bring myself to believe all the things that they believe." Malcolm adds: "I think that in this remark he was not disparaging their belief. It was rather an observation about his own capacity."[28]

Such remarks about religion as appear in his principal writings are allusive and indirect. To find a direct application of his ideas to religion, one must study his three lectures on religion in *Lectures and Conversations* and his brief critical remarks on Frazer's great work *The Golden Bough*. In both these places Wittgenstein cautions, with specific examples, against the error of approaching an alien form of life, whether primitive society or religion, with the canons of one's own society and one's own unexamined criteria of rationality and scientific respectability. Such a course is bound to lead to a misunderstanding of the alien grammar, however coherent it might be. Such an encounter must keep in focus one's own criteria of rationality as well as probing the criteria of rationality embodied in the alien form of life. If someone should charge that "Wittgenstein is trying to undermine reason", he would, he avows, reply, "This wouldn't be false"![29] Nor would it be the first time, for his rejection of the *Tractatus*, although hardly an attempt to undermine rea-

---

[28]Malcolm, *Ludwig Wittgenstein: A Memoir*, p. 72.
[29]Wittgenstein, *Lectures and Conversations*, p. 64.

son, certainly battered one important *theory of rationality*.

One may easily miss the entire point of religious discourse, Wittgenstein warns, if one fails to consider that all the key terms involved—"believe", "contradict", "understand", "opinion", "error", "evidence", "prediction"—are being used outside what is for the investigator their *normal* use in nonreligious grammar. Those who participate in religious forms of life, Wittgenstein maintains, are frequently in the grip of a kind of picture; for instance, that of the rewards and punishments connected with the Last Judgment. Yet one would seriously distort one's understanding of the grammar of this form of life were one to say, "These people rigorously hold the opinion (or view) that there is a Last Judgment."[30] For it is no "opinion" of the sort that is used in nonreligious discourse, subject to the usual canons of evidence, testability, and high probability—which is why words like "dogma" and "faith" are likely to be used instead of "hypothesis" or "opinion".

In criticism of Wittgenstein it may well be urged that while some religious believers do use their key words in such an extranormal sense, there have been and still are many believers who hold, or claim to hold, their religious beliefs as sorts of hypotheses, subject to evidential support and canons of scientific testability. Wittgenstein is well aware that such persons exist, but he finds them ludicrous. Such a believer, he says, "I would definitely call unreasonable. I would say, if this is religious belief, then it's all superstition. But I would ridicule it, not by saying it is based on insufficient evidence. . . . You can say: this man is ridiculous because he believes, and bases it on weak reasons."[31]

At this point Wittgenstein is not even consistent. For is that category of believers who, at least from a "normal" point of view, *misuse* scientific canons not to be allowed to do just that if that is part of *their own form of life*? And if not, is this not after all *philosophical* interference in a possible

---

[30]*Ibid.*, p. 56.
[31]*Ibid.*, p. 59.

form of life? It could be rash indeed to attribute such a form
of life to self deception, even assuming that that were an
unproblematic concept, for as Wittgenstein himself admon-
ishes: "These statements would not differ just in respect to
what they are about. Entirely different connections would
make them into religious beliefs, and there can easily be
imagined transitions where we wouldn't know for our life
whether to call them religious beliefs or scientific beliefs."[32]

This weakness in Wittgenstein's treatment of religion,
while submerged in his three lectures on religion, comes
strongly to the surface in his brief treatment of Frazer's
Golden Bough. While Wittgenstein is sensibly concerned to
object to the snobbish assumption that "superior" nineteenth-
century European cultural canons could evaluate, criticize,
analyze the many religions that Frazer treated, Wittgenstein
has neither evidence nor satisfactory theory to counter, except in a wholly *a priori* manner, the mine of facts and
connections on which Frazer draws to link a religion's *opinions* with its *rituals*.

Dismissing Frazer's explanation of rituals in terms of
erroneous beliefs, opinions, and interpretations of nature,
Wittgenstein coolly sets down an alternative account lacking
any supporting evidence. Religious customs are, he pro-
claims, instinctual responses to an inner need for release
and satisfaction, unconscious and with no other purpose.
"When I am angry about something", he explains, "I sometimes beat on the ground or against a tree with my cane. But
I do not, for that matter, believe that the earth is guilty or
that beating is of any help. 'I ventilate my anger.' *And all rites
are of this sort*. Such actions could be called instinctual".[33]

Even when he is being facile, as he is here, Wittgenstein
is fascinating and, if unwittingly, speaks to the point. For
how would an anthropologist or psychologist interpret that

[32]*Ibid.*, p. 58.
[33]Wittgenstein, "Bemerkungen über Frazers *The Golden Bough* ", p.
244. (My italics.) Rush Rhees omitted this passage when he reprinted this
essay as *Remarks on Frazer's* Golden Bough in 1979. But see C. G. Luckhardt,
ed., *Wittgenstein: Sources and Perspectives* (London: Harvester, 1979), p. 72.

ritual for releasing tension that Wittgenstein adopted in the early 1920s after losing his precious rod and refusing to answer the call of his dream? Might he not wonder whether that beating of the feminine earth and the masculine tree with the phallic cane might not have something to do with some unanalyzed picture or interpretation of the world formed by a small boy growing up in the Palais Wittgenstein in the 1890s, trying to play his games among seven older, bigger, and brilliantly talented children in a home whose very walls—as those who were there report—trembled when old Karl Wittgenstein strode through the front portal and mounted up the crimson staircase? Had young Ludwig examined more closely the tree that he beat with his cane, he might even have looked up to find a golden bough.

Such speculation is also a form of life—and Wittgenstein acknowledged Freud as "my teacher".

XII

In his last years, despite his growing physical weakness and his almost constant depression, there remained around Wittgenstein in Cambridge a group of talented and energetic students. No other philosopher of the past two centuries had formed a school so devoted, so responsible, or so loyal. Or so bullied: Wittgenstein tyrannized his friends and disciples, played off one against another, made cruel fun of their talents.[34] Yet somehow he was able to preserve their loyalty without cultivating their affection.

In the autumn of 1949, shortly after a summer's visit to his former student Norman Malcolm at Cornell University, Wittgenstein learned that he was dying of cancer. Without letting his family know of his illness, he gathered together

---

[34]On Wittgenstein the teacher, see Peter Munz, "Transformation in Philosophy through the Teaching Methods of Wittgenstein and Popper", in *Proceedings of the 10th International Conference on the Unity of the Sciences* (New York: ICF Press, 1982), pp. 1235–62.

his disciples and executors-to-be and put his papers and affairs in order as best he could. That he wished some of his writings, especially his still uncompleted *Philosophical Investigations*, to be published is clear; that he ever expected they would is not. He could not possibly have imagined the reception they would receive.

At Christmas 1949 he returned one final time to Vienna to be with his family and friends, to talk, to make music with Koder and Postl again, and to wait with Mining as she died of cancer. Not long after her death in February 1950, he left Vienna forever. Most of the rest of the year he spent in England, but that autumn he went again briefly to his hut in Norway and in a moment of optimism considered settling there. In February 1951, growing weaker, he moved into his doctor's house in Cambridge, where he died on April 29.[35]

Throughout this time his disciples saw him regularly, and they continued to discuss philosophy until a few days before his death. He was, about himself, as lighthearted as he could be, but for the most part he maintained gloom about his written work, expressing to his friends the sort of pessimism he had already set down in the Preface to the *Investigations*: "I should have liked to produce a good book. This has not come about, but the time is past in which I could improve it ... These remarks ... I make ... public with doubtful feelings. It is not impossible that it should fall to the lot of this work, in its poverty and in the darkness of this time, to bring light into one brain or another—but, of course, it is not likely. ... I should not like my writing to spare other people the trouble of thinking. But, if possible, to stimulate someone to thoughts of his own."

---

[35]He is buried in St. Giles's churchyard, Cambridge. A brief account of Wittgenstein's death and burial appears in M. O'C. Drury's "Conversations with Wittgenstein", in Rhees, ed., *Ludwig Wittgenstein: Personal Recollections*, p. 184.

Epilogue

Wittgenstein is so famous for his knack of teaching by catching one off guard that his technique has, misleadingly, been compared to that of a Zen master. Certainly he took me by surprise, for prior to my encounter with his old elementary school pupils I had had no intention of writing a book about him. No one who has read this brief study will doubt my respect for Ludwig Wittgenstein. Yet it would be wrong to part from the reader without cautioning him that this study has not been written by a disciple: I reject the main tenets of his early and later work. Should it be said that his significance lies not in any tenets but in a new style or method of philosophizing, I should have to confess that I consider the styles and methods of philosophical analysis advocated and practised by Wittgenstein sometimes useful but quite overrated. This comment is only for the record; although I have criticized his views here and there in the preceding chapters, no critique or comprehensive assessment of his work has been given, nor was any such envisioned. Before one may criticize a philosopher responsibly, one has to determine quite precisely what his problems were and what he had to say about them. With Wittgenstein, this is still far from easy; and all too many writers, both defenders and critics, have already used his work as a kind of Rorschach blot for their own predilections.

I hope that I have not added to their number, but have, rather, encouraged someone or other to pursue some of the leads about his life and work that I have mentioned, and thereby come to a clearer understanding of him.

In any case, the progress of Wittgenstein scholarship in recent years gives some hope that the possibility of the sort of exegetical projection that has gone on since his death is nearing its end. To mention two examples, the demonstration that the *Tractatus* is concerned primarily with logical questions and only peripherally with epistemology has corrected a forty-year-old misreading. One may wonder how the philosophy of the past half century would have differed had that misinterpretation never taken place. Again, the publication of Wittgenstein's correspondance with Paul Engelmann and Ludwig von Ficker has brought into proper highlight his view of the "unwritten but more important" half of the *Tractatus*, dealing with the ethical and "the mystical"—showing more dramatically than any exegesis how far Wittgenstein was removed from logical positivism, a movement which he is still occasionally, and ridiculously, credited with having fathered.

Although Wittgenstein published only one brief philosophical book during his lifetime, and one tiny philosophical paper that he repudiated almost as soon as he had posted it to the printer, he wrote voluminously. This work, much of which has been preserved, is being published posthumously by his literary executors. Perhaps another decade or more will pass before all his work—including his remarkable correspondence—has been published, and made available in English as well as German. I mention the correspondence because so little of it has been published, despite the vivid sense not only of the man but also of the pace and atmosphere of philosophical dialogue and humane concern that some of it conveys.[1]

Also needed are some ambitious works in biography and intellectual history—not simply more memoirs—both from those who knew him intimately in his later years and have cared faithfully for his literary estate and those quite outside this circle of philosophers. Both kinds of biography, to be satisfactory, will have to wait on two conditions: first, the eventual accessibility—together with permission to publish

---

[1] For the correspondence that has been published, see the Bibliography to this book.

—of the total corpus of the man's work and related papers; and second, the reconstruction and restoration of the most important links between Anglo-American and Austro-German philosophical traditions, links sundered by two world wars.

A man can bare himself before others only out of a particular kind of love. A love which acknowledges, as it were, that we are all wicked children. . . .

Hate between men comes from our cutting ourselves off from each other. Because we don't want anyone else to look inside us, since it's not a pretty sight in there.

—*Ludwig Wittgenstein, 1944[1]*

It's difficult to think well about "certainty", "probability", "perception", etc. But it is, if possible, still more difficult to think, or try to think, really honestly about your life & other people's lives. And the trouble is that thinking about these things is not thrilling, but often downright nasty. And when it's nasty then it's most important.

—*Ludwig Wittgenstein, 1944[2]*

If you think I'm an old spinster—think again!

—*Ludwig Wittgenstein, 1945[3]*

Afterword, 1985
On Wittgenstein and Homosexuality

I

A POLEMICAL REPLY TO MY CRITICS

Wittgenstein's homosexuality is mentioned very briefly in this book—on about four or five pages. The information given there is, as stated, based on confidential reports from

---

[1]Ludwig Wittgenstein, *Culture and Value*, ed. G. H. von Wright (Chicago: University of Chicago Press, 1980), p. 46e.

[2]Norman Malcolm, *Ludwig Wittgenstein: A Memoir* (London: Oxford University Press, 1958), p. 39.

[3]Ibid., p. 45.

his friends. On the first publication of this book, in English, these reports were vehemently challenged by other of his friends. Since that time, however, Wittgenstein's homosexuality has been corroborated by his own written statements in his coded diaries. *Thus there is no longer any ground for controversy about the fact of Wittgenstein's active homosexuality.* Yet it continues to be denied, and the controversy continues.[4]

Having treated the matter so briefly in this book itself, I am ambivalent about entering into a more extended discussion of the matter in this Afterword. There are two reasons for this. First, I do not want to attach undue importance to it. And I find—and here my own experience matches Wittgenstein's—that many people do not "think well" or at all forthrightly when dealing with such issues. And yet, as Wittgenstein himself cautions, "when it's nasty then it's *most* important". And it is clearly necessary to treat the controversy briefly on the occasion of this new edition. Otherwise further misunderstanding and controversy will inevitably occur.

* * *

Homosexuality is unlikely to be treated with any equanimity until sexuality itself is so treated. There seems little likelihood, despite the developments of the past century, that that shall soon occur. The original reception of this book, in its publication in 1973 and 1974 in New York and London, illustrates this as well as anything.

Part of the reception was refreshing. I had in no way blamed or criticized Wittgenstein for his sexual preferences

---

[4]See Desmond Lee's review of Rush Rhees, ed., *Ludwig Wittgenstein: Personal Recollections* (Totowa, N. J.: Rowman & Littlefield, 1981), in *The Times Literary Supplement*, January 15, 1982, p. 46. Perhaps the most comical of these denials is that of Ian Hacking, in his "The Uncommercial Traveller", *Times Higher Education Supplement*, April 8, 1983. Hacking concedes that Wittgenstein "was no heterosexualist" but implies that he must then have been a virgin. See my reply to Hacking in *Times Higher Education Supplement*, April 29, 1983, p. 35.

or activities; and many readers seemed to absorb this information in the same calm and understanding spirit in which they took similar revelations about Lytton Strachey, E. M. Forster, John Maynard Keynes, Virginia Woolf, Vita Sackville-West, D. H. Lawrence, and other eminent British thinkers who are commonly associated, directly or indirectly, with Wittgenstein through Cambridge and the Bloomsbury Group, and who also happened to be homosexual.[5] In any case, the book was tolerably well reviewed. Thus *The British Journal for the Philosophy of Science* described it as "extraordinarily concise", "enthrallingly written", "profound", and "more interesting and provocative than anything else written about Wittgenstein".[6] And C. P. Snow in his review described my treatment of Wittgenstein's homosexuality as "temperate and unusually detached ... written with neutrality".[7]

But this was only a small part of the story. Several of Wittgenstein's literary executors and relatives threatened legal action to suppress the publication of this book, and also

---

[5]Among the many books dealing with these matters, see Michael Holroyd, *Lytton Strachey*, 2 vols. (London: Heinemann, 1967); P. N. Furbank, *E. M. Forster: A Life* (New York: Harcourt Brace Jovanovich, 1978); E. M. Forster, *Maurice* (New York W.W. Norton, 1971); Nigel Nicholson, *Portrait of a Marriage* (New York: Atheneum, 1973). See also the *Letters* and the *Diaries* of Virginia Woolf.

[6]Professor I. C. Jarvie, review in *British Journal for the Philosophy of Science*, vol. 25, no. 2 (June 1974), pp. 195-98. See also *The Economist*, April 6, 1974, p. 107; *Review of Metaphysics*, vol. 27, March 1974, pp. 601-2; *Times Literary Supplement*, August 17, 1973, pp. 953-54; *Los Angeles Times*, July 30, 1973; *The Christian Century*, December 19, 1973, p. 1255; *Philosophy and Phenomenological Research*, 1974, pp. 289-90; *Cross Currents*, Spring 1975, p. 84: See also N. Wendevogel, "Wittgenstein, Psychopompos", *Berlin Tagesspiegel*, November 1983; Peter Friedl, "Der Philosoph als Gärtner", *Nürnberger Nachrichten*, November 25, 1983; Eckhard Nordhofen, "Philosophie oder Leben", *Frankfurter Allgemeine Zeitung*, November 22, 1983; "Lieber Volksschullehrer als Professor", *Die Welt*, January 28, 1984; and "Philosophen: Alles, was der Fall ist", *Der Spiegel*, January 9, 1984, pp. 142-51.

[7]C. P. Snow. "Bounds of Possibility", *The Financial Times*, London, 11 April 1974, p. 32.

called on my British publishers to attempt to persuade them
to stop publication.[8] Controversy raged in the columns of
The Times Literary Supplement, and in several other publications. Thus Professor G. E. M. Anscombe, of Cambridge University, one of Wittgenstein's literary executors, published
two letters suggesting that I could not have known and ought
not to have claimed the things I did.[9] Wittgenstein's close
friend M. O'C. Drury, after explaining that, since he was a
psychiatrist, it is "in the nature of my work to be alert to
problems of homosexuality whether latent or active", wrote
that "Bartley is in error when he supposes that Wittgenstein
was at any time 'tormented by homosexual behaviour' . . .
sensuality in any form was entirely foreign to his ascetic
personality".[10] Another of Wittgenstein's literary executors,
Mr. Rush Rhees, of the University of London, uses words
and phrases like "novellette" and "at the level of gossip
columns" to describe my book.[11] A letter-writing campaign
was set up: those whom I had mentioned in my acknowledgements were contacted, asked to disassociate themselves
from me, and to withdraw permission to use their names.
One of those contacted, an eminent British literary critic,
wrote to me: "My respect for you and your work are such

---

[8]See my letters to *The Times Literary Supplement*, January 11, 1974 and
February 8, 1974; and G. E. M. Anscombe's letter of January 18, 1974.

[9]*The Times Literary Supplement*, letters as follows: G. E. M. Anscombe,
November 16, 1973 and January 4, 1974; W. W. Bartley, January 11, 1974
and February 8, 1974; F. A. von Hayek, February 8, 1974; M. O'C. Drury and
Irina Strickland, February 22, 1974; Peter Johnson, December 14, 1973;
Brian McGuinness, January 18, 1974; Rudolf Koder, February 8, 1974;
William Miller, January 18, 1974.

[10]*Times Literary Supplement*, February 22, 1974. See also Drury's essays "Some Notes on Conversations with Wittgenstein" and "Conversations
with Wittgenstein", in Rhees, ed., *Ludwig Wittgenstein: Personal Recollections*, p. 135, where Drury's point goes uncorrected.

[11]Rush Rhees, "Wittgenstein", in *The Human World*, February 1974,
pp. 66-78. (See also John Stonborough's remarks in the same issue, pp.
78-85.) Numerous writers—without examining the matter—blindly followed Rhees. Thus Professor Rudolph Haller, of the University of Graz,
writes of my book: "This thesis remains without a trace of proof." See his
review in *Conceptus*, vol. 11, 1977, pp. 422-24.

that I will write in complete frankness. I wonder whether you have a clear notion of the ugliness which followed on the publication of your book here. . . . The general line here is that you are to be drummed out of the trade and that no academic invitation of any kind will be extended to you from the United Kingdom henceforth. . ."

This ugliness has continued over the years. Thus in the Wittgenstein Documentation Center in Kirchberg am Wechsel, Austria, the site of the annual international Wittgenstein congress, two display cases are devoted to arguing that Wittgenstein was *not* a homosexual, and that my account is "verfälschend".[12]

This entire attack on my book, and on my own *bona fides*, has been based on bluff, on projection, and on plain naïveté.

First, as to bluff. The documents confirming Wittgenstein's homosexuality—his own coded diaries—have been in the possession of the Wittgenstein literary estate all along. During the height of their attack, the Wittgenstein literary executors had coded notebooks, in Wittgenstein's own hand, written in a very simple cipher and long since decoded and transcribed, corroborating my statements about his homosexuality. There is also an allusion to his homosexuality in

---

[12]I should, however, report that Dr. Adolf Hübner, the director of this Center, has undergone an interesting transformation in this regard, and has now recanted (though privately). In his "Bartley Refuted" (Schriftenreihe der Österreichischen Ludwig-Wittgenstein Gesellschaft, 1978), Hübner denied that Wittgenstein was homosexual. By the time he published his book *Wittgenstein*, with Kurt Wuchterl (Hamburg: Rowohlt, 1979), Hübner had modified his opinions, and although still denouncing my book, now himself wrote of Wittgenstein's "homoerotic tendencies" (p. 67). By September 9, 1979, Hübner wrote to me to say that he "would not again write an article in defense of his [Wittgenstein's] personality against reproaches such as yours. I am rather sure, that his literary executors know that Wittgenstein suffered from homosexual tendencies". Hübner goes on to say that his article was written in a period in which his admiration for Wittgenstein was "still boundless". But there is no reproach in my own book; and *my* admiration for Wittgenstein was in no way affected by my discoveries about his sexuality.

a letter from Wittgenstein to his sister Mining written as early as his days as an engineering student at the University of Manchester (1908-11).

Only two of the coded notebooks appear to have been preserved. It is known that several of his notebooks were destroyed, by Wittgenstein's own order, in 1950, and these appear to include the notebooks for the period 1918-28, the period with which my own book was chiefly concerned.[13] At any rate, they are missing. Of the two books that are preserved, the first dates from the period of the First World War, ending prior to 1918. In it, Wittgenstein explicitly discusses his homosexual wishes and longings, recurrences of "sensuality", and the way in which he is tormented by them.[14] But there is as yet no unequivocal evidence of homosexual *activity*, and thus one cannot judge with certainty whether Wittgenstein's relationship with his friend David Pinsent—

---

[13]See my letter "Wittgenstein and Homosexuality", *Times Literary Supplement*, February 8, 1980, p. 145. I am, incidentally, not the only person to have discussed Wittgenstein's homosexuality. Discussion also appears in A. L. Rowse, *Homosexuals in History* (New York: Macmillan, 1977), pp. 328-50; and George Steiner, *After Babel* (Oxford: Oxford University Press, 1975), p. 40. See also George Steiner, "The Language Animal", in *Encounter*, 1969, reprinted in his *Extraterritorial* (London: Penguin, 1972), pp. 66-109; and Steiner's "Rare Bird", *The New Yorker*, November 30, 1981, pp. 196-204, esp. p. 202. See also Paul Levy, *Moore: G. E. Moore and the Cambridge Apostles* (London: Weidenfeld & Nicholson, 1979), p. 270. That other persons judged Wittgenstein to be homosexual as early as 1915, we now know from G. E. Moore's diary. In his biography of Moore, Paul Levy reports: "7 August 1915, when Moore was visiting the Wedgwoods and was asked by their great friend Richard Curle (who edited Julia Wedgwood's letters and was also a friend of Joseph Conrad) to talk about his quarrel with Wittgenstein. It was then that Curle and Iris Wedgwood bluntly asked Moore 'about [Wittgenstein's] being normal (about women) which I don't like'." See Levy, *Moore: G. E. Moore and the Cambridge Apostles* (London: Weidenfeld & Nicolson, 1979), p. 274.

[14]Brian F. McGuinness, who is writing the official biography of Wittgenstein (which has been announced several times since the early 1970s but has never been published), refers to this very indirectly in his "Wittgenstein's 'Intellectual Nursery-Training' ", in *Wittgenstein, the Vienna Circle and Critical Rationalism, Proceedings of the 3rd International Wittgenstein Symposium* (Vienna: Hölder-Pichler-Tempsky, 1979), p. 39.

which is often supposed to have been a homosexual one —involved active sexual relations.

The second notebook dates from a later period, following 1928, and reveals both that Wittgenstein was involved in homosexual activities and that this brought him great distress of mind. In these pages Wittgenstein finds it abhorrent that he should have such desires, yet also comments that he cannot blame himself for having them and that it is not bad to have them. This notebook also reveals that active homosexual practice was involved in Wittgenstein's relationship with his friend Francis Skinner.[15]

So much for bluff. And so much for Drury's "alertness" to homosexuality.

Then there is projection. I am using the word "projection" in the psychological sense, in which internal subjective states lead to radical misperceptions of the external world. To illustrate how unreliable people often become in the presence of information about homosexuality, I have selected two descriptions of my book by authors who are friendly to it. Any reader of its first chapter will be able to confirm that I do not claim or imply that Wittgenstein's sexual partners were prostitutes or that he despised them. What I *do* say (pp. 40) is:

> By walking for ten minutes to the east ... he could quickly reach the parkland meadows of the Prater, where rough young men were ready to cater to him sexually. Once he had discovered this place, Wittgenstein found to his horror that he could

---

[15]This testimony by Wittgenstein himself is contrary to that of Fania Pascal, in her discussion of the relationship between Skinner and Wittgenstein in "Wittgenstein: A Personal Memoir", *Encounter*, August 1973, pp. 23-29. Pascal's version is, however, not corrected in the version reprinted in Rhees, ed., *Ludwig Wittgenstein: Personal Recollections*. If Pascal does not *correct* her remarks, at least she *mentions* Skinner. Although Wittgenstein and Skinner were, in Pascal's words, "inseparable", Norman Malcolm completely omits mentioning Skinner in his *Memoir*. This omission—as serious as Roy Harrod's omission of the question of homosexuality from his biography of John Maynard Keynes—seriously flaws the portrait that Malcolm draws of Wittgenstein.

scarcely keep away from it. . . . Wittgenstein found he much preferred the sort of rough blunt homosexual youth that he could find strolling in the paths and alleys of the Prater to those ostensibly more refined young men who frequented the Sirk Ecke in the Kärntnerstraße and the neighboring bars at the edge of the inner city.

Out of this statement, W. D. Hudson conjures up—for his book *Wittgenstein and Religious Belief*—the following report:

Bartley's book openly states that Wittgenstein's perpetual bad conscience arose, in part at least, from the fact that he regularly consorted with the most repellent kind of male prostitute in London and Vienna.[16]

And Ben-Ami Scharfstein, in his book *The Philosophers*, writes of Wittgenstein, referring to my book:

His whole situation would be more intelligible, as would his frequent attacks on his own decency, if he suffered, as has been claimed, from his attachment to rough homosexual men whom he despised.[17]

It is as if the matter is made less threatening by introducing, in the imagination, something which was, to the best of my knowledge, never there: the repellent, despised prostitute.

Finally, a word about the quite extraordinary naïveté that has attended the reception of this book. I will mention only two of the many preposterous arguments that have been published purporting to establish that I could not possibly have obtained the evidence I had for the details of Wittgenstein's homosexuality. First, it is alleged that anyone who could have known about Wittgenstein's sexual activities

---

[16]W. D. Hudson, *Wittgenstein and Religious Belief* (London: Macmillan, 1975), p. 102.

[17]Ben-Ami Scharfstein, *The Philosophers: Their Lives and the Nature of Their Thought* (New York: Oxford University Press, 1980), p. 334.

shortly after the First World War would be either dead or too old to remember. Yet when I obtained my information in the early and mid-1960s, my informants were of course in their early and mid-sixties.[18] Is it seriously suggested that men in their sixties cannot remember the sexual escapades of their youth—particularly when so distinctive a personality as Wittgenstein is involved?

Second, it is often argued that Wittgenstein could not have been homosexual since anyone so well known and so distinctive in voice and dress, and so rich, would—had he been homosexual and done the sorts of things described in this book—have been recognized and been blackmailed.[19] This is a very odd argument. Of course Wittgenstein was recognized: otherwise I could not have obtained my original information. Moreover, although homosexual practice was illegal in Austria prior to and following the first world war (indeed until 1970), and although there was sporadic enforcement of the law, there was little active, serious or sustained persecution or legal prosecution of homosexuals prior to the Hitler period. Thus Count Harry Kessler reports in his diaries the following story about Count Leopold Berchtold, the Imperial Austrian foreign minister:

> On 31 July 1914, when the whole world was waiting for the Serb reply to the Austrian ultimatum, he [Kuh] saw Berchtold in the fun-fair part of the Vienna Prater standing by a merry-go-round notorious as a meeting-place for male prostitutes. An extremely pretty youth, in white trousers and white pullover, winked broadly every time the merry-go-round carried him past a very smartly-dressed man whose eyes never left him. When the merry-go-round halted, the youth stepped down and went up to the gentlemen, who greeted him and took him along. The gentleman was Berchtold. At the moment that the

---

[18]My first trip to the lower Austrian villages where Wittgenstein taught was much later. My research on all the matters discussed in this book extended over a decade.

[19]Thus, Rhees and Stonborough in *The Human World*, February 1974, pp. 67 and 80.

two were leaving, newspaper sellers rushed on the scene with shouts of "Serb Answer to the Ultimatum! War with Serbia! Austrian Invasion of Serbia!" The start of the World War which Berchtold had precipitated.[20]

Berchtold was obviously a far better candidate for black-mail than was Wittgenstein. Yet blackmail is far rarer than is homosexuality. And this is the same Prater where Wittgenstein's nephew John Stonborough suggests that homosexual importuning is hardly to be found.[21]

II

THE QUESTION OF THE RELEVANCE OF HIS HOMOSEXUALITY TO WITTGENSTEIN'S PHILOSOPHY

> *It is sometimes said that a man's philosophy is a matter of temperament, and there is something in this.*
>
> —*Ludwig Wittgenstein*[22]

Although Wittgenstein's homosexuality is, it seems obvious to me, of central importance in understanding the man and

---

[20]Graf Harry Kessler, *In the Twenties: The Diaries of Harry Kessler* (New York: Holt, Rinehart & Winston, 1971), p. 457. If these reports are to be believed, Berchtold seems to have spent quite a bit of time on public view that summer. See Max Graf's vignette in his *Legend of a Music City* (New York, 1945), pp. 69-70: "I can still see the distinguished Count Berchtold on a summer's day in 1914, standing in the doorway of a Ringstraße hotel. He had just signed the declaration of war on Serbia. Now he stood here, slender, laughing ironically, a gold-tipped cigarette in his well-manicured fingers, watching the crowds and conversing with the passersby." For comparable information about homosexual assignations, see the Victorian novel *Teleny, or the Reverse of the Medal* (London: Leonard Smithers, 1893), or Brian Reade, *Sexual Heretics* (New York: Coward-McCann, Inc., 1970), pp. 223-45. Another example of a prominent homosexual during this period is that of Count Brockdorff-Rantzau, Germany's chief delegate to the Versailles conference.

[21]Stonborough, in *The Human World*, February 1974, esp. pp. 79-82.

[22]Wittgenstein, *Culture and Value*, p. 20.

his influence, I made no attempt in my book to explain his *thought* in terms of it. This too has been criticized. Thus George Steiner, who gave my book a generous welcome, nonetheless suggested that I had evaded the "crux of the matter", and that Wittgenstein's sexual life and theory of language are closely related.[23]

This is a question that I wish to confront in this section.

*　*　*

I have a good friend named Ben-Ami Scharfstein, who is professor of philosophy at the University of Tel-Aviv, and the author of some splendid books on art and aesthetics, on Chinese and comparative studies, on mysticism, and on the lives of the philosophers. Most philosophers, Scharfstein contends, hide behind façades: their ideas are indeed constructions intended to make those façades the more difficult to penetrate.[24] And sometimes their ideas are the façades themselves.

Such a claim is of course difficult to evaluate fairly. For we are, all of us, so adept at turning a profit out of whatever comes our way, that it is often hard to tell whether we have brought about something to our advantage, or whether we have simply *turned* it to our advantage. Doubtless anyone clever enough to invent a philosophy would be clever enough to find a way to hide behind it—if he wanted to hide. Such is the very stuff and prerequisite of any ability to manipulate ideas to corrupt or to confuse understanding.

However this may be, Scharfstein's view would hardly have been advanced were there not at least some philoso-

---

[23]Steiner's notices of my book appeared in *The New Yorker*, July 23, 1973, p. 77, and in *The Listener* (with Anthony Quinton), March 28, 1974, pp. 399-401.

[24]See Scharfstein, *The Philosophers*, for an account of his views. Steiner seems to argue in a similar vein in *After Babel*, pp. 32-33, when he writes that "languages conceal and internalize more, perhaps, than they convey outwardly. Social classes, racial ghettoes speak at rather than to each other".

phers to whom it seemed, at least on the surface, to apply. Wittgenstein might appear to be a good example, and I can see how Steiner also could take him to be so. Certainly in his early theory of language Wittgenstein does insist that everything of real importance is unsayable, and he also says that the interior of a person is impenetrable by language. From Scharfstein's perspective, this would be façade, a façade all too conveniently deflecting the gaze of the curious inquirer (and perhaps Wittgenstein's own attention as well) away from Wittgenstein. As if in confirmation of this, it has been recorded that Wittgenstein "would above all abhor anybody enquiring into his personal life".[25] Wittgenstein himself wrote: "Don't play with what lies deep in another person."[26] And although he himself seriously entertained the idea of becoming a psychiatrist, he advised his disciple M. O'C. Drury— who did become a psychiatrist—that "he [Wittgenstein] would not want to undergo what was known as a training analysis. He did not think it right to reveal all one's thoughts to a stranger."[27] (One cannot know whether Drury is reporting Wittgenstein accurately here either. But if he is, a psychiatrist would likely accuse Wittgenstein of irresponsibility. He would say that anyone who presumes to treat others without having undergone something like a training analysis himself does indeed *play* with his patients' depths.)

In any case, Wittgenstein's friends and literary executors have taken care to carry out his apparent wishes where possible. One of them has written: "If by pressing a button it could have been secured that people would not concern themselves with his personal life, I should have pressed that button."[28] Another executor, when publishing a selection from

---

[25]Pascal, "Wittgenstein: A Personal Memoir", p. 26.

[26]Wittgenstein, *Culture and Value*, p. 23.

[27]See Drury's "Conversations with Wittgenstein", in Rhees, ed., *Ludwig Wittgenstein: Personal Recollections*, p. 151.

[28]G. E. M. Anscombe, quoted by Paul Engelmann in *Letters from Ludwig Wittgenstein, with a Memoir* (Oxford: Basil Blackwell, 1967), p. xiv. In 1953 the Wittgenstein literary estate refused to permit F. A. von Hayek, Wittgenstein's second cousin once removed, the distinguished Nobel-prize-winning economist and biographer of John Stuart Mill, to publish some

Wittgenstein's notes, "excluded from the collection notes of a purely 'personal' sort—i.e., notes in which Wittgenstein is commenting on the external circumstances of his life, his state of mind and relations with other people ...".[29] The "love that dare not speak its name", that which is "among Christians not to be named", needed to be shielded from view.

Scharfstein's thesis—that a man's philosophical product is a disguised expression of his inner state—is a sophisticated variant of "epistemological expressionism",[30] the popular idea that a man's work, whether of art or of philosophy, is an expression of his inner state, of his emotions, of his personality. Thus the philosopher and psychologist John Oulton Wisdom has argued that Bishop Berkeley's philosophical idealism is an expression of his internal state as discoverable by psychoanalysis. Berkeley's idealism, his denial of the existence of matter, is, Wisdom argues, linked to and an expres-

---

letters of Wittgenstein until they themselves had first published them. As a result, to our common loss, Hayek abandoned his own biography of Wittgenstein. Later, Anscombe denied that this occurred. See her letter to *The Times Literary Supplement*, January 18, 1974, and F. A. von Hayek's letter in the same journal, February 8, 1974. See also Hayek's "Remembering My Cousin Ludwig Wittgenstein", *Encounter*, August 1977, pp. 20-22. The hostility of Wittgenstein's literary executors to biographical and historical investigation has been effective; they have been able to deflect numerous researchers—with the result that every portrait drawn of Wittgenstein is false; not to mention that it is thereby also almost impossible to tell the story of—or to direct critical attention to—the formation of his school and the creation of its influence.

[29]See G. H. von Wright, in his Preface to Wittgenstein's *Culture and Value*.

[30]The term "epistemological expressionism" comes from Karl R. Popper, *Objective Knowledge* (Oxford: Oxford University Press, 1972), pp. 146-47. My discussion here is based on my essay "Ein schwieriger Mensch: Eine Porträtskizze von Sir Karl Popper", in Eckhard Nordhofen, ed., *Physiognomien: Philosophen des 20. Jahrhunderts in Portraits* (Königstein/Ts.: Athenäum, 1980), pp. 43-69. On expressionism see E. H. Gombrich, *The Sense of Order* (New York: Phaidon, 1979), pp. 42-44, and *Meditations on a Hobby Horse* (New York: Phaidon, 1963), pp. 56-69 and 78-85. My discussion is much inspired by Gombrich's work. See also Karl R. Popper, *Unended Quest* (London: Fontana, 1976), sections 13 and 14.

sion of the same unconscious anality which caused him, physically, to suffer from colitis![31] Elsewhere, Wisdom has argued that Hegel's philosophy is an expression of his isolation, loneliness, and depression.[32]

But can *Wittgenstein's* thought be understood in this way? And if so, what does it express? And what precisely is its connection, if any, with his homosexuality?

Before raising such questions, we need to ask whether *anyone's* thought is appropriately so interpreted. This is a question worth raising, for expressionism is widespread, shifting attention from the quality of the product to the character of the producer, and thereby also encouraging the romantic preoccupation with personality that is so prevalent in, if not an expression of, our culture. It is also an approach—often in the past called physiognomy—sanctioned by age. In the eighteenth century it is found in J. J. Winckelmann, who regarded the impassive marble fronts of classical statues as an expression of the "noble simplicity and quiet grandeur" of the Greek soul; and also in Johann Casper Lavater's *Physiognomische Fragmente* (1775-78), which sought to decipher characters from portrait silhouettes. The approach was later ridiculed by Georg Christoph Lichtenberg who, in his delicious parody of Lavater, showed that those who followed Lavater lost the capacity to discriminate between Goethe's pigtail and Goethe's *Faust*. An even earlier example is G. B. della Porta, in *De humana Physiognomia* (1586), who sought to develop a science of physiognomics by comparisons between human types and particular animals. Thus a man with an acquiline nose would be noble of spirit, and one with a sheepish face would be sheepish.

Such expressionism might seem palatable to Wittgen-

---

[31]J. O. Wisdom, *The Unconscious Origin of Berkeley's Philosophy* (London: 1953).

[32]J. O. Wisdom, "What Was Hegel's Main Problem?", Royal Institute of Philosophy Lecture, London, February 2, 1962. See also Wisdom's *Philosophy and Its Place in Our Culture* (New York: Gordon & Breach, 1975). For a somewhat similar approach see Morris Lazerowitz, *The Language of Philosophy: Freud and Wittgenstein* (Dordrecht: D. Reidel, 1977).

stein himself, in that he once wrote, in a physiognomical mood, that "The human body is the best picture of the human soul".[33] More important, such expressionism is often found intertwined with contemporary studies of language; and language is the focus of all Wittgenstein's work. Thus George Steiner asks, "In what measure are sexual perversions analogues of incorrect speech?", whether there are affinities between pathological erotic compulsions and the obsessive search for a private language, and "Might there be elements of homosexuality in the modern theory of language (particularly in the early Wittgenstein), in the concept of communication as an arbitrary mirroring?"[34]

> Eros and language mesh at every point. Intercourse and discourse, copula and copulation, are sub-classes of the dominant fact of communication. . . . Sex is a profoundly semantic act. . . . To speak and to make love is to enact a distinctive twofold universality: both forms of communication are universals of human physiology as well as of social evolution. It is likely that human sexuality and speech developed in close-knit reciprocity. Together they generate the history of self-consciousness. . . . We can only prohibit that which we can name. . . . The seminal and the semantic functions . . . together they construe the grammar of being. . . . If coition can be schematized as dialogue, masturbation seems to be correlative with the pulse of monologue. . . . The multiple, intricate relations between speech defects and infirmities in the nervous and glandular mechanisms which control sexual and excretory functions have long been known. . . . Ejaculation is at once a physiological and a linguistic concept. Impotence and speech-blocks, premature emission and stuttering, involuntary ejaculation and the word-river of dreams are phenomena whose interrelations seem to lead back to the central knot of our humanity. Semen, excreta, and words are communicative products. They are transmissions from the self inside the skin to reality outside. . . . The grounds of differentiation (between the speech of men and

---

[33]Ludwig Wittgenstein, *Philosophical Investigations*, ed. G. E. M. Anscombe and Rush Rhees (Oxford: Basil Blackwell, 1967), p. 178.
[34]Steiner, *After Babel*, pp. 39-40.

women) are, of course, largely economic and social. . . . But certain linguistic differences do point towards a physiological basis or, to be exact, towards the intermediary zone between the biological and the social. . . . Are there biologically determined apprehensions of sense data which precede and generate linguistically programmed conceptualizations?[35]

This is a delight to read. But is what it says true? For that matter, what exactly *does* it say?

It is easy to mock such approaches: to produce, say, examples of realists who suffer from colitis and happily extraverted Hegelians—or to recall Winston Churchill's description of a political opponent as "a sheep in sheep's clothing". It is also easy to remark that Steiner's brilliant discourse insinuates an expressionism which he is too sophisticated to state outright—insinuates by the use of provocative questions which are posed and then abandoned, as if the answers to them were obvious. It might even be important to remark that, although Steiner's discussion suggests the contrary, Wittgenstein's early work does *not* contain any "concept of communication as an arbitrary mirroring", and that Wittgenstein, far from obsessively searching for a private language, firmly maintained that such a language was impossible.

In the following, however, I do not wish to make fun of physiognomy or expressionism, and certainly not of Steiner's provocative and brilliantly suggestive studies of language and translation. Rather, I wish to begin to identify some of the basic *scientific* objections to expressionism and to all attempts to reduce human speech and its content to the circumstances—physiological, psychosexual, and otherwise—of the individuals who use and create that speech.

We may begin by placing human expression in a somewhat wider context.

For this purpose, I draw on Karl Bühler's famous work, *Sprachtheorie*, concerning the theory of human language. Bühler,[36] who was from 1922 to 1938 Professor of Philoso-

---

[35]*Ibid.*, p. 38-39, 43. See also Steiner's *Extraterritorial*, esp. pp. 66-109.
[36]Karl Bühler, *Sprachtheorie: Die Darstellungsfunktion der Sprache* (Leipzig, 1934; 2nd edition, Stuttgart: Gustav Fischer, 1965).

phy and Psychology in the University of Vienna, and whose possible influence on Wittgenstein's later philosophy is discussed in chapters 3 and 4 above, analyzed the communicative function of a language into three components: (1) the *expressive* function, where the communication serves to express the internal states of the speaker; (2) the *signalling* or stimulative or release function, where the communication serves to stimulate or to release certain reactions in the hearer; (3) the *descriptive* function, which is present to the extent that the communication aims to describe some state of affairs. At this third level, the regulative idea of truth emerges, assessing descriptions according to whether they fit the facts. These first three functions are separable in so far as each is accompanied by its preceding one but need not be accompanied by its succeeding one(s). That is, one may express without signalling; one may express and signal without describing. But one cannot signal without expressing, or describe without both expressing and signalling. Another function has been added to Bühler's set by my teacher Sir Karl Popper (who was Bühler's student in Vienna), and on whose work I shall also draw in the several paragraphs that follow: namely, (4) the *argumentative* function. In terms of this, descriptive statements are appraised with regard to the regulative standards of truth, content, and truthlikeness; and arguments are appraised with regard to their validity. The same hierarchical ordering applies here: one cannot argue without describing, signalling, expressing.[37] The first two functions apply, of course, to animal languages. But the second two functions may be characteristically human—although some of those who research into the life and languages of animals hope for discoveries which will modify some accepted views about the limits of animal communication.[38]

---

[37]See Karl R. Popper, *Conjectures and Refutations* (London: Routledge and Kegan Paul, 1962), pp. 134 and 295; Popper, *Objective Knowledge* (London: Oxford University Press, 1972), pp. 41, 120, 160, and 235; and Popper, *The Self and Its Brain* (New York: Springer, 1977), pp.57-58. See also chapter 2 of my book *Morality and Religion* (London: Macmillan, 1971).

[38]Frisch's bees are a possible example.

As an aid in the understanding of his ideas, Bühler developed this diagram:

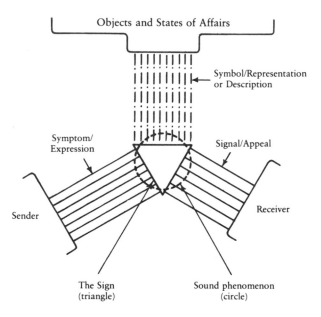

The triangle in the middle denotes the linguistic sign, whatever its character. This sign may be used by the sender or speaker to express himself; it may be received by the receiver or listener as a signal or appeal which may or may not have been intended by the speaker. And the same sign again may be used—by sender, receiver, or both—to symbolize some objective state of affairs independent of the receiver and sender.

The analysis obviously may be applied to contemporary art, music, and poetry—and to a variety of theories about them. Let the sign include not only language but also works of art. Such a work may express certain subjective states of mind (conscious or unconscious) or intentions on the part of the artist; those who receive or respond to the work of art may or may not decode it (consciously or unconsciously) as it was intended by its sender. And the work of art may or may not be representational.

But let us not pursue this but, instead, with Bühler's account in mind, return to our question: can a philosopher's theories be reduced to the expressive level? Philosophers' ideas are of course self-expressive; in a trivial sense, anything that one does is self-expressive. (And this observation should make us, right from the start, somewhat sceptical of the explanatory power of expressionism: if expression characterizes everything that one does, it can have little hope of explaining the particular features of some specific things that one does—such as art or philosophy.) But the question is whether such ideas can (as is maintained in expressionist accounts of philosophy—and of art) be reduced to the expressive level, whether they are, ultimately, *only* expression.

The answer to this question is emphatically negative—for a variety of reasons, logical, physical, biological. I shall cite three such reasons or arguments—two very short ones, and another rather longer one.

The first argument is that expressionism is quite contrary to everything we know from biology and from evolutionary theory. It removes the biological function from our descriptive statements, and thus leaves the important role that description plays in human life go quite ignored and unexplained; unchecked self-expression (i.e., self-expression unchecked by description) in the dangerous environments in which human beings have evolved and continue to live would be biologically lethal.

The second argument is that it is in any case impossible to reduce the descriptive and argumentative levels of language to the expressive and signal levels: *no causal physical theory of the descriptive and argumentative functions of language is possible.* Popper shows that the name relationship—which is the simplest case of a descriptive use of words—cannot be causally realized.[39] That is, any purely causal

---

[39]Popper has shown this in "Language and the Body-Mind Problem", in *Conjectures and Refutations*, pp. 293-98. See also his *The Open Universe: An Argument for Indeterminism*, vol. II of his *Postscript to the Logic of Scientific Discovery*, ed. W. W. Bartley, III (Totowa, N.J.: Rowman & Littlefield, 1982), especially sections 20-24, and the three Addenda: "Indeterminism is Not Enough: An Afterword", "Scientific Reduction and the Essential

model of naming is intrinsically defective, in that no causal chain alone can represent or realize the relation between a thing and its name. Rather, *interpretation* (which itself cannot be causally realized) must be added, in order to pick out or select and to name some *parts* of the total physical situation. It follows from this that, to the extent to which a philosopher's theories contain representational descriptive statements intended to be true or false, and arguments intended to be valid or invalid, those theories cannot be reduced to the expressive level. This argument was originally constructed to refute physicalism and behaviorism, not expressionistic theories of art and philosophy; yet it applies to the latter just as much as to the former.

The argument is strong and general; and *it suffices* to refute the related family of philosophies (materialism, mechanism, determinism, expressionism, etc.) that attempt to reduce the human self, language, and theory to the conditions under which they arise, whether economic, psycho-sexual, physiological, genetic, or otherwise.

But I promised another argument. One which is not only easier to understand but which is also, I believe, particularly revealing, relates to the logical and informative content of theories. When we affirm a theory, we also propose its logical implications (otherwise we should not have to retract it when these come to grief), all those statements that follow from it—as well as those further implications which result from combining this theory with other theories which we also propose or assume. But this means that the informative content of any theory includes an infinity of unforeseeable nontrivial statements; it also makes clear that the content of an idea is far from identical with some particular person's thoughts about it. For there are infinitely many situations,

---

Incompleteness of All Science", and "Further Remarks on Reduction 1981". See my discussion in "The Philosophy of Karl Popper, Part II: Consciousness and Physics: Quantum Mechanics, Probability, Indeterminism, The Body-Mind Problem", in *Philosophia*, vol. 7, July 1978, pp. 675-716; and my "On the Criticizability of Logic", in *Philosophy of the Social Sciences*, vol. 10, 1980, pp. 67-77.

themselves infinitely varied, to which the theory may be applicable. Yet many of these situations have not only not even been imagined at the time the theory is proposed; they are also, literally, *unimaginable* at that time, in terms of the information then available. For example, part of the informative content of Newton's theory is that Einstein's theory is incompatible with it; yet this could not possibly have been imagined at the time Newton proposed his theory; nor could the test situations or applications that eventually decided against Newton's theory have been imagined then—since such possibilities of observation and testing of Newton's theory became conceivable only after the invention of Einstein's theory.[40]

This startling result means that, literally, "we never know what we are talking about".[41] Even the inventor of a theory cannot possibly fully have understood it—as many historical examples attest. Thus Erwin Schrödinger did not understand the "Schrödinger equations" before Born gave his interpretation of them; and the content and application of these equations is, indeed, still a matter of controversy. Since it is logically impossible, consciously or unconsciously, to anticipate such matters on the basis of what we know about the inventor or discoverer of a theory, it is absurd to think of them in terms of "self-expression".

Developing this result, we shall find that expressionist accounts must then fail in three fundamental ways. First, they suppose that there is a fixed core to the individual, of which his work and thought is an expression. Second, they neglect the objectively unfathomable depths of the product. And third, as a consequence, they are unable to capture the nature of the relationship between a man and his work (any more than they capture the "name relationship"). In sum, expressionism misunderstands the nature of the individual

---

[40]There is the related problem that the growth of knowledge is unpredictable in principle. See Karl Popper, *Poverty of Historicism* (Boston: Beacon Press, 1957), Preface; and Popper, *The Open Universe*, chapter 3.

[41]See Popper, *Unended Quest*, section 7.

self; the nature of intellectual work and creativity; and the nature of the relationship between the two. The result is altogether too passive and one-directional.

We have already discussed the second point—the objectively unfathomable content of intellectual products or ideas—on which the entire argument hangs. To take the first and third points in turn: the human self, while no doubt in part resulting from inborn dispositions, is also at least in part held together by theories. These help to provide its unity, its individuality, and its continuity; and it is rich, unfathomable, and growing to the extent to which these theories enjoy these characteristics.[42] Once one has acquired descriptive language, one becomes not only a subject but also an object for oneself: an object about which one can reflect, which one may criticize and change. Self-transcendence is a familiar and all-important characteristic of human life and is attained in large part through the reflective criticism and examination of the theories that hold the self together, the destruction of some of those theories, and the creation of new theories in their place. Hence, for the reasons already mentioned, we can never fully know ourselves any more than we can know what we are talking about in other areas. For both poles are anchored in descriptive language.

The relationship between this unfathomable self and the unfathomable theories which it has somehow produced can then hardly be one of expression of the one by the other! Such an account fails to take account either of the nature of language and of theory, or of the constantly changing flame-like quality of the individual, as expressed in his *active* cybernetic relationship with his cultural world, including his own cultural products, and the creative, unpredictable character that is intrinsic to that relationship. This relationship is one of give-and-take between the individual and his work; it depends upon "feedback" amplified by conscious self-criticism. Such feedback is, as is evident from evolutionary theo-

---

[42]See Popper, *The Self and Its Brain*, chapter P4, esp. section 42, and *Objective Knowledge*, pp. 146-50.

ry, part of any growth process; so it is hardly surprising to find it here.[43]

When one produces an idea—whether about oneself, about the nature of the world, about human society, or language, or whatever—this idea, being formed in descriptive language, takes on an objective life of its own, and particularly so when it is written down and published and thus made available to others. It has unexplored and sometimes also *unwanted* potential transcending what could possibly have been intended, or expressed, in the moment of its utterance. As one's understanding of such an idea unfolds, it may literally alter the econiche in which one dwells by introducing into it new potentialities and problems. The cultural world, which contains one's self-conceptions and one's theories about the external world, is thus an objective natural exosomatic product, comparable in certain respects to a spider's web. This web of ideas is autonomous in the sense that it generates its own problems and that its content is largely independent of our wishes, existing independently of being realized in the subjective consciousness of any individual.[44] As Nietzsche found: "I discovered and ventured divers answers; I distinguished between ages, peoples, degrees of rank among individuals; I departmentalized my problem; out of my answers there grew new questions, inquiries, conjectures, probabilities—until at length I had a country of my own, a soil of my own, an entire discrete, thriving, flourishing world, like a secret garden the existence of which no one suspected."[45]

In this setting, the unexpected ramifications of one's own ideas about the world, about society, about the individual,

---

[43]See my "Biology and Evolutionary Epistemology", in *Philosophia*, vol. 6, September-December 1976, pp. 463-94, esp. pp. 469-77. See also my "Knowledge Is a Product Not Fully Known to Its Producer", in Kurt Leube and Albert Zlabinger, eds., *The Political Economy of Freedom* (Munich: International Carl Menger Library, Philosophia Verlag, 1985).

[44]For a different sort of example, take the table of logarithms or the problem whether there are highest twin prime numbers.

[45]Friedrich Nietzsche, *On the Genealogy of Morals*, Preface, section 3.

about one's own aims and preferences, may—as one pursues them, as one works with them, as one adopts them as problems—have a radical impact on one's self-conception, and also on one's instinctive life. Far from expressing one's old self and self-conceptions, they may be radically at odds with them. They may *work against* one's self-expression.[46]

Some persons of course exploit this potential rather little. Yet in his interaction with and contribution to this cultural world—and with the descriptive and argumentative levels of language—a person has at least the opportunity to form himself, to transcend his origins, the conditions of his birth, his genes, his instincts, his self-expression. In this interaction, one's self is constantly being transcended, together with its expressions of itself.

In the case of an individual such as a scientist or philosopher who is distinguished by his interaction with the world of intellect, one might even be tempted to say that he expresses his ideas, rather than that his ideas express him. Some persons have taken this sort of thinking to an extreme: I am thinking, for instance, of physical therapists in the United States, in the school of Ida Rolf for example, who contend that one's whole body, even the very curvature of the spine and the fascia of one's muscles, express one's thoughts. But this too will not do: although the impact of the world of ideas on any person—even on the most original—exceeds the impact which any individual can make on it, the whole model of expression is too passive.

Many other arguments against such attempts at reduction could be added here, serious scientific arguments which are generally ignored in the loose popular talk—literary, historical, and philosophical—about "influences" from the psyche, and such like. Such influences of course exist, but it would, for the reasons indictated, be quite impossible for them to work in the direct ways in which they are commonly alleged to work.

---

[46]For a good example, see J. D. Unwin's amusing Introduction to his *Sex and Culture* (London: Oxford University Press, 1934) .

* * *

In view of these facts about language, thought, and culture, it is hard to take seriously the project of reducing a philosophy to its inventor's personal circumstances, to his personal psychopathology, or to think of it simply in terms of expression. One must set aside such biography, which "explains everything and therefore explains nothing", as empty and unscientific. Such is not biography motivated by the search for deeper understanding; it is biography by recipe.

To understand a philosophy, one must study its content and the constellation of objective problems that stand behind its creation; and one must not be distracted unduly by the personal circumstances of the philosopher. To do otherwise, to follow an expressionistic program, is for the intellectual historian or biographer to risk turning himself into a kind of graphologist: grasping for insight in deviations from copybook drill; dubiously expressing (or disguising!) his own individuality in his projection-laden interpretations of the scribblings of others. The personal circumstances of the philosopher may *sometimes* play an important role in the network of problems and theories within which he is working; and *sometimes they may play no role at all.*

Sometimes they don't; *and sometimes they do.* In arguing against facile forms of expressionism, I do not want to suggest that sexuality *never* decisively shapes the content of the work of a philosopher or scientist. For there are no doubt some cases where this apparently has happened.[47]

_____

[47]Walter Kaufmann has contended that this is true of C. G. Jung—that some of the positive content of Jung's psychology, and particularly the argument of his *Answer to Job,* can be understood best in terms of his failure to resolve his own Oedipal conflicts. See Walter Kaufmann, *Freud versus Adler and Jung,* vol. 3 of *Discovering the Mind* (New York: McGraw-Hill, 1980), esp. Part IV.

III

SOME ATTEMPTS TO LINK THE HOMOSEXUALITY AND THE THOUGHT

After this review—which ought to form a prolegomenon to any psychologically oriented intellectual history or biography—it is high time to return to the specific case of Wittgenstein.

I know of one interesting detailed attempt to explain the content of Wittgenstein's thought in terms of his homosexuality. It is due to Professor A. W. Levi, of Washington University.[48]

Inspired by Nietzsche's remark that "systems of morals are only a sign language of the emotions", Levi recalls the deep consciousness of personal guilt that runs through Wittgenstein's letters to Engelmann "like a trail of blood". The words Wittgenstein uses to refer to himself, over and over again, are Unanständigkeit, Schlechtigkeit, Schweinerei, Niedrigkeit, Gemeinheit (indecency, badness, filthiness, baseness, vileness). The state in which he finds himself, Wittgenstein writes, "is the state of *not being able to get over a particular fact*", the only remedy for which, so Wittgenstein suggests, is suicide. Wittgenstein had the conviction, as he sometimes said, that he was "doomed".[49]

Levi's argument is straightforward: Wittgenstein's account of ethics is a kind of reaction formation, aimed at assuaging this heavy burden of guilt.[50] Just as in his daily life

---

[48]A. W. Levi, "The Biographical Sources of Wittgenstein's Ethics", *Telos*, vol. 38, Winter 1979, pp. 63-76. See also A. W. Levi, "Wittgenstein as Dialectician", *The Journal of Philosophy*, vol. 61, no. 4, February 13, 1964, pp. 127-39; Thomas Rudebush and William M. Berg, "On Wittgenstein and Ethics: A Reply to Levi", *Telos*, vol. 40, Summer 1979, pp. 150-60; Steven S. Schwarzschild, "Wittgenstein as Alienated Jew", *Telos*, vol. 40, Summer 1979, pp. 160-65; and A. W. Levi, "Wittgenstein Once More: A Response to Criticism", *Telos*, vol. 40, Summer 1979, pp. 165-73.

[49]G. H. von Wright, in Malcolm, *Wittgenstein: A Memoir*, p. 20.

[50]Information about Wittgenstein's views on ethics is rather sparse: it includes the last three pages of the *Tractatus*, his "Lecture on Ethics", (1929-30), and brief remarks in his notebooks and correspondence, in his

he sought out milieux in which he would be protected from his homosexual urges, so "his moral philosophy was unconsciously constructed to protect himself against the moral condemnation which those inclinations might be expected to call out". His theory of ethics is, Levi says, "the subtle strategy of a proud but guilty homosexual who has with great perspicuity and care placed himself beyond the condemnation of rational speech—that is to say—beyond the moral judgment of his fellow men". To do this, Wittgenstein simply created an account of language which rendered moral condemnation meaningless (because it went beyond a statement of the factual).

Wittgenstein does this by sharply excluding from ethics anything of a factual character, or anything that may be reduced to factual statements. For example, judgments of value as a means to an end, or as meeting a standard, have nothing to do with ethics since, according to Wittgenstein, they can be translated into factual statements. For the same reason, statements of "tastes or inclinations", Wittgenstein stresses and repeats, are not matters of ethics.[51] Likewise, although "preferences" can be stated in meaningful language, "the fact of being preferred has equally little claim to be something valuable in itself".[52]

In short, personal tastes, inclinations, and preferences—and hence, presumably, sexual tastes and preferences—are not matters of ethics. The "particular fact", the particular state of affairs, of being homosexual—or of being heterosexual, or of acting as preferred by the majority of society, or

conversations with Waismann and Schlick, and in the collection of remarks published as *Culture and Value*. (See Wittgenstein, "Lecture on Ethics", *The Philosophical Review*, January 1965, pp. 3-12.) For Wittgenstein's conversations with Schlick and Waismann, see Friedrich Waismann, *Ludwig Wittgenstein and the Vienna Circle* (Oxford: Blackwell, 1979); these are conversations recorded by Waismann. Levi takes all except *Culture and Value* (which was not published when he first wrote) into account, and concentrates his attention on the "Lecture on Ethics".
[51]Wittgenstein, "Lecture on Ethics", p. 7.
[52]Waismann, *Ludwig Wittgenstein and the Vienna Circle*, p. 116.

of acting otherwise—has no coercive moral power, and it is not necessary, Wittgenstein states quite explicitly, to feel guilty about matters of taste or inclination.

So far, Levi's interpretation might seem to hold. Such a view of ethics could indeed give at least intellectual relief to a guilty homosexual—or, for that matter, to a heterosexual who was deviant in some way and was inclined to feel guilty about that.

Yet I do not think that Levi's interpretation works. For there is another dimension to Wittgenstein's thought which, it seems to me, Levi's explanation does not capture at all— although he is of course well aware of it, and tried hard to fit it in.

True ethical judgments—what Wittgenstein calls judgments of "absolute value"—transcend the factual, and are *supernatural*. "What is good", he wrote in 1929, "is also divine. Queer as it sounds, that sums up my ethics. Only something supernatural can express the supernatural".[53] As he puts it, the absolute good, if it were a describable state of affairs (and it is not), would be one which "everybody, *independent of his tastes and inclinations*, would necessarily bring about or feel guilty for not bringing about".[54] However, no such state of affairs exists: "No state of affairs has, in itself, what I would like to call the coercive power of an absolute judge."[55]

Here we find Wittgenstein himself talking about the supernatural and absolute value. People are not at all deterred from talking about the supernatural, and about the absolute value which is its prerogative, by accounts such as Wittgenstein's which contend that such talk is meaningless. *And Wittgenstein knows this very well.* Moreover, he himself is not deterred. Quite the contrary, as he writes: "My whole tendency, and I believe the tendency of all men who ever tried to write or talk about Ethics or Religion was to run

---

[53]Wittgenstein, *Culture and Value*, p. 3e
[54]Wittgenstein, "Lecture on Ethics", p. 7. my italics.
[55]*Ibid.*, p. 7.

against the boundaries of language."[56] Such an attempt is hopeless; no knowledge can ever come from it. "But it is a document of a tendency in the human mind which I personally cannot help respecting deeply and I would not for my life ridicule it."[57]

What sorts of things do such people thereby want to express? Wittgenstein offers three concrete personal examples: (1) wonder at the existence of the world; (2) the experience of feeling absolutely safe; and (3) the experience of guilt, particularly that God disapproves of one's conduct. To put these experiences into language, Wittgenstein says, *points to something,* yet leads to nonsense. Nonsensicality is at their very heart: for when we use such expressions *we intend to go beyond the factual* and beyond significant language, and to point to the absolute, the supernatural.

Now a number of serious problems arise here. If people are not deterred from talking about the supernatural by Wittgenstein's theory of the limits of language, they are not likely to be deterred from making moral judgments in matters of taste or inclination either. And thus Wittgenstein's theory of language and ethics—*if devised to protect himself from such judgments* — would be a failure.

Levi tries to circumvent this problem, and to draw Wittgenstein's discussion of the supernatural and the absolute within his interpretation by arguing that Wittgenstein's three experiences place one "in the very center of the moral nightmare of Wittgenstein's moral universe". Thus he says that Wittgenstein's wonder at the existence of the world is really a moral horror at the brute givenness of his "moral deformity". And his concern for absolute safety stems from his fear of the wild homosexual desires raging within him, as well as from the very real threat of physical danger to which he exposed himself in the pursuit of those desires. The third experience, that of guilt, is "obviously" a consequence of his life situation.

---

[56]*Ibid.,* pp. 11-12.
[57]*Ibid.,* p. 12.

But Wittgenstein's discussion simply does not bear Levi's interpretation. Nor would Levi's interpretation work even if it did.

First, there is no evidence that Wittgenstein means moral horror where he speaks of wonder: Wittgenstein chose his words, including his metaphors and his expressions of emotion, carefully. Morever, the pregnant yet bewildering question why there is anything at all, although formulated in a variety of ways, is familiar in German-language philosophy and goes back at least to Schelling. Karl Jaspers concerned himself with such a question in the 1920s and eventually published a book on Schelling (1955) whose central section is devoted to it. The question also arises in Heidegger, in Tillich, and in numerous other writers (including Sartre). I do not know whether Wittgenstein knew the work of Schelling, Jaspers, Sartre, or Tillich; but he did know something of Heidegger, and referred to him briefly in his discussions with Schlick and Waismann.[58] Nowhere in these discussions is there any discussion of or reference to moral horror; and although Wittgenstein adds something new to the discussion—namely, an argument concerning its nonsensicality—he nowhere suggests that he intended anything so radically different from these other writers.

Second, there is no reason to suppose that Wittgenstein had the dangers, either subjective or objective, of homosexuality in mind when he referred to the feeling of absolute safety. Such an idea of safety is of first importance in Christianity in connection with salvation and the immortality of the soul, with no specific reference to homosexuality; and it also appears, in a different context, in Buddhism, in the striving for liberation from the circumstances of the world. There is no reason to suppose that, when Wittgenstein mentioned this experience, he had in mind other than what he

---

[58]Waismann, *Ludwig Wittgenstein and the Vienna Circle*, p. 68. See however Henry LeRoy Finch's argument in his *Wittgenstein—the Later Philosophy* (New York: Humanities Press, 1977), p. 265, where it is denied that Wittgenstein and Heidegger have the same experience or question in mind.

said he had in mind: *religious* experience.

Moreover, there is some further, rather specific evidence that goes contrary to Levi's interpretation, quite apart from the "Lecture on Ethics". Around 1910 Wittgenstein attended and was deeply affected by a performance of the Austrian playwright Ludwig Anzengruber's play, "Die Kreuzelschreiber". At the beginning of the third act, one of the characters states: "Whether you are lying six feet deep in the earth beneath the grass or whether you have to face this many more thousand times again—nothing can happen to you—you belong to all of it and all of it belongs to you. Nothing can happen to you. And this was so wonderful that I hollered to all the others around me: Nothing can happen to you. . . . Now be joyful, joyful—Nothing can happen to you."[59] Wittgenstein was struck by this thought, and later described it to Malcolm as a turning point in his attitude toward religion.

The most important objection is that Wittgenstein's third experience simply refutes, rather than supports, Levi's interpretation. For the third experience appeals explicitly to *divine* disapproval. And divine disapproval is precisely what Wittgenstein's account of language would not remove—even though it made discussion of it meaningless, and even if it had succeeded (as we have seen is doubtful) in removing human disapproval.

For if Wittgenstein conjured up a theory of language and an account of ethics from his unconscious need to deflect human condemnation of his actions, surely his unconscious was ingenious enough to conjure up a philosophy or theology to deflect divine judgment as well! Without this second step, his view is hardly the "protective device of incontestable power" that Levi claims it to be.

Levi acknowledges that his argument is problematic, but does not seem aware how problematic it is. We have (1) the

---

[59]Ludwig Anzengruber, *Gesammelte Werke* (Stuttgart, 1898), vol. 7, p. 279. See also Norman Malcolm's account in his *Ludwig Wittgenstein: A Memoir*, p. 70.

fact of Wittgenstein's feelings of guilt; (2) his theory of language and account of ethics; (3) the "factually meaningless" yet nonetheless powerful images of God as a terrible judge; (4) the powerful human desire, which Wittgenstein shares and respects, to point to a transcendent realm of some sort. (Levi even suggests that Wittgenstein might have held something like a "culpalogical argument" to argue from the fact of his moral corruption to the need for a Last Judgment and a divine judge.) We are apparently asked to believe that Wittgenstein's ethics functions to *assuage* his guilt, whereas his implicit theology and his account of a human tendency to "run up against the limits of language"—which would also, on such an account, have to be part of a reaction formation—work to *aggravate and increase* it. All this is—as a form of psychopathology—within the realm of possibility. But there is no reason to believe it, as it does not form an economical whole. A deeper account of Wittgenstein's psychopathology, uniting these two disparate strains, would be needed before such hypotheses would, individually, have anything to recommend them.

There is a straightforward alternative explanation that makes much more sense. Wittgenstein's account of ethics was more or less dictated by his theory of language; it was indeed *an unintended consequence of it*, in the sense explained in the previous section. And the theory of language, in turn, was dictated by the network of thinking that he shared with Russell and the logical positivists. Similar views of ethics were adopted (although without the residual theology) by other philosophers, such as Carnap, who were quite heterosexual. Wittgenstein may well have noticed the limited effect his account of ethics could have in freeing him from the condemnation of his fellow men; and this may account, say, for his explicit mentioning of tastes and preferences in this connection. If he did notice any such thing, this could have been of only very limited significance for him. For his guilt continued, and was associated, throughout his life, with images of divine punishment that were not effectively removed by his philosophy.

Levi's attempt to link Wittgenstein's homosexuality to his

philosophy focuses on his early work, as represented by the
Tractatus, and on the "Lecture on Ethics". I could imagine
a similar argument being made on the basis of Wittgenstein's later philosophy, as discussed in chapter 4 above,
sections VII to XI. There Wittgenstein suggests that understanding is rooted in and does not occur without shared
practice and a common or shared form of life. Thus members or participants in one practice have no basis for criticizing or for judging good and bad those who engage in other
practices. If we consider homosexuality as a "form of life",
then such a philosophy also effectively insulates it from the
moral criticism of others, although the protective umbrella
is now constructed rather differently.

Possibly this aspect of his later philosophy, had he noticed it, would have appealed to Wittgenstein. But, once again,
it is hard to accept the suggestion that he was *motivated* to
construct his position by such a consideration. There are
two reasons why. First, he was forced into such a relativistic
position by what I have elsewhere called the "Wittgensteinian problematic", by the objective intellectual problem situation in which he found himself.[60] Many other persons who
were neither homosexual nor in any serious moral difficulty
also found themselves forced by this intellectual problem
situation to accept similar relativistic stances.

More important—and this is a fact about Wittgenstein
which Levi's entire discussion neglects—all the biographical evidence suggests that Wittgenstein was never much
motivated by or afraid of the opinions of other persons.
He repeatedly behaved in disregard of ordinary social convention, and appears to have been singularly self-willed
and independent. As he expressed the matter in his notebooks: "Don't take the example of others as your guide, but
nature!"[61]

---

[60]See my "A Popperian Harvest," in Paul Levinson, ed., *In Pursuit of
Truth* (New York: Humanities Press, 1982); and my "On the Differences
between Popperian and Wittgensteinian Approaches", in *Proceedings of the
10th International Conference on the Unity of the Sciences* (New York, 1982).
[61]Wittgenstein, *Culture and Value*, p. 41e.

IV

WITTGENSTEIN AS PSYCHOPOMP

Much of his life will remain forever unknown to his closest friends.

—*Fania Pascal*

I have rebutted or cast doubt on various attempts to link Wittgenstein's homosexuality and his thought. Now I must return to explain the important connection which I do see between the homosexuality and the man and his influence—a connection which some might not expect.

The connection that I see relates to the fact that Wittgenstein, although not a thinker of great originality, exerted, and continues to exert, immense influence. If one wanted his ideas, one could go to any number of other, clearer, writers. Those who have been influenced by him, particularly those who were close to him (two of his literary executors and several of his closest students are converts to Roman Catholicism; several other of his closest students are Anglicans), have responded to him as if to a *psychopomp*, to an *anima mundi*, a spiritual guide of almost supernatural character, to a shaman, priest, and medicine man, to a hermetic figure or *spiritus mercurialis*—a spirit concealed or imprisoned in matter. *Wittgenstein fascinates.*[62]

Thus J. N. Findlay expresses this mood when he writes of Wittgenstein:

At the age of 40 he looked like a youth of 20, with a godlike beauty, always an important feature at Cambridge, . . . awesome in its unearthly purity. . . . The God received him . . . in an ascetic room, beautiful in its almost total emptiness, where

---

[62]Thus note the ancient, metaphorical meaning of *fascinem* as *membrum virile*. Incidentally, it is not only close disciples of Wittgenstein who respond to him in this way: all sorts of persons claim to be followers of Wittgenstein and to do the "sort" of things that he was doing—though they rarely can state what he *was* doing.

a wooden bowl of fruit on a table made the one note of colour. . . . The God was all he had been described as being: he looked like Apollo who had bounded into life out of his own statue, or perhaps like the Norse God Baldur, blue-eyed and fair-haired, with a beauty that had nothing sensual about it, but simply breathed the four Greek cardinal virtues, to which was added a very exquisite kindness and graciousness that bathed one like remote, slightly wintry sunshine . . . what Wittgenstein himself was thinking was of little importance, only much superior to the confusions and half-lights in which most philosophers of his acquaintance lived, despite their very great excellence as *men*. . . . There was . . . an extraordinary atmosphere that surrounded him, something philosophically saintly that was also very distant and impersonal: he was the *philosophe Soleil.* One had walked in his sunlight but one had not at all been singled out by the Sun. . . . the tea one drank with him tasted like nectar.[63]

For our purposes, three things are important in connection with such responses to Wittgenstein. First, such a response seems to work on the instinctual level; it is archaic, and what C. G. Jung calls archetypal, independent of individual training. Second, in the Pythagorean tradition, and in the alchemical and hermetic writings which probe this response, such a shamanic figure is seen as a *sufferer*, "the sufferer who takes away suffering", "the wounded wounder who is the agent of healing". Third, in these same ancient traditions and writings—and elsewhere, as in Plato's myth of lost androgynous unity—such a figure is frequently *hermaphroditic.* Thus for the Neopythagoreans, hermaphroditism is an attribute of deity; so Hermes Trismegistus is said to incorporate the masculine-spiritual with the femine corporeal, and Hermes Psychopompos is the *filius hermaphroditus.* One could also mention the divine bisexuality often attributed to Brahma and Siva, to Adam, to Baal and Mithras, to Dionysus and Apollo. Thus what are seen as the two great powers of nature, the masculine and the feminine, are combined in one being.[64]

---

[63]J. N. Findlay, "My Encounters with Wittgenstein", *The Philosophical Forum*, vol. 4, 1972-73, pp. 171-74.

[64]There is an immense literature here. See for examples: Francis A.

For a human figure, such as Wittgenstein, to have such traits and powers projected on him by his admirers, it is necessary that the homosexuality be there; that it be known or sensed subconsciously by his followers; but that it not be admitted consciously. *Indefiniteness is essential:* the taboo and the temptation must be there together; both must be exploited. Thus what Drury and Pascal both sensed and recorded—Wittgenstein's *noli me tangere* and foreignness to sensuality (and his intense suffering from this)—must be there: so far they told the truth. As did Julian Bell, when he rhymed, in 1930:

> I pity Ludwig while I disagree,
> The cause of his opinions all can see
> In that ascetic life, intent to shun
> The common pleasures known to everyone.[65]

Yates, *Giordano Bruno and the Hermetic Tradition* (London: Routledge & Kegan Paul, 1964); Heinrich Zimmer, *The King and the Corpse* (New York: Pantheon, 1948), esp. the discussion of Merlin, pp. 181-201, and Part II, on the Kalika Purana; David Stacton, *Kaliyuga* (London: Faber & Faber, 1965); H. G. Baynes, *Mythology of the Soul* (London: Methuen, 1949), pp. 186, 227, 240; C. G. Jung, *The Psychology of the Unconscious* (New York: Dodd, Mead, 1937), pp. 33-34, 299; C. G. Jung, *Symbols of Transformation* (Princeton: Princeton University Press, 1956), pp. 125-26, 160n, 221-22; C. G. Jung, *Mysterium Conjunctionis* (Princeton: Princeton University Press, 1963), *passim*; C. G. Jung, *Psychology and Alchemy* (London: Routledge & Kegan Paul, 1953), *passim*; C. G. Jung and C. Kerényi, *Essays on a Science of Mythology* (New York: Pantheon, 1949), pp. 74, 90, 93, 107, 128, 130, 132, 138, 148, 204; Edward Carpenter, *Intermediate Types among Primitive Folk* (New York: Arno Press, 1975), p. 71. One should also, in this connection, study the libertine tradition in early Christianity, the understanding of which has been greatly aided by the discovery of the "secret gospel" of Mark. See Morton Smith, *The Secret Gospel* (New York: Harper & Row, 1973), esp. pp. 17 and 115-38; Morton Smith, *Clement of Alexandria and a Secret Gospel of Mark* (Cambridge: Harvard University Press, 1973), pp. 254-63, 167-88 (esp. p. 185), and 217-29. See also his *Jesus the Magician* (New York: Harper & Row, 1978). For an especially valuable treatment, see John Boswell, *Christianity, Social Tolerance, and Homosexuality: Gay People in Western Europe from the Beginning of the Christian Era to the Fourteenth Century* (Chicago: University of Chicago Press, 1980).

[65]From Julian Bell, "An Epistle on the Subject of the Ethical and Aesthetic Beliefs of Herr Ludwig Wittgenstein (Doctor of Philosophy) to

But equally required, in order for the mystique to hold, is the subconscious awareness that that is not the whole story.[66]

This indefiniteness must also be present in the message of such a figure, particularly in that aspect of it which relates most closely to issues of morality. So it is not surprising that Wittgenstein's doctrine of ethics is so hard to state: that there is so much weighty controversy about what he said—or meant—in saying that what is said in these matters is meaningless ... and yet of immense importance. As Wittgenstein wrote to Ficker: "My work consists of two parts: the one presented here plus all that I have *not* written. And it is precisely this second part that is the important one."[67] This, of course, concerned ethics.

Where everything is obscure—the personality, the sexuality, the content of the thought—anything may be projected.[68] And thus, *from his friends and disciples*, Wittgenstein

---

Richard Braithwaite Esq. MA (Fellow of King's College)", a long poem in Drydenesque couplets. Originally printed in *The Venture*, February 1930; quoted from T. E. B. Howarth, *Cambridge Between Two Wars* (London: Collins, 1978), pp. 71–72. See also Peter Stansky and William Abrahams, *Journey to the Frontier: Julian Bell and John Cornford: Their lives and the 1930's* (London: Constable, 1966), pp. 60–61.

[66]My colleague Theodore Roszak has pointed out to me, after reading this Afterword, an interesting connection to Iris Murdoch, herself one of Wittgenstein's students. One of her novels, *Nuns and Soldiers*, opens with the name "Wittgenstein", and references to him crop up occasionally elsewhere in her work as well. An important image recurring throughout Murdoch's novels is that of the enchanter, obscure but tantalizing, who transforms the lives of those about him. Often there is a vaguely sexual fascination and an elusiveness masking this figure. Did Wittgenstein inspire this image?

[67]Ludwig Wittgenstein, *Briefe an Ludwig von Ficker* (Salzburg: Otto Müller, 1969), pp. 35–36.

[68]I do not believe that such *construction* of Wittgenstein is at all restricted to his later disciples in Britain. A similar process seems to have been at work in Vienna with the members of the Vienna Circle. Thus Heinrich Neider writes of "Wittgenstein ... the half-mythical 'patron saint' of the Vienna Circle. ... I remember that even two years later, during an animated discussion at the philosophers' congress in Prague, a German participant said: 'Herr Wittgenstein, should he be a real person or rather, as I believe, a synthetic figure invented by the Vienna Circle as a mouthpiece for their theses? . . .' ". See Marie Neurath and Robert S. Cohen, *Otto Neurath: Empir-*

rejected all overtures: interpretations of his thinking were rejected emphatically and even cruelly. And similarly, *noli me tangere* ruled out in advance most overture-interpretations of his sexuality.

Nothing more is needed to explain the response to the first edition of my book.[69] Thus—as discussed in the first section above—the bluff and coverup, the projection, the naïveté. And the pain, affront, and shock. For when this preserve of unnamable privacy was breached, when the details of Wittgenstein's sexuality were reported—however "neutrally"—the mystery was gone. Then it was "just sex".

I wonder then whether eagerness to prevent such aspects of Wittgenstein's life from being explored does not stem from some source such as this? With unconscious prudence and savvy,[70] the "unnamability" of this area is kept safe in

---

icism and Sociology (Dordrecht: D. Reidel, 1973), p. 47. In his biography of G. E. Moore, p. 9, Paul Levy suggests that Wittgenstein's followers may provide a comparatively rare instance of the "cult of personality" operating within philosophy. See also J. N. Findlay, who writes of Wittgenstein's "magic of personality" and "personal enchantment" in his "My Encounters with Wittgenstein".

[69]There is of course more to the explanation than this. Thus any great thinker or artist tends to be romanticized by his followers. Every several years, with remarkable regularity, some outraged doctor or other writes an article denying that Beethoven or Schubert suffered from venereal disease. See Heuwell Tircuit, "Knocking the 'Great Immortals' Back to Earth", *Review*, August 9, 1981, p. 17. See also Maynard Solomon, *Beethoven* (New York: Schirmer Books, 1977), p. 262; and John Reed, *Schubert's Final Years* (London: Faber, 1972). It seems that a heroic effort is made to overcome one's basic distrust of intellectual and artistic effort by making it into a "higher" calling in which the artist must take an elevated role, not prone to the temptations of ordinary mortals. The reverse of the coin here is the tendency to see all artists as libertines.

[70]I say "unconscious" prudence; and so it no doubt would have to be. It could not have worked better to the advantage of Wittgenstein's posthumous reputation had it been conscious and deliberate. For by preserving silence about these things, one could avoid affronting the extensive repressed homosexuality and homophobia of American professional academics, and at once titillate and influence them. Hence Wittgenstein's extraordinary influence throughout the arts subjects of American academia. This is not surprising: American children have for years been schooled on the Minnesota Multiphasic Personality Inventory Test, which can assign

order to preserve the power and appeal, the magic, of the man.

_____

one a higher "femininity quotient" if one prefers going to the museum or reading a book to playing football or selling brushes door to door. In the circumstances, it is hardly surprising that many American professors in the arts live with the not quite irradicable fear that they may be not simply homosexual but downright *queer*.

Addendum
On Wittgenstein's Descent

The following brief account sets down what is known about Wittgenstein's descent. As mentioned at the beginning of the book, he was partly Jewish although this was not widely known outside the family.

When, in 1969, I mentioned his Jewish background to Rudolf Koder, one of his closest surviving friends, a friend also of the family, I was assured that it was preposterous to think of Wittgenstein as Jewish, even though it was *possible* that his paternal grandmother, Fanni Figdor, was partly so. In fact, Wittgenstein went to some lengths to conceal his Jewish connections: he pleaded with a cousin living in England not under any circumstances to reveal his descent; and on his death several important obituaries, including that in *The Times* of London, stated that he was descended from the princely German family of Sayn-Wittgenstein. His only Jewish friend seems to have been the interior decorator Paul Engelmann, whose acquaintance he made while on army duty in Olmütz during the First World War.

Only since Wittgenstein's death has it become customary for biographical accounts, following that of Georg Henrik von Wright, to mention the Jewish descent, the usual account now being that he was three-quarters Jewish. This account is probably, but by no means certainly, true. Within the family itself there exist sharp divisions of opinion, some of its members claiming that both his paternal grandfather and his paternal grandmother had converted from Judaism, whereas other members stoutly maintain that his grandfather Hermann Christian Wittgenstein was a Gentile, the illegitimate offspring of some members of the Sayn-Wittgenstein family.[1] To add to the confusion, some members of the Sayn-Wittgenstein family have on occasion indicated that they are related to Ludwig Wittgenstein's family. The Nazis, unable to establish the origins of the Wittgensteins of Vienna, eventually classified them as *Mischlinge* (non-Jewish but of "mixed Jewish blood") under the Nuremberg laws. Thus the property and persons of those members of the family—such as Wittgenstein's sister Hermine (Mining)—who remained within the Reich during the Second World War were unharmed. During the war, some of Wittgenstein's nephews served in the German army, others in the American army.

The truth of the matter appears to be something like this. In 1935 a family tree prepared by a source outside the family was deposited in the Vienna City Archives. According to this account, which the Nazis later used, Hermann Christian Wittgenstein was the son of a certain Hirsch Wittgenstein, a Jew of Bielefeld. A thorough search of the Bielefeld records, however, gave no evidence to connect Hirsch Wittgenstein with Hermann Christian Wittgenstein; indeed, the Nazis were unable to prove any Jewish connection in the descent of Hermann Christian Wittgenstein himself, although his wife was demonstrably Jewish, just as the wife of their son, Karl Wittgenstein, was demonstrably half-Jewish.

Another family tree, however, prepared in Jerusalem since the war, reports that Hermann Christian Wittgenstein was the son of Moses Meier Wittgenstein, Jew of Korbach, and the grandson of Moses Meier, Jew of Laasphe and Korbach. Although the records of the Jewish community in Korbach were destroyed when the SS burned the Korbach synagogue in November 1938, family tradition, comments in the diary of Hermine Wittgenstein, and significant facts—such as that

---

[1]Wittgenstein himself was of the opinion that he was three-quarters Jewish in descent. So at any rate he confessed in a series of "confessions" made in January 1937 to persons in England and Austria. See Fania Pascal's account in "Wittgenstein: A Personal Memoir", in Rush Rhees, ed., *Ludwig Wittgenstein: Personal Recollections* (Totowa, N.J.: Rowman & Littlefield, 1981), p. 48.

the Wittgenstein family in Vienna possess portraits of Moses Meier and his wife Brendel Simon—suggest that this line of descent is correct.

If so, Ludwig Wittgensein was indeed three-quarters Jewish, the family name having been changed from Meier to Wittgenstein in 1808 when Napoleonic decrees required that Jews adopt a surname. By the mid-1830s, almost all members of the family had converted to the Protestant religion. The history of the Meier-Wittgenstein family, in Korbach and Bielefeld, in Berlin, Leipzig, and Vienna, from their first appearance in European history toward the end of the eighteenth century until the present day, is an extraordinary—and complicated—story of remarkable talent, energy and success which well deserves study in its own right.[2]

---

[2]My sources for the above account are, apart from conversations with members and friends of the family, the following: (a) Wiener Stadtarchiv Ahnentafel, 1935; (b) Jerusalem Ahnentafel, 1961; (c) Wittgenstein family Ahnentafel, required by Nazis, 1938, in possession of the family; (d) *Synagogen Buch der Jüdischen Gemeinde zu Bielefeld*, by J. Posner, Staatsarchiv Detmold and Stadtarchiv Bielefeld; (e) *Kirchenbücher der Neustädter Marienkirche, ev. A.B.*, in Ev. Landeskirchenamt Bielefeld; (f) gravestones in the Jewish Cemetery of Korbach; (g) *Ein- und Auswanderung Bielefeld 1763–1874*, Stadtarchiv Bielefeld; (h) List of inhabitants of Bielefeld in 1828, Stadtarchiv Bielefeld; (i) Lutheran Church records in Vienna; (j) "Aus der Geschichte der Juden in Waldeck: Jakob Wittgenstein", in *Zeitschrift für Geschichte, Literatur, Kunst und Bibliographie*, Preßburg, January-February 1935, vol. 56, pp. 4–8; (k) *Korbach, die Geschichte einer deutschen Stadt*, by W. Medding, Korbach Stadtarchiv; (l) Gütersloh Liste, 1808.

Acknowledgements

The help of the following persons has been invaluable. Needless to say, they are in no way responsible for my conclusions and have in several cases disagreed with them. I am also indebted to several persons who, for reasons of their own, do not wish to be mentioned. My most sincere thanks go to: Professor Joseph Agassi, Professor Hans Albert, Frau Dir. Georg Berger, Frau Margarete Bicklmayer, Mr. Kenneth Blackwell, Professor I. M. Bochenski, Herr Franz Brenner, Professor Sylvain Bromberger, the late Professor Charlotte Bühler, the late Professor Rudolf Carnap, Professor Robert S. Cohen, Frau Anny Eder, Professor Herbert Feigl, Professor Paul K. Feyerabend, Professor Henry LeRoy Finch, Professor Antony Flew, Herr Karl Gruber, Herr und Frau Konrad Gruber, Professor Eugene C. Hargrove, Professor F. A. von Hayek, Professor Jaakko Hintikka, Professor Merrill Provence-Hintikka, Dr. Adolf Hübner, Professor Kurt Hübner, Dr. W. D. Hudson, Dr. Hanns Jäger, Professor I. C. Jarvie, Herr Bürgermeister Emmerich Koderhold, the late Professor Viktor Kraft, Professor Larry Laudan, Mr. Michael Lebeck, Frau Gerda Leber-Hagenau, Dr. Gustav Lebzeltern, Dr. F. Lenz, Professor Werner Leinfellner, Dr. Elisabeth Leinfellner, Professor Konrad Lorenz, Mr. Harry Margolis, Professor John Moran, Professor Peter Munz, Mr. Wallace Nethery, Professor George Pitcher, Professor R. H. Popkin, Professor Sir Karl Popper, Dr. Günther Posch, Professor Gerard Radnitzky, Mr. Dolf Rijkers, Herr Norbert Rosner, Professor Ben-Ami Scharfstein, Herr Johann Scheibenbauer, Herr. Dir. Martin Scherleitner, Professor Steven S. Schwarzschild, Mrs. Carol Southern, Professor Herbert Spiegelberg, Herr Georg Stern, Dr. Thomas H. W.

Stonborough, Professor George Steiner, Professor Marx Wartofsky, Professor Albert Wellek, the late Mrs. Jane West, Professor J. O. Wisdom, Professor Elizabeth Wolgast.

I am also indebted to the staff of the following institutions for their cooperation and help: Landesarchiv für Niederösterreich, Vienna; Stadtbibliothek, Vienna; Kriegsarchiv, Staatsarchiv, Vienna; Pädagogisches Institut der Stadt Wien; Pädagogisches Zentralbücherei, Vienna; Stadtschulrat für Wien, Vienna; Stadtarchiv Bielefeld; Stadtarchiv, Korbach; Historisches Museum der Stadt Wien; Wittgenstein Documentation Center, Kirchberg am Wechsel.

I am also indebted to Interlit, B.V.I., and to the Research Committees of the University of Pittsburgh; Gonville and Caius College, Cambridge; the University of California; the California State University; and of the Hoover Institution, Stanford University, which at various times have supported my investigations into German and Austrian intellectual history. I am also indebted for generous support to the American Council of Learned Societies, the American Philosophical Society, the Institute for Humane Studies, the Fritz Thyssen Stiftung, and the Deutscher Akademischer Austauschdienst.

It is a pleasure to thank André Carus, David Ramsay Steele, Sue Olson, and Leslie Auerbach for making this new Open Court paperback edition possible.

For photographic permissions I am grateful as follows: For page 1, Professor F. A. von Hayek; for pages 2, 3 upper, 4, 5 upper, 6 upper, 8, 10, an anonymous friend of Wittgenstein; pages 2 and 3 upper are also printed by permission of the Kriegsarchiv, Vienna; for page 3 lower, Bildarchiv d. Öst. Nationalbibliothek, Vienna; for page 5 lower, Museen der Stadt Wien, Vienna; for 6 lower, Plan und Schriftenkammer der Stadt Wien, Vienna; for page 7 upper, Bildarchiv d. Öst. Nationalbibliothek, Vienna; for page 7 lower, Staatsgalerie, Munich. The photographs on page 9, 12, and 13 are by the author; for page 11, Armando Armando, Rome; for page 14 (Kraus and Boltzmann), Museen der Stadt Wien; for page 14 (Glöckel), Bildarchiv d. Öst. Nationalbibliothek, Vienna; for page 15 (Loos), Museen der Stadt Wien; and for page 15 (Weininger), Bildarchiv d. Öst. Nationalbibliothek, Vienna; for page 16, *The New York Review of Books.*

Acknowledgements

Finally, I am particularly indebted to my dear friend, the late Professor Walter Kaufmann—for his inspiration as well as for his radical yet constructive criticism of the original manuscript of this work.

Bibliography

Note: This guide to Wittgenstein's own writings is intended mainly for English-language readers. Wittgenstein wrote most of his work in German, and much of it was first published either in German or in an edition with both German and English on facing pages. Most of his writings were not published until long after their original composition. The following indicates the probable date of composition (in whichever language) and an English-language edition wherever available.

For a guide to the vast secondary literature on Wittgenstein, the reader is directed to the footnotes to this book and also to François H. Lapointe, *Ludwig Wittgenstein: A Comprehensive Bibliography* (Westpoint, Conn.: Greenwood Press, 1980).

The splendid picture book about Wittgenstein should also be mentioned: Michael Nedo and Michele Ranchetti, *Wittgenstein: Sein Leben in Bildern und Texten* (Frankfurt: Suhrkamp Verlag, 1983).

WORKS BY WITTGENSTEIN
(in approximate order of writing):

"On Logic, and How Not to Do It", review of P. Coffey, *The Science of Logic*. Published in the *Cambridge Review*, March 6, 1913. Reprinted in Eric Homberger, William Janeway, and Simon Schama, eds., *The Cambridge Mind* (Boston: Little, Brown, 1970), pp. 127–29.

Notebooks 1914–16. Edited by G. E. M. Anscombe and Georg Henrik von Wright. (Oxford: Basil Blackwell, 1961).

Prototractatus (1918). An early version of *Tractatus Logico-Philosophicus* (London: Routledge & Kegan Paul, 1971).

Bibliography

Tractatus Logico-Philosophicus (1918). (London: Routledge, 1923). New English translation by D. F. Pears and Brian F. McGuinness (London: Routledge & Kegan Paul, 1961).

Wörterbuch für Volksschulen (1925). (Vienna: Hölder-Pichler-Tempsky, 1926). Reprinted by the same publishers in 1977, edited by Adolf Hübner and Werner and Elisabeth Leinfellner, with an Introduction in English and German by Hübner, and containing Wittgenstein's Preface, which had been omitted from the original edition.

"Some Remarks on Logical Form", *Proceedings of the Aristotelian Society, Supplementary Volume*, 1929.

"A Lecture on Ethics" (1929–30). *The Philosophical Review*, January 1965, pp. 3–12.

Philosophical Remarks (1930). Edited by Rush Rhees. (Oxford: Basil Blackwell, 1975).

Remarks on Frazer's Golden Bough (1931 and later). Edited by Rush Rhees. (Retford, Nottinghamshire: The Brynmill Press, 1979). Also published earlier in a slightly different form in *Synthèse*, 1967, pp. 233–45.

Philosophical Grammar (1932–34). Edited by Rush Rhees. (Oxford: Basil Blackwell, 1974).

"Letter to the Editor", *Mind*, 1933.

The Blue and Brown Books (1933–35). Edited by Rush Rhees. (Oxford: Basil Blackwell, 1958).

"Cause and Effect: Intuitive Awareness" (1937). Edited by Rush Rhees. *Philosophia*, vol. 6, nos 3/4, September-December 1976, pp. 391–445.

Remarks on the Foundations of Mathematics (1937–44). Edited by Georg Henrik von Wright, Rush Rhees, and G. E. M. Anscombe. (Oxford: Basil Blackwell, 1956).

Philosophical Investigations (1945 and 1947–49). Edited by G. E. M. Anscombe and Rush Rhees. (Oxford: Basil Blackwell, 1953).

Zettel (1945–58). Edited by G. E. M. Anscombe and Georg Henrik von Wright. (Oxford: Basil Blackwell, 1967).

Remarks on the Philosophy of Psychology (1946–49). Edited by G. E. M. Anscombe, Georg Henrik von Wright, and Heikki Nyman. (Oxford: Basil Blackwell, 1980). In two volumes.

Remarks on Colour (1950–51). Edited by G. E. M. Anscombe. (Oxford: Basil Blackwell, 1977).

On Certainty (1949–51). Edited by G. E. M. Anscombe and Georg Henrik von Wright. (Oxford: Basil Blackwell, 1969).

Culture and Value (1914–1951). Edited by Georg Henrik von Wright. (Oxford: Basil Blackwell, 1980).

Last Writings On the Philosophy of Psychology (1951). Edited by G. H. von Wright and Heikki Nyman (Oxford: Basil Blackwell, 1982).

LECTURES BY WITTGENSTEIN,
as transcribed by his students:

Wittgenstein's Lectures: Cambridge 1930–32. Compiled from notes taken by John King and Desmond Lee. Edited by Desmond Lee. (Totowa, N.J.: Rowman and Littlefield, 1980).

Wittgenstein's Lectures: Cambridge 1932–35. Compiled from notes taken by Alice Ambrose and Margaret Macdonald. Edited by Alice Ambrose. (Totowa, N.J.: Rowman and Littlefield, 1979).

Lectures & Conversations on Aesthetics, Psychology and Religious Belief (1938–46). From notes taken by Yorick Smythies, Rush Rhees, and James Taylor. Edited by Cyril Barrett. (Berkeley: University of California Press, 1967).

Wittgenstein's Lectures on the Foundations of Mathematics: Cambridge, 1939. From the notes of R. G. Bosanquet, Norman Malcolm, Rush Rhees, Yorick Smythies. Edited by Cora Diamond. (Hassocks, Suffolk: The Harvester Press, 1976).

LETTERS BY WITTGENSTEIN:

W. Eccles, "Some Letters of Wittgenstein, 1912–1939", *Hermathena*, Dublin, 1963, pp. 57–65.

Letters to Russell, Keynes and Moore (1912–48). Edited by Georg Henrik von Wright. (Oxford: Basil Blackwell, 1974).

Paul Engelmann, *Letters from Ludwig Wittgenstein with a Memoir* (Oxford: Basil Blackwell, 1967).

Briefe an Ludwig von Ficker (1914–20). Edited by Georg Henrik von Wright. (Salzburg: Otto Müller, 1969).

Letters to C. K. Ogden (1922–33). Edited by Georg Henrik von Wright. (Oxford and London: Basil Blackwell, and Routledge & Kegan Paul, 1973).

MISCELLANEOUS:

"Notes for Lectures on 'Private Experience' and 'Sense Data' " (1934–46), edited by Rush Rhees, *Philosophical Review*, vol. 77, 1968, pp. 271–320.

Bibliography

Friedrich Waismann, *Ludwig Wittgenstein and the Vienna Circle*. Conversations 1929–32, recorded by Friedrich Waismann, edited by Brian McGuinness. (Oxford: Basil Blackwell, 1979).

Index

Adler, Friedrich, 50
Adorno, T., 56
Aesthetics, 48, 50, 53, 55, 66, 68, 70
Aiken, Henry David, 63
Analytical philosophy, 9
Anscombe, G. E. M., 62, 63n, 67n, 149n, 151, 162 & n, 170n, 171n, 173n
Anzengruber, Ludwig, 189 & n
Apostles, the, 14–15 & n
Arbeitsschule, 79
Architecture, 54
Associationism, 78–79, 127–128, 138
Atomic facts, 62
Atomic (elementary) propositions, 61–62, 128, 141, as unneeded for meaningful communication, 133–138, as needed to demarcate legitimate claims, 133
Atomism (logical and philosophical), 128–129, 131, 136
Atomism (in learning theory and psychology), 127, 129, 131–133, arguments against, 132–133
Augustine, Saint, 73, 130
Austria, Chapter 1, 3, and *passim*

Barrett, Cyril, 24n
Behaviorism, 46, 128, 178
Bell, Julian, 194n, 195n
Berchtold, Leopold, 167–168 & n
Berger, Georg, 87–89, 91, 93, 94, 95
Berkeley, George (Bishop), 171

Biography, 183–184
Bloomsbury group, 15, 161
Blue Book (Wittgenstein), 125, 130, 133
Boltzmann, Ludwig, 36
Born, Max, 179
Boswell, John, 194n
Brahms, Johannes, 76
Braithwaite, Richard B., 195n
Broad, C. D., 121 & n, 136
Brockdorff-Rantzau, Count, 168n
Brome, Vincent, 27n
Brouwer, L. E. J., 73 & n
Brown Book (Wittgenstein), 73, 125, 130, 133
Brunswik, Egon, 129
Bühler, Charlotte, 127, 130
Bühler, Karl, 17–18, 113, 127 & n, 128–131, 137–138, 143 & n, 174 & n, 175–177
Buxbaum, Eduard, 99

Cambridge University, Wittgenstein at, 20–21, Chapter 4, 161
Carnap, Rudolf, 21, 53, 190
Carnegie, Andrew, 76
Carpenter, Edward, 194n
Carroll, Lewis (the Rev. C. L. Dodgson), 59 & n, 60n
Categories, 139–140, 145
Category mistake, 141–142, 145–146
Child psychology, Chapters 3 and 4 *passim*
Chomsky, Noam, 46, 47, 140n
Church, Alonzo, 67, 68n
Churchill, Winston, 174

Index

Kreisel, Georg, 42n, 43n
Krupp family, 76
Külpe, Oswald, 128, 137–138, 143
Kundt, Wilhelm, 86–88, 95, 110

Language:
  abuse of, 51,
  abstract words in, 128,
  acquisition of, 46, 73, 74, 130,
  animal, 175
  attitudes toward, 51,
  as bewitching intelligence, 141,
  as creating reality, 139,
  convention in, 128, 131,
  functions of, 175–183,
  international (pictures), 143 & n,
  Jewish attitudes to, 56–57,
  logic of, 60,
  limits of, 48, 53, 57, 142, 187, 190,
  meaningfulness, 46,48, 60, 131, 187,
  ordinary, 134, 141,
  possibility of, 46,
  primitive, 74, 126,
  private, 74, 126, 174,
  of morality, 55–56,
  representative, picturing, mirroring, 131, 138, 173–174,
  refinement of, 55–56,
  and sex, 173–174,
  simples of, 137, 139,
  systems of, 139,
  theory of, 129
  usage, 133,
  Wittgenstein's ideas on, Chapter 4,
  Wittgenstein's method of teaching, Chapter 3
Language-games, 138–154,
  change and development of, 147
Lavater, Johann Casper, 172
Lawrence, D. H., 161
Lazarsfeld, Paul, 129

Leavis, F. R., 28n
Lectures and Conversations on Aesthetics, Psychology and Religious Belief (Wittgenstein), 24n, 143
Lee, Desmond, 160n
Leinfellner, Elisabeth and Werner, 73n
Leitner, Bernhard, 37n, 118n
Lenin, V. I., 50
Levi, A. W., 67n, 184 & n, 185 & n, 186–191
Levy, Paul, 15n, 164n, 196n
Lewin, Kurt, 128
Liar Paradox, 22, 59
Lichtenberg, Georg Christoph, 172
Logic, mathemathical, 14n, 48,
  foundations of, 58,
  of different kinds of discourse, 139–154,
  laws of, 139
Logical analysis, 59
Logical paradoxes, 58–60, 67
Logical positivism, 47, 50, 53, 128, 157
Logical structure, scaffolding, 64–66, 139
Logical terms, 65
Loos, Adolf, 54, 77, 117
Lorenz, Konrad, 129
Love, 159
Lukasiewicz, Jan, 59
Lynd, Helen Merrell, 55

Mach, Ernst, 50, 128, 138
MacIntyre, A., 149n
Mahler, Gustav, 76
Malcolm, Norman, 16 & n, 18, 19, 151 & n, 154, 159n, 165n, 189 & n
Marx, Karl, 50
Marxism, 50
Materialism, 50, 178
Mauthner, Fritz, 51 & n, 54
Mautner, Herr, in Trattenbach, 86
McGuinness, Brian, 75n, 130, 162n, 164n

211

scientific, 138
Pseudopropositions, 61
Psychiatry, 170
Psychoanalysis, 55
Psychology: child, Chapter 3,
112n, Chapter 4,
use of, in explaining
philosophical ideas, 11
Puchberg, Wittgenstein in, 18,
72, 91, 100, 104, 106, 114–116
Putré, Josef, 117 & n
Puzzlement, philosophical, 141

Quine, W. V., 59–60
Quinton, Anthony, 46 & n, 47,
63, 169n

Ramsey, F. P., 114, 120, 124, 125
Ranchetti, Michele, 105n
Rationality, criteria of, 151–153
Religion, 48, 53, 66, 68, 70, 90,
100, 149, 150, 186–191
Reality, nature and structure of,
61,
access to, 139, 144,
as discoverable through
analysis of language, 63,
simples of, 137
Reductionism, 128, 177 & n, 178,
183
Relativism, 139
*Remarks on the Foundations of
Mathematics* (Wittgenstein),
125
Rhees, Rush, 24n, 28n, 38n, 41n,
67n, 107n, 150n, 153, 155n,
160n, 162 & n, 165, 167n,
173n, 199n
Richard, J., 58
Riddle, 67–68
Rilke, Rainer Maria, 55, 77
Rolf, Ida, 182
Rosenzweig, Franz, 57 & n
Rosner, Norbert, 73, 100, 115
Roszak, Theodore, 195n
Rottenhan, Count, 78
Rowse, A. L., 164n
Russell, Bertrand, 14 & n, 26, 26n,
34, 36, 45, 49, 58, 60, 62, 65, 66,

72, 81, 82 & n, 83, 84, 88, 90,
113, 115, 119 & n, 120–123 & n,
136, 140, 145, 190,
letters from Wittgenstein, 39n,
43n,
paradox of, 14n, 59
theory of types, 59, 66–68,
on Wittgenstein's character,
83, 121,
on Wittgenstein's philosophy,
67, 120–123

Sackville-West, Vita, 161 & n
Safety, absolute, 187–191
Salzer, Helene (sister of
Wittgenstein), 34, 39
Sartre, Jean-Paul, 188
"Sayable", the, 48–53
Sayn-Wittgenstein family,
198–199
Scaffolding, logical, 64
Scharfstein, Ben-Ami, 166 & n,
169 & n, 170–171
Scheibenbauer, Johann, 20
Schelling, F. W. J., 188
Schenk-Danzinger, Lotte, 129
Scherleitner, Martin, 37, 87–88
Schiller, Franz, 73n
Schlick, Moritz, 15, 53 & n, 118,
125, 126, 130, 185n, 188
Schönberg, Arnold, 54
School-reform movement
(Austrian), 17, 37–38, Chapter
3, 126–131, 143n,
influence on Wittgenstein, 11,
112 & n, 113–114,
principles of, 95, 126–131,
psychology and, 128–131,
Wittgenstein in, 11, 73, 80
Schrödinger, Erwin, 179
Schumann, Clara, 76
Schwab, Charles M., 76 & n
Science, versus nonscience, 45,
47–50, 61, 138, 153,
as not authoritative, 142,
and criteria of meaning, 48,
61,
language of, 140
Secession, 76

Index

Wertheimer, Max, 128
Whitehead, Alfred North, 140
Winckelmann, J. J., 172
Wisdom, J. O., 118 & n, 146, 171, 172 & n
Wittgenstein, this book,
  criticisms of, Afterword, section 1,
  editions and translations of, 11 & n
Wittgenstein, Hans (brother), 35
Wittgenstein, Hermann Christian, 198–199
Wittgenstein, Hermine (Mining) (sister), 21, 34, 35, 37 & n, 38n, 39 & n, 77, 94–95, 99, 155, 164n, 199
Wittgenstein, Hirsch, 199
Wittgenstein, Karl (father), 14, 34–35, 76, 81 & n, 102, 154
Wittgenstein, Frau Karl (Poldy) (mother), 34, 116, 119, 199
Wittgenstein, Kurt (brother), 34–35
Wittgenstein, Ludwig (uncle), 35, 39
Wittgenstein, Ludwig: *passim*,
  appearance, 15,
  army service of, 15, 16,
  as Austrian figure, 20–22,
  birth, 13,
  at Cambridge University, 15,
  character, 15–16,
  correspondence of, 157–158,
  cruelty, alleged, 83, 107–112,
  death, 13, 154–155,
  descent, 16, 39, Addendum,
  diaries of, 25n, 163–165,
  disciples, 16, 154,
  dreams, 24–25, 29–33,
  education, 14,
  engineering and, 14,
  fortune, 38–39,
  friendships, 42, 43,
  gift to Ficker, 76 & n, 77,
  Gospels, knowledge of, 72,
  house designed for his sister, 116–118
  influence of, 13, 120,

Jewish descent, Addendum,
  literary executors of, 161–163 & n, 170–171 & n, 192,
  logical theory of, 67 68,
  "lost years", "mystery years" of, 9, 13, 17,
  mathematical work of, 14,
  as philosopher, standing, 25, 192,
  philosophy of, 11, 15, 17, 156, 170,
    background of, 131,
    early philosophy of, 17, Chapter 1,
    later philosophy of, 17, Chapters 3 and 4,
    new direction in, 9, 120–123, Chapter 4, 131,
    writing about, "Wittgensteinian", 124,
  psychological state, 33–40, 108, 124–125, 184–191,
  as psychopomp, 192–197,
  publications of, 15,
  quest for sublimation and, 25, 26, 27,
  religion, 16, 100,
  "research formula or program" of, 144–146,
  as schoolteacher, 15, 17, 28, 37, 70, Chapter 3, 131,
  school of, 171n,
  self–protection, patterns of, 42,
  sexual life, homosexuality, 22, 25, 26, 30, 33, 40–44, 72, 111, Afterword,
  students, 85, Chapter 3, 154–155,
  suicide, thoughts of, 35–40,
  as teacher, 16, Chapter 3,
  trial, 19, 107–112,
  writings, *see under titles and in Bibliography*
Wittgenstein, Margarete, *see* Stonborough, Margarete
Wittgenstein, Moses Meier, 199
Wittgenstein, Paul (brother), 21, 34–35, 39

215

About the Author

WILLIAM WARREN BARTLEY, III is Senior Research Fellow of the Hoover Institution, Stanford University, where he is writing the biographies of Sir Karl Popper and F. A. von Hayek.

Born in Pittsburgh, Professor Bartley prepared at Harvard College and at the London School of Economics and Political Science, where he wrote his doctoral dissertation under Popper's supervision.

His previous appointments include the Warburg Institute of the University of London; the London School of Economics and Political Science; the University of California (Berkeley and San Diego); and Gonville and Caius College, Cambridge University. From 1967 to 1973, he taught at the University of Pittsburgh, where he was Professor of Philosophy and of History and Philosophy of Science. Professor Bartley is the author of *Lewis Carroll's Symbolic Logic*; *The Retreat to Commitment*, a major work in the theory of rationality that has been translated into five languages; *Morality and Religion*; *Werner Erhard: The Transformation of a Man*, the best-selling biography of the founder of *est*; as well as of *Wittgenstein*. He is a contributor to *The Times Literary Supplement*, *New York Review of Books*, *Scientific American*, *Commentary*, *Encounter*, and many other journals. He is the Editor of Sir Karl Popper's *Postscript to the Logic of Scientific Discovery* and of *The Collected Works of F. A. von Hayek*.

He has held fellowships from the United States Educational Commissions in the United Kingdom and in New Zealand; the American Council of Learned Societies, the American Philosophical Society, the Deutscher Akademischer Austauschdienst, the University of California Institute for the

Humanities, the *est* Foundation, the Danforth Foundation, the Vera and Walter Morris Foundation, the Institute for Humane Studies, the Thyssen Foundation, and other bodies. He has lectured widely in the United States, Europe, and the Orient, and is a member of the Mont Pèlerin Society.